ASK
THE LAWN
EXPERT

ASK
THE LAWN
EXPERT

by Paul N. Voykin,

GOLF COURSE SUPERINTENDENT

MACMILLAN PUBLISHING CO., INC.

NEW YORK

COLLIER MACMILLAN PUBLISHERS

LONDON

Macmillan Publishing Co., Inc.
866 Third Avenue, New York, N.Y. 10022
Collier Macmillan Canada, Ltd.

Library of Congress Cataloging in Publication Data

Voykin, Paul N   1931–
Ask the lawn expert

Includes index.
1. Lawns.   I.   Title.
SB433.V66   635.9′64   75–29232
ISBN 0–02–622170–5

FIRST PRINTING 1976

Printed in the United States of America

To my dear mother Julia for all her love,
to Bob Cromie for opening the door,
and
to Herb Luthin
for all his help and encouragement.

Contents

viii

Preface

SHORTLY AFTER THE publication of my first book, *A Perfect Lawn the Easy Way,* I began to be deluged with letters from homeowners all over North America writing to tell me how much they appreciated my down-to-earth facts on home lawns. All of them ended by asking me questions based on their own particular lawn problems. Many of the things they asked about either were not covered in my first book or were not covered as thoroughly as they might have been. I answered all inquiries, and hope they will keep coming in.

So, that is how the idea for this book originated—with my readers. I thought, Why not write a simple question-and-answer book based on my correspondence? And why not add the most pertinent questions that have come up during my countless lectures to garden clubs and in interviews for radio, TV, and newspapers? And finally why not ice the cake with the answers to twenty years' worth of home lawn questions from members of golf courses where I have worked as well as from friends and neighbors? There is just one more thing to add. My answers will be as simple as I can possibly make them without sounding like a textbook; *but they will cover the questions as completely and extensively as possible*

—unlike most question-and-answer books, periodicals, and articles. The reader will not be scratching his head at a too-terse, five-word answer.

In view of worldwide scarcity, let's remember that home lawns comprise the biggest single crop in this country and that grass is now even used in the manufacture of protein.

I hope that in this book you finally find the answers to your lawn problems. Let's keep America green . . . and beautiful!

PAUL N. VOYKIN

Acknowledgments

MY SINCERE THANKS to the following friends who helped me avoid gross error. Any disagreements between us is only because in certain instances I decided to stay with my own views and opinions.

Jerry H. Cheesman, Lake City Community College, Florida; Dr. Bill Daniel, Purdue University, Indiana; George M. Kozelnicky, University of Georgia; Dr. Bill Meyer, plant pathologist, Hubbard, Oregon; Louis E. Miller, golf course superintendent, Louisville Country Club, Kentucky; Charles G. Wilson, Milwaukee Sewerage Commission,
and
most of all, my special thanks to Dr. Jack D. Butler, Colorado State University and Dr. Al Turgeon, University of Illinois.

ASK
THE LAWN
EXPERT

I

Lawn Grasses and
Where They Grow Best

THE FIRST DUTY of this book will be
to divide the lawn grasses of the United States and Canada into
cool-region and warm-region grasses. This will help the reader
understand the grasses in the area where he is living. An ex-
planation can easily be made without the aid of cumbersome and
costly marked-up maps. Simply remember that Canada and the
northern United States (you know where you live) will be called
the cool grass region and the southern states will be called the
warm grass region. Of course there are areas in some of the
southern states (California, Arizona, etc.) where cool-season
grasses will grow, but these are exceptions, and the homeowner
can use whatever is applicable in our discussion of cool-region
grasses for these areas. The transition grass zone is the states that
cannot be logically called northern or southern. Frankly, this area
is the most difficult of all places for growing and maintaining
grass, even for experts. We will deal carefully with this "twilight
borderline" zone, for it is too far north for warm-climate grasses
and too far south for cool-climate grasses to do well in. Therefore,
getting the right grass to adapt itself to this frustrating area is
sometimes most difficult. But I have seen some outstanding lawns

1

in this zone, so it is possible. Furthermore, encouraging progress has been made recently in developing new, adaptable varieties of grasses as well as up-to-date methods of maintenance, including more effective disease and insect control methods.

COOL-SEASON GRASSES

The prime cool-season grass in the United States is Kentucky bluegrass, *Poa pratensis*. It is the most popular species of turf grass grown throughout the northern United States and Canada. This beautiful grass plant, with its enduring perennial nature, came to North America from Europe and Asia and can now be found in natural stands along roadsides, railroad right-of-ways, virgin pastures, and other noncultivated areas. Kentucky bluegrass is the most widely tested turf grass species, because of its popularity and broad adaptation, at least 100 varieties are being tested by experimental stations. Many of these are already available to homeowners. A few years ago, available varieties of Kentucky bluegrass could be counted on the fingers of your hands. The choice today is almost unlimited.

One of the most frequent questions asked of me is, What variety of Kentucky bluegrass seed do you consider to be superior? There are so many varieties available today in lawn and garden stores, supermarkets, department stores, hardware stores, and even drugstores, that an anxious homeowner is often confused and bewildered. So let's get right down to business and start this book with the question most often asked of me: *What type of Kentucky bluegrass seed should I buy to plant a top-quality, new home lawn?*

Answer.—Provided you live in a cool-season climate and your yard is exposed to the sun, the seed that I recommend you purchase from a neighborhood lawn and garden store is a top-quality blend of several Kentucky bluegrass varieties. Be sure no other turf grass, such as ryegrass or fescue, is included in the package. We want to start your lawn off with a pure stand of Kentucky bluegrass, and *nothing* else will do. Fescues and ryegrasses are fine cool-season grasses, but they have other functions and purposes, which we will discuss later.

Q.—What exactly do you mean by a blend of Kentucky bluegrass varieties? Can you give me an example?

A.—Certainly. A store shelf blend* might consist of Merion, Fylking, and Nugget; or Pennstar, Fylking, and Sodco; or Merion, Windsor, and Victa; or a dark green formula such as either Nugget, Adelphi, and Merion, or Pennstar, Fylking, and Prato.** Most of these Kentucky bluegrass varieties are considered to be in the all-star class, and like a good hockey forward line, they usually work well together.

With so many varieties on the market, I sometimes get the urge to recommend to my frustrated friends that they take a pound of each strain, mix them together, and see what they come up with. But this is risky and better left to the seed companies and their professionals, whose job is to try to combine varieties of Kentucky bluegrass in terms of appearance, color, height, and resistance to disease. Many other factors are also considered in working out a combination that will form a thick green carpet of turf and also withstand the ravages of nature.

Q.—Why not use only one variety of Kentucky bluegrass, like Merion or Fylking, instead of a composite?

A.—Experience has indicated that no variety is perfect. For this reason lawn grass specialists often suggest formulas including more than one variety of Kentucky bluegrass, and sometimes other kinds of grass as well. The admitted weakness of all currently available bluegrass varieties has caused some turf specialists to recommend the use of Kentucky bluegrass blends but not single variety plantings. It is hoped that the weakness of one variety will be compensated for by the complementary strength of another variety and that the combination will result in a good lawn for all seasons. The safety-in-numbers syndrome works well here. But let me enlighten you a little further so you can better understand the subject of Kentucky bluegrass varieties (or any grass variety for

* From here on we will use the word *blend* to mean a combination of varieties (mixing two or more varieties of the same species) and the term *mixture* to mean a composition of two or more species (e.g., Kentucky bluegrass and ryegrass).

** All these blends mentioned are actual recommendations by turf specialists or seed companies.

that matter). In order for a new Kentucky bluegrass variety to be placed on the market, it should have some outstanding trait or characteristic, such as resistance to a major disease, deep color, low growth, hardiness, or an aggressive root system. Such a characteristic supposedly could make it superior to other available varieties. The choice of the "number one" bluegrass can be compared to the selection of the outstanding rose each year or to picking the finest young lady in a Miss America contest. Each has to have extraordinary talents or traits to be a winner. Seed companies have found out that by blending together some of these varieties, they can give the homeowner an improved grass for his lawn.

Q.—What are the drawbacks, if any?

A.—Well, there is a major one if the homeowner suddenly loses interest in his lawn. These high-quality blends of Kentucky bluegrass varieties generally require fairly consistent care to be kept in beautiful condition (no matter what the ads say), and as long as the American homeowner gets spring fever only once a year (and then for just a short time), these new and more expensive strains *may* suffer readily from insufficient care. As a result these blends can end up looking very bad after a couple of seasons, or even sooner. Superior types, as a rule, require better-than-average attention and sometimes perform no better than "common" types under neglectful management. Now is a good time to mention that the new varieties normally grow best with up to 4 pounds of actual nitrogen per 1,000 square feet. Some varieties like Merion need even more nitrogen to do well. "Common" needs only 2 pounds of actual nitrogen per 1,000 square feet and usually gets even less from the average homeowner.

Q.—Whatever happened to old, reliable, cheaply priced, common Kentucky bluegrass? Why all the expensive blends?

A.—I am glad you asked that question, because I love "common" Kentucky bluegrass and prescribe it for the average homeowner, who usually doesn't worry too much about his lawn after he goes through the rites of spring fever. "Common" Kentucky tolerates neglect better than any other variety that I know. And it comes up smiling at the sun each spring, though admittedly it has more leaf spot problems during some summers than other varieties. It's damned ironic that for years turf experts have been down-grading common because of its low resistance to leaf spot; because the fact is that some of the heralded "prima donna" strains get diseases such as fungi that are much more devastating than common's leaf spot. I think that's a bum rap.

Q.—Here you are saying common Kentucky bluegrass is the grass of our forefathers, of our fathers, the grass we grew up on! So why didn't you recommend common in the first place?

A.—First, it's not easily available, and secondly, we didn't place as much emphasis on manicured lawns back in those days as we do now. There are so many of the newer and supposedly better varieties for sale that you don't see common Kentucky bluegrass on the shelves as much as I would like to see it. Ten years ago it was no problem to buy common; now you must know what to look for. It has been augmented by improved selections, and any common that is for sale now is labelled simply Kentucky blue-grass. Common also comes under different labels. Seed companies and turf specialists, the men who discover the new, improved varieties of Kentucky bluegrass, tend to spend a lot of time promoting the higher-priced superior varieties; but I adamantly state that very few homeowners can distinguish the difference between common and other kinds of Kentucky bluegrass. Some Kentucky bluegrass that is now sold as common is actually the old Newport, a high seed producer from Oregon that was released as a pure strain in 1958. Newport is a good mixture when planted with other varieties. However, with the passing of time this grass deteriorates; it is not the grass we thought it was. Perhaps that's the reason it has been sluffed off as common. I think Park (released in 1957) is one of the varieties of Kentucky bluegrass that comes closest, in appearance and growth habit, to the old common, because Park is a conglomerate of many varieties of Kentucky bluegrass. Both of the above-mentioned varieties do well in the Midwest if leaf spot is not severe. Another similar strain is Delta. In fact, when it comes to the nitty-gritty, the many wild strains of Kenblue and South Dakota Certified are perhaps closest to the old-fashioned common bluegrass. But let's be realistic. Remember, these "cheapy commons" are something less than desirable for modern luxury lawns. They're for homeowners who don't give a hoot about their lawns. Buy the improved varieties of Kentucky bluegrass, but make up your mind to give your lawn consistent love and care throughout the growing season (April–October). Even though you will have to open your wallet a little oftener and work a little harder, it will be worth it.

More and more of the higher-priced improved varieties are being blended, because it's been admitted that they don't do well by themselves. However, because the majority of them have been derived from the old common Kentucky bluegrass (and Grandpa still continues to beget offspring), to my way of thinking, we end up with a higher class of common Kentucky bluegrass. This class is a composite of types elevated in stature and performance, considerably better in all-around disease resistance and adaptation to local conditions than the old customary blends, but still to me common. Many many years from now, when seed companies and governmental groups get a little wiser, we may once again find reconstituted common on market shelves with the simple title "Quality Kentucky Bluegrass": an all-around "super" blend with the sought-for ideal of 100-percent purity and germination, and having no weed or crop content (a term I'll explain later on), which will guarantee its superiority to all others. This would end all consumer confusion. But until it happens, your decision comes down to how much lawn care you want to devote to keep the higher-priced, improved varieties attractive. And since people who read books and articles on lawns usually want the best, not average or below, your decision shouldn't be hard to make.

Q.—What is the basic difference in growth between common-type Kentucky bluegrass and some of the new varieties?

A.—The newer strains are mostly low-growing and not upright, like a high percentage of the individual common seeds. Most of the new strains on the market were chosen after they were compared under various maintenance levels with common and Merion Kentucky bluegrass. These levels entailed experiments and practical observations of ten years or more.

Q.—Why did you change your mind about planting a *new* lawn with several varieties of Kentucky bluegrass rather than with just one pure strain?

A.—Everybody is entitled to a change of mind, especially if the change is for the better. And since I don't work for seed or sod companies, I believe I can be objective. After a decade of evaluation, I have changed my mind about planting a new lawn or golf fairway with only a pure strain. I have just explained that common Kentucky bluegrass is no longer readily available and that furthermore some of the newer individual pure-strain seeds aren't living up to par (or should I say to their advertising?) as hoped for. Therefore, blends of Kentucky bluegrass varieties are *now* your best bet. Another reason for going with the blends is that some of the great varieties, like Merion (which I will talk about in the next answer), are exhibiting ominous signs that have turf scientists puzzled. In some parts of the country, Merion has developed a disease called stripe smut that is fatal to this once-great strain. This confounded smut is due to a fungus that is serious on some varieties but not on others. Turf scientists are discovering that minor diseases can become major ones, and also that disease resistance can break down in time, sometimes owing to a buildup of new strains of disease causing fungus. Thus the choice between a blend of bluegrass varieties and a pure stand of Kentucky bluegrass deserves careful consideration. The modern concept of blending involves selection of superior components that are compatible to produce a superior turf with better adaptation to wide variations in environmental conditions and generally better disease resistance.

Q.—Please list the many varieties of Kentucky bluegrass presently available to a homeowner. Which are the best to buy? It seems every seed company has varieties and brands that I never heard of before.

A.—Such a list would be quite impossible, for new varieties are popping up almost as frequently as grocery prices are changing. Some good ones are just test numbers at universities and turf grass supply companies, and by the time this book is published the numbers will have names and my list of varieties will be inadequate. Even so, I'll name some of the older varieties that I know about plus a few of the new varieties. Put the teakettle on and let's go through them. But first let me tell you this: I will discuss the varieties of Kentucky bluegrass pro and con, unlike so many articles that make them all sound faultless.

Merion. When Merion (discovered in 1936) first came out in

1947, fistfights broke out among impatient homeowners waiting in car lines backed up for blocks at nurseries to purchase this heavily advertised "wonder" grass. It was the first release of an improved elite variety of Kentucky bluegrass; heralded as faultless, it was an absolute success with homeowners. It is interesting to know how this beautifully colored, sun-loving grass was first discovered—and here, I am somewhat prejudiced forever in its favor. I'll tell you why. In the mid-thirties, a talented Italian greenkeeper (golf course superintendent) by the name of Joseph Valentine observed at the Merion Golf Club in Ardmore, Philadelphia, what the turf world knows today as Merion Kentucky bluegrass. It was truly the first of the wonder bluegrass varieties, which all other cultivars followed.

Although Merion is now having problems with stripe smut, a devastating disease requiring expensive control, it is an excellent grass with a wide leaf and an outstanding color if fertilized heavily. It doesn't do well under thatched or droughty conditions, and its seedling stage has a slow development. During prolonged dry weather, the mature grass deteriorates if not soaked heavily once a week (but frankly, so do other varieties). Because of its enemy stripe smut (dark black vertical lines along the leaf blade), it should not be grown alone, but should be mixed with a smut-resistant Kentucky bluegrass variety such as Fylking, Pennstar, or Nugget.

Adelphi. I am much more partial to dark green grasses than to lighter shades of green because any attacking fungus always will look bad on light green turf. The public, I'm sure, prefers the dark green color. Adelphi, the first man-made grass hybrid, is one of the best-looking grasses, and is now the United States government's standard for the color of dark green for all future bluegrasses. It has good resistance to leaf spot disease as well as to fusarium blight. Adelphi can withstand a low-mower cut. It blends well with glade and merion grasses. A combination of the three would definitely produce a superior lawn.

Fylking. Here is a superior, low-growing bluegrass, one of the first. It has a ground-hugging habit (prostrate) and a somewhat interlacing leafy growth. Fylking has a bent-over style of growth (almost 90 degrees) and arched narrow leaves; it grows fast and shows excellent resistance to some diseases (but is subject to powdery mildew and fusarium blight). Like many other Kentucky bluegrasses, this regal grass has an outstanding root development, called a rhizome development, whereby rootlike stems send leafy shoots above the surface of the ground and at the same time send roots down from the stems' lower side.

Fylking needs nitrogen fertilization to perform well and should be mowed low for best performance. Like other Kentucky bluegrasses, it doesn't require more than 1 to 2 pounds of seed per 1,000 square feet to establish a good turf. Use a sharp mower and give this grass the time that it deserves, and you can have an outstanding lawn. Keep in mind, though, that some turf specialists report that Fylking has a rather poor wear tolerance, especially on lawns with a lot of use. In my opinion, Fylking is best suited to golf courses and professionally maintained courts and estates. Incidentally, by now that bikini-clad gal in the Fylking advertisements has surely called your attention to this grass. However, contrary to such signals of warmth, it doesn't do well in the cold winters of the Canadian prairie provinces. Also I might add that in the warmer climates of the cool region, Fylking has been showing ominous signs of being susceptible to *Rusarium roseum,* which—more foreboding still—is moving northward within the region (very serious from central Illinois to Michigan). However, this grass has good resistance to both melting out (*Helminthosporium*) and stripe smut,* which is a very important credit. Fylking was chosen as the official grass for Expo 74, the first world's fair ever to celebrate the environment. The fair was held on a 100-acre site in Spokane, Washington. The architectural committee chose this variety to please an estimated five million visitors.

Pennstar. A good Kentucky bluegrass variety released from Penn State in 1968 and placed on the market shelves in 1971. Pennstar has a low growth habit that permits low mowing. It is highly resistant to several of the bluegrass diseases, such as stripe smut, rust, and melting out. This grass has a pleasing, medium green color that blends extremely well with other varieties of the low-growing bluegrasses. Pennstar can be kept looking well with

* See the chapter on diseases.

moderate management, which means it can be used successfully in most areas of the Kentucky bluegrass country. However, in cold places like Saskatoon, Saskatchewan, where I was born, it winter-kills severely (as do Merion and Fylking). Though I have perhaps characterized Fylking and Pennstar differently, I truthfully see no differences between them; they are both good performers, although Pennstar has a slightly better adaptation to low fertility.

Warren's A-20 Kentucky. This grass is not yet propagated from seed, but is grown from sod or sod plugs. According to my friend Ben Warren, A-20 will possibly be available as seed in two or three years. This excellent grass produces a dense, weed-free turf. It is highly resistant to melting out and leaf smuts and has an above-average resistance to fusarium blight and powdery mildew. It is an aggressive, low-growing variety. A-20 has found a perma-nent place on both golf courses and home lawns. I have this carpet-like grass on some of my closely cut fairways. Another strong recom-mendation comes from my barber, who has this grass on his front lawn. The deep green color is outstanding. One drawback with any lawn grass is how to repair an open spot that is worn or damaged; you can't seed it, since that would cause off-color spots, so for uni-formity you must repair it with sod or plugs (that is, if you want to keep a pure variety of a vegetatively produced grass species). Several varieties, such as Merion, Adelphi, and Windsor, will blend very well with Warren's A-20. Otherwise use a "weak sister" like Sodco in spring, and A-20 will probably crowd it out eventually.

Nugget. This attractive lawn grass came out of Alaska about ten years ago. Nugget produces a dense turf; it can be mowed quite low and still produce a good dense sod. Mow this grass 1 inch with a sharp mower. Its winter hardiness is excellent, but its winter color is poor. Nugget is a good lawn grass for northern portions of the bluegrass belt. It has good shade tolerance, but greens up later in the spring than other commercial varieties. Nugget is very susceptible to dollar spot and needs to be fertilized in August to reduce disease incidence.

Sodco. This strain comes from Indiana's Purdue University. Sodco also has good disease tolerance against stripe and flag smut and dollar spot. It is, however, a very slow grower. This drawback hinders its establishment in lawns and limits its competitive ability with weeds and other grasses. Sodco is another lawn grass with good color that tolerates close mowing, but like all other improved strains, it needs good nutrition and lawn management. Sodco is best used as a filler in a seed blend.

Windsor. One of the pioneers in the field of improved Kentucky bluegrass, Windsor is a good overall performer, especially during the first few years after its establishment. Windsor is a trifle susceptible to everything, but with careful management, it is a good grass for home lawns; it has a texture finer than Merion and it needs only moderate fertility to look attractive. However, it is *very susceptible* to stripe smut; therefore, a homeowner must be prepared to inaugurate a vigorous disease prevention program. At lower fertility levels, weeds may invade this grass. So give it lots of plant food. (This goes for all improved strains.) I must mention this variety if for no other reason than that it originated from O. M. Scott & Sons Co., which has done such an excellent job of making the public aware of good home lawns and their care. Of course, if a lawn is planted well and cared for diligently, the need for turf chemicals (excepting fertilizer) greatly diminishes.

O. M. Scott was also the first company to serve customers with attractive packaging and lawn care newsletters. Scott's gigantic advertising and sales promotion has made its turf products by far the most popular on the market. The massive advertising for Windsor had quite a bit to do with the decline of common Kentucky bluegrass, though in reality Windsor isn't that much better. According to sod growers, Windsor has another drawback; it loses color in early fall, before any of the other varieties. Windsor turns brown early. Nevertheless, in the high plains of the United States, Windsor produces an exceptionally fine turf—just one more argument for choosing a grass or blend of grass for your particular region. Another area where Windsor does very well (and I know this from personal observation) is central Illinois—provided, of course, that satisfactory fertilization is given.

Delta. A Canadian lawn grass developed in the capital city of Ottawa, Delta is a good replacement for common because it is one of the more vigorous seedling bluegrasses, it develops quickly, and it keeps right on growing. Along with fair color and a rapid vertical growth rate, it has low temperature tolerance, but its spring green-up is good. It has poor sod strength, though. Mow Delta high or it will thin out and become quite weedy. It is very susceptible to *Helminthosporium* (melting out). Its growth habit and appearance are similar to those of common, but it doesn't have the genetic diversity of common.

Baron. A new variety, which was developed in the Netherlands and has been extensively tested during the last two or three years in Canada and the United States, Baron is moderately dark green in color and has medium-coarse texture and a moderately low growth habit. Like many of the Kentucky bluegrasses, it has good low temperature hardiness and color retention. Its spring green-up is fair to good. This new variety establishes rapidly, which helps crowd out weeds and other undesirable grasses. It has a fair to good resistance to melting out and is reported to have good resistance to stripe smut. In my opinion, Baron Kentucky bluegrass is "a real comer."

These, then, are some of the major strains of Kentucky bluegrass. Others on the market include Prato, Victa, Sydsport, Glade, Arboretum, Nu-Dwarf, Arista, Campus, Primo, and Bonniblue. Many others are still only numbers. No seed supplier can possibly carry all varieties. A discriminating seed company will carry only those varieties that in the company's opinion grow well in the territory where it is located. It should be pointed out here that all of the Kentucky bluegrass strains I've mentioned above are cool-region grasses. Some strains, as experimental stations have proved time and time again, do better than others in particular parts of the cool grass region. You the homeowner should keep uppermost in mind that the best varieties of Kentucky bluegrass to purchase are those having a good resistance to both stripe smut and *Helminthosporium* leaf spot. It's very important that such varieties be included in any bluegrass mixtures or blends you buy. (Check a county extension advisor for varietal recommendations.)

Q.—What are some other important characteristics, besides low growth, deep color, and disease resistance, that turf scientists are hoping to breed or tailor into future varieties of Kentucky bluegrass?

A.—Turf scientists are seeking to develop further and further south better winter color, hardiness, seedling strength, and adaptability. In the North, they are trying to build in winterkill survival. In other words future varieties will be better suited to a broader range of soils and environments. Two other sought-for qualities are drought tolerance and better *wear* resistance, not only for athletic fields but for lawns used by large, active families. Finally, scientists are always seeking more information about how new varieties perform when blended together. Though good progress has been made, the science of turf grass blending is not fully developed yet, and so much of it is still largely a matter of guesswork. Future blends will give much better long-term performance.

Q.—Seed and some other turf products seem to be cheaper at chain drugstores, supermarkets, and department stores than at lawn and garden stores. Where do you recommend I buy my seed?

A.—Buy prescriptions at drugstores, groceries at supermarkets, and clothing at department stores. Give your seed business to the local lawn and garden centers. (I like hardware stores, also.) The owner is usually an independent who lives the year round in your community. He is trying to make a living and survive against the "super stores." And in this day and age of conglomerates, it isn't easy. So give him your business. If the lawn and garden independent fails, he goes out of business. If the "chains" fail, it's usually in just one phase of their merchandising. Stick with your local lawn and garden store. It will be to your benefit; he is more of an expert. His products are usually of quality, his prices are always competitive, and he won't let you down. He must live with you and stand behind what he sells you. Unlike ordinary run-of-the-mill clerks, he has the knowledge and willingness to help you with lawn problems. And here is a special economy-size hint for you: if you ask the owner of the lawn and garden store, he will probably be able to order you straight common Kentucky bluegrass seed. But remember this about any quality seeds: they may be the most expensive per pound, but they are always the best buy. Fast-cover, cheap seed packages are high in annual ryegrass. You don't want this for your lawn.

Q.—Please tell me in simple language what the terms *germination, purity, weed content, inert,* and *crop content* mean on the seed packages. Do the terms indicate high or quality seed content? I am confused.

A.—This question is frequently asked of me from all parts of our country. However, before answering the question, I should make certain things clear. The price of seed has gone up so much each year that I am afraid homeowners this year are more likely than ever to be purchasing more and more bargain-rate, inferior seed—and getting nothing for their money except serious lawn problems well after the great buy they got or the cheap seed is forgotten. Don't be tempted by bright-colored seed packages or by bags with hornswoggling phrases and convenient grip handles. Just make sure the seed you purchase is fine-textured and is a premium certified* seed or mixture. The law requires seed to be labelled fine-textured if it is, so pick the fine-textured package if you want the best for your lawn. Bargain-rate, fast-cover seed (with beautiful home lawns pictured on the package) is often the most costly, because the seed's purity and germination are lower than what is desired for a superior lawn. Usually these packages are high in temporary grasses.

Years ago the United States Department of Agriculture established standards that the seed industry must meet in order to sell seed. This important consumer law (state and federal) clearly states what must be printed on seed packages by the seed companies, and I will now acquaint you with pertinent facts about the terms used. Seed laws are definite and well conceived, although in most cases they were worded for farm seeds and not for lawn seeds. They need to be reconsidered for turf use.

Purity indicates quantity, *not quality*. This seeming contradiction often confuses the homeowner. Purity is the percentage by weight of a particular seed variety labelled on the package. This also applies to mixtures of more than one variety of grass species in a seed package. In such mixtures of grass seeds, each variety or species has to be listed with a separate percentage.

Germination indicates the percentage of pure seed that should develop into seedlings under standard laboratory testing (that is, grow in a prescribed time). The higher the germination percentage

---

* Guaranteed by the original developer to be a pure strain that meets stringent physical standards and has a known genetic history. In simple words, certified seed is produced from known parents and assures the homeowner top performance.

the better. You might ask, Why can't the germination be 100 percent? It seems that, according to laboratory tests, this just doesn't happen. Regardless, it is still impossible for every seed in your lawn to germinate anyway. But 100-percent germination is the ultimate goal turf scientists and turf seed companies are trying to reach, and someday we just might be able to accomplish it. Now, though, a warning: the older the seed, the lower the germination that is stated on the package. This is why it's important for you to always buy seed with the test date printed legibly on the package. Selling seed a year (often less) after dating is breaking the law. Seed that isn't sold within a year's (or season's) time, according to law, has to be sent back to be retested and relabelled. The stores can still sell it, but the germination test must be updated. The test dates look like this: 1/2/76.

Weed content. Be careful, please. The weed content should be under one-half of one percent. The lower the better. Weed content is the percentage by weight of all seeds in the package that are not pure seed (purity) or other crop content. Try to remember that the smallest possible percentage of weed content can still mean literally thousands of undesirable seeds coming up as weeds in your lawn.

Crop content. This doesn't mean wheat, oats, or barley. It really means weed seeds. Crop content could mean other crop grasses, such as bentgrass, fescue, rye, or *Poa annua,** which are not desirable in a bluegrass blend. Conversely, in a pure bentgrass seed package, Kentucky bluegrass or roughstalk bluegrass crop seed would be equally undesirable. Again, let me repeat: even the smallest percentage of crop could mean thousands of undesirable seeds. The weed content or crop content, depending on the nature of contamination, means that you are asking for trouble and wasting time and money.

Noxious weed is defined by state law. Beware. This percentage should be *zero, zero, zero* in any quality seed package. Many of the noxious weeds survive at lawn grass mowing heights, and could include other crops—*Poa annua* (also called annual blue-

---

* Annual bluegrass, a black sheep of the bluegrass family that dies out in the summer. Poa is considered a weed grass.

grass), clover, dandelion, crabgrass, chickweed, knotweed, and many more. Let me warn you now never to buy seed that has the harmless-sounding name of annual bluegrass under any of the previous headings. This annual bluegrass is none other than the notorious weed *Poa annua*. It will take over your lawn beautifully and then quickly die in the first hot spell of summer, leaving ugly spots of yellow green and eventually a brown lawn. *Poa* has driven many golf course superintendents (some of whom are now mowing grass with hand push mowers at state mental institutions) out of business. Another dangerous weed grass to avoid is tall fescue, also called Kentucky-31. Don't be deceived. This becomes unsightly clumps of grass with broad leaves and a terrific root system, which tends to lie close to the ground and so is hard to mow. (However, in the transition zone and in parts of the southern states, tall fescue makes an acceptable turf. See chapter 3.)

Inert. This simply means the remaining percentage by weight of material that is nothing more than a carrier, like chaff or corn cobs ground to a fluff. These carriers won't germinate, no matter how much you sprinkle. Thus, your only consideration is the fact that you are buying something and getting nothing. Often inert material is added to bargain seed to meet weight requirements. Inert matter should be under 5 percent of the total weight of the seed.

Well, there you have it. That's the way "goodness" and "badness" are measured in a seed container. Too bad people can't be labelled similarly. Just imagine how many politicians would be out of jobs—or in jail.

Now, after reading through this chapter, I would like to end it with a question (yes, another one!) I am frequently asked at garden clubs.

Q.—My lawn is full of heaven knows what type of grasses. Can you please tell me how I can tell Kentucky bluegrass plants from other species?

A.—A long time ago, when I was just a wild young "farmer" from Saskatchewan, a wonderful old greenkeeper, "Pops" Brinkworth, with whom I apprenticed at Jasper National Park golf course and who turned my life to turf grass maintenance, told me shortly before his death the simplest way to recognize Kentucky bluegrass. I'll tell it to you now. Take what you think is a bluegrass plant and look at it closely. If you see a set of fine, perfectly formed "railroad tracks" (veins) coming down the middle of the leaf, you have a bluegrass. Frankly, the technical description will only confuse you, except where it states that the leaf blade tip of Kentucky bluegrass is pointed like the bow of a boat.

2

Cool-Region Grasses for Shade and Lawn Restoration

Iɴ ᴛʜɪs ᴄʜᴀᴘᴛᴇʀ we will deal primarily with the shade turfgrasses and the grasses a homeowner should use for renovation of old lawns and bad spots. The questions I am asked most frequently by worried homeowners concern shade and lawn restoration. Both are serious problems to the homeowner. Therefore, we will deal extensively with the subjects of shade and restoring old and spotty lawns in this very important chapter. I will also make some comments on grass mixtures.

Shade lawn grasses and other lawn covers. Trees and lawn grasses complement each other in beautifying a yard. However, in about one out of four home lawns, trees in a landscape present problems to the homeowner because of the difficulties in maintaining the grass in the shade beneath these trees. So the major point to be made in this chapter is how to select proper grass species to compensate for the light reduction under trees. Two outstanding shade grasses in the cool region are the creeping red fescues and *Poa trivialis*. Each can serve a different function when sown in the shade areas of your yard. In addition to these two, I am happy to say, there are now other shade grass performers derived from Kentucky bluegrass that are available for the first time as sod and seed. We will discuss all of these shade lawn grasses in the questions and answers in this chapter. But there are some significant factors I would like to bring out before we begin. In twenty-five years as a golf course superintendent and lawn consultant working with various types of species of grasses, I have made a few important observations. One is that in lightly shaded lawns, Kentucky bluegrass varieties do well, so it isn't usually necessary to include a shade grass in such areas. (For certain questionable cases, I will discuss mixing Kentucky bluegrass with a shade species.) Another observation is that even the best shade grasses won't perform well in *deep shade* under a dense tree canopy. This is one honest observation that other turf experts sometimes just won't face, and they continue to recommend shade grasses. Homeowners have as much chance of growing a lawn in deep shade as I have of swimming the English Channel. For homeowners with deeply shaded yards, I am going to recommend other ground covers, which are available in both the southern and northern regions of North America.

Our discussion of shade grasses, then, will deal only with recommendations for lawns having *medium-to-heavy** shade, that is, lawns having dim or partially sunny areas where some sort of shade grass can be grown with a fair degree of success. I have always felt that horticultural authors never really cover the many problems that homeowners encounter with shade grasses. Let's see if we can do so in this chapter.

The question asked more and more frequently by homeowners who hope that there may be an ultimate grass or solution for their long-suffering shady lawn is: What shade grass shall I use for my lawn with *medium-to-heavy* shade that has both dry and moist areas?

A.—This question is best answered first with a preamble on the shade grasses that are available to homeowners.

Fescues. It's too bad people have never become familiar with fescues for use in their home lawn. This probably is because there are fine and coarse fescues (the latter grow in clumps or bunches).

---

* In this book we will describe shade areas as light, medium, heavy, and deep, in that order of shade cover.

Fine and coarse fescues are used primarily as a mixture with Kentucky bluegrass for shady areas. I love the fine fescues. This extraordinary type of grass, in my opinion, is almost the perfect turf grass. Too bad fescues don't take to modern care. They need very little maintenance. Fescues like to be left alone. Fescues grow in both deep shade and sunlight, and even poor soils aren't a hindrance to them. I have rarely seen weeds in a good stand of fescue; it is one turf grass that holds them back successfully once it gets established. Fescues usually grow well under trees. They are disease-resistant in the more northern states, except to leaf spot (the further south the worse it gets), and take *minimal care*. With other grasses, tree competition for soil nutrients and moisture is sometimes a critical problem. But not with fescues. In fact, if you overwater or fertilize them more than very little, especially when they begin to go into their summer dormant stage, they will be damaged and fade out.

The dormant stage's color isn't very attractive, and as a result the homeowner won't leave it alone; he'll try to pep it up, which is a mistake with this particular shade grass. Chemicals are often damaging to fescues. In other words, tender loving care is not necessary and *not recommended*. In my opinion, a 100-percent fine fescue lawn would be the perfect lawn for the lazy man or the busy golfer. Remember also that any watering, except once in a great while, is especially bad on poorly drained soils in hot weather. One disadvantage of fine-leaf fescue is poor summer color, which is usually a green grey (and don't try to improve it with fertilizer). Fine fescue is also not available in sod by itself. And it doesn't like children running all over it making trails. Believe it or not, the fine fescues were used on putting greens by greenkeepers before creeping bent was found to be a better species for this close-cut special use.

Creeping red fescues are still mowed very low on flat, treeless areas in England, but don't try it in the Midwest if you are a homeowner. Mow it high. Fine fescues love the north country best. Their leaves are folded compactly together in a delicate, toothpicklike appearance to conserve moisture. If you carefully flatten the leaf, you'll find to your surprise that it is almost as wide as a Kentucky bluegrass leaf. I recommend fine fescues for areas where it is dry and where the shade cover is medium to heavy. Fine fescues do well in sandy and droughty areas.

If you have wet and dry shady areas, use a composite mixture of fine fescues and *Poa trivialis* (rough-stalk bluegrass or rough bluegrass; the English call it rough-stalk meadow grass). The fescue will grow in dry shady spots and the *Poa trivialis* will grow in the moist areas. *Poa trivialis* is a grass neither frequently used nor extensively advertised, and so is often overlooked by the homeowner. It shouldn't be. Nothing beats it for wet, shady areas (provided the areas have minimal traffic). Most garden centers now have *Poa trivialis* in combination with the fescues. It grows quite well, but tends to separate out in patches by itself and therefore is not the best mixer in a lawn. Buy this package if you have the conditions I have just described. But keep in mind that *Poa trivialis* is sold by its Latin, or generic, name, rather than by its common name, which is rough (it really isn't) bluegrass. The lower leaf sheath is roughened on mature shoots (has an onion skin appearance). So much for your newly discovered wet friend, *Poa trivialis*. Let's go back to the fescues now.

Good types of creeping red fescue are Pennlawn (cultivated from a strain found on a golf course long ago), Rainer, Illahee, Highlight, Dawson, and Ruby. Other fine-leaved old fescue varieties are Chewings fescue varieties (even finer-leaved than the creeping red fescue), but these types grow in bunches or tufts similar to the coarser fescues. Because of this, I don't recommend the use of old-type Chewings fescue alone or in a mixture. However, two new strains recently developed are a considerable improvement over the old Chewings fescue varieties. Their names are Jamestown and Wintergreen. Both do a commendable job. Buy them for shade lawns and impoverished lawns.

Q.—We have just seeded our new lawn and it has *light medium* shade. We planted a mixture of Kentucky bluegrass and creeping red fescue. Did we do the right thing?

A.—Provided your seedbed preparation was correct (see chapter 4), I think you're on the right track. You aren't taking chances with this mixture. Remember, a mix essentially provides environmental adaptability, which is desirable in a location characterized by variability in sunlight intensity. My experience with light shade, as I said earlier in this chapter, indicates that Kentucky bluegrass will grow by itself quite well with good management—especially the newer varieties. However, the homeowner frequently can't distinguish between light shade, medium shade, and heavier shade.

I have observed thousands of lawns where exactly this inability to judge shade density resulted in poor-looking lawns. One homeowner planted pure stands of sun-loving Kentucky bluegrass seed or sod in dark shade, and then began wondering what happened to the grass two years later (or even sooner) when it started to thin out owing to lack of sunlight, which the bluegrass needs.

In your case, the Kentucky bluegrass will do okay in the light shade areas, and the fescue should take over where the shade is more intense. But there is one disadvantage in mixing bluegrass and fine-leaved fescues for home lawns: given high management or ultra-care, home lawns with fescue will soon disappear. They will thin out or become invisible. The reason is that the more you water and fertilize fescues (which Kentucky bluegrass requires for best results), the worse they get.

So let me repeat, fescues have poor tolerance to the fertility and moisture of luxury bluegrass management. Fescues like to be left alone. So be careful in your management of these two excellent grasses when they are mixed. You can have both grass species growing in your yard only if you know their strengths and requirements.

Q.—Is there one grass now, besides fescues or a mixture of Kentucky bluegrass and fescue, that I can safely use in light-to-medium shade and give it top attention?

A.—Yes, there is. One good new shade variety of the bluegrass species is called Warren's A-34. It is a relatively new discovery that supposedly stands shade up to 60 percent quite well. Its paramount forte is that it's resistant to powdery mildew. A-34 is available in sod form as well as seed.

A couple of years ago, a young superintendent friend of mine sodded some of this Kentucky blue shade grass under a maple tree where nothing else would grow, and so far it is doing beautifully. So it looks like A-34 can also grow in shades darker than just light to medium. But my recommendation is to use it only in shade areas similar to that described in your question. Warren's A-34 is also guaranteed.

Sod dealers and seed dealers throughout the bluegrass country are blending shade-tolerant varieties. A nursery in the Chicago area is combining five new varieties of Kentucky bluegrass, three of which will stand light-to-medium shade; the nursery will have it in sod form soon. The five blends are Fylking, Adelphi, and the three alleged shade-resistant grasses—Glade, Nugget, and Victa (Nugget especially has been getting glowing reports). But let's wait and see. There is no doubt in my mind that turf scientists will continue to breed new and better Kentucky bluegrass strains to withstand shade. This is excellent news for the homeowners who have been suffering long enough with problems of shade lawns.

Q.—What are the areas where you specifically recommend mixtures of bluegrass and fescues?

A.—I recommend them in sunny areas of low-to-medium intensity of lawn management, as well as in dry light shaded areas with similar care. Good examples of areas where the bluegrasses and the fescues, at 2½ to 3 inches mowing height, make valuable companions are small or nonirrigated parks, memorial gardens, cemeteries, large industrial lawns, golf course roughs, estates, golf course clubhouse lawns, pastures, and some athletic fields. And oh yes, they are good for all golfers who don't like lawn work and for people who just don't have the time. Technically speaking, a shaded lawn should be mowed *higher* because the root system is shallower. Also, a shade lawn has a lower density and its carbohydrate resource is less.

Q.—Is there a grass I can grow in deep shade? I'm having terrible problems. My shaded lawn is thin and sickly looking. I feel like giving up.

A.—Give up. It's the only sensible thing to do, no matter what other opinions you might hear. I have to honestly state that trying to grow lawns successfully in deep shade just can't be done by homeowners. Damn few experts can succeed. Frankly, it is nearly impossible because the grass plant needs at least some sunlight to grow vigorously and stay healthy. When this very important element is lacking, even the best grass won't grow. Of course you can try trimming lower branches, pruning some crown branches, or even root-pruning to reduce shading and competition between trees and turf. But unless it's done expertly, you can do more damage than good.

Q.—What would you describe as deep shade?

A.—Deep shade (it sounds like an X-rated greenkeeper's movie!) is an area where the sun doesn't hit the ground at all during the hours of daylight, or perhaps just sporadically here and there in a few open spots.

Q.—What ground cover, then, do you recommend for a deeply shaded lawn? The grasses recommended by various seed companies and turf experts have been damn expensive, and I'm not getting any younger.

A.—Since grass will never grow successfully in this type of shade, quit trying. I'll be happy to recommend low ground covers that can be successfully planted in deep shade.

There are two possible ways of replanting your shaded yard with ground covers other than grass. One method is more expensive, though, and it deals with spot cover only in areas that are completely grassless or weak looking. In these areas, I suggest that you blend low-foliage ground cover other than grass with any existing shade grass that may be thriving in a few areas where it gets some spot sunlight. You can separate the surviving grass and the new low-foliage ground cover by means of a metal edging. Also, if you have moss, leave it alone. Moss looks nice. I love it in a shaded yard, but it's very sensitive to heavy traffic.

A long time ago, I made a mistake that I will forever regret. A dear friend of mine had a deeply shaded lawn with lots of weeds, little grass, and fluffy green moss, which my friend loved. But he hated weeds with a passion, especially when they started to interfere with his silly old moss. So one day he asked me to get rid of the unsightly weeds but to please save the moss if at all possible (I suspect because the moss cover meant he had to mow his lawn only four times a year or less). Well, to make a long story short, I made one slight miscalculation (that's all you need) with the chemical formulation and killed not only the weeds and all the scraggly grass, but also the sensitive, fairylike playground moss that my friend liked so much. Of course the lawn never looked the same, nor did it ever recover. There was nothing left after I got through with it. After that, we had a hard time establishing a shade lawn, and finally he gave up and moved away—I think because he had lost his beloved moss.

Now let's discuss the other method of establishing your deep-shade lawn with a low ground cover other than grass. Completely planting the whole yard from one end to the other with new tolerant shade cover would be hard on your pocketbook and perhaps even somewhat ridiculous. Instead, I recommend that you establish paths or trails in between the low ground covers and play areas. Use materials like tanbark, cocoa hulls, wood blocks, wood chips, or cheaper materials like red gravel, sand, or other stone aggregates. In the deep shade of my small back yard I have placed a layer of red gravel over 2 inches of sand, which is on plastic paper (to keep out the weeds). All I do is rake once a week, to level and smooth out the gravel, and it looks great. No upkeep.

Q.—What low-foliage growing ground covers do you recommend for deep, deep shade?

A.—There are many low-growing foliage plants that will do well in deep shade and yet be aesthetically tasteful. Some of these are pachysandra (Japanese spurge), *Vinca minor* (periwinkle, myrtle), Euonymus (especially *colorata*, or purple leaf winter creeper, and *vegetus*, or big leaf winter creeper), and *Polygonum reynowtica* (also called fleece flower, with reddish pink flowers and brilliant foliage in the fall). Ferns and ivy (English or Baltic) may also be used.

All of these may be interspersed with such shade-loving flowers as begonias, day lilies, and impatience, or bright-leafed coleus or caladiums. Low bush shrubs can also be used with success.

Some ground covers for shade in the South are *Helxine loleirolii* (baby's tears), *Planipetal vancouveria* (inside-out flower), sedum, partridge berry, *lippia* (in the Southwest), carpet bugle, common thrift, and sweet woodruff. Another good one is mondo for under spreading oak trees. Mondo comes from China and is an evergreen perennial. Extremely shade-tolerant, it is sometimes called lily grass.

A few of the cheaper and wilder forms of ground covers that I have seen homeowners successfully transplant from a natural habitat to their yards are wild strawberry and gill-over-the-ground (sometimes called creeping Charlie, and boy! does this weed spread in moist shade areas). Another one you can't beat for damp areas is an herb called mint, or spearmint.

Q.—What can I do for my bluegrass lawn where I have a trouble area of heavy shade and problems with powdery mildew? (It is white and powderlike in appearance.)

A.—Thin out the heavy-shade area by careful pruning of your trees to give the area more sunlight and better air circulation. But do this only if it's feasible. For heaven's sake, don't cut down any trees (unless they were planted too close together initially, a not uncommon problem). Just prune them. Get a professional tree expert if it's a difficult job. All of your trees probably need pruning anyway, so here is an opportunity for you to kill two birds with one stone. But please remember, it takes only a few minutes to down a tree, but a lifetime to grow one.

Another method is to take out or completely renovate the shaded area and sow a shade-tolerant grass species like creeping red fescue. If you don't want to do this, then a good solution is to spray the powdery mildew with a chemical available at lawn garden stores. Follow the instructions carefully. Do not try to whip the heavy mildew off with a bamboo pole or a long bendable stick in the early morning, as I have seen done. It's best to buy the right chemical to kill this organism. Just whipping it off is not an effective remedy. This will only spread it and inoculate the rest of the grass with powdery mildew.

Q.—What about mowing a shady lawn? At what height do you suggest I set my mower? We are presently mowing at 1½ inches with a reel-type mower, and the lawn looks dreadful afterward. To further compound the problem, roots are protruding all over, with bumps and depressions, and the ground stays muddy a long time after even the slightest rain. In spring, it's impossible to walk on the lawn or to mow it. Everything is squishy and scalped. Where do I go from here?

A.—If you persist with your present mowing program, you'll soon be without a lawn. Mowing height is a problem that I am glad to set straight once for all in this book. Low mowing, in my opinion, whether on a shaded lawn or *otherwise,* is the one *major* mistake homeowners make in North America. A long time ago, when we were a little more sensible (at least our fathers and grandfathers were), we mowed lawns at reasonable heights (2½ inches or longer) and the grass seemed to thrive splendidly (or was I too young to remember?). Sadly, however, somewhere along the line we lost whatever sense of horticulture we had and started to mow grass shorter and shorter, which is only proper on the golf course, where the stoloniferous creeping bentgrass can tolerate low mowing. Did our low mowing result from watching Arnold Palmer too much on TV and maybe craving a home lawn like a golf green or fairway, nice and short, or was it the result of too much promotion through the news media? Let me tell you something. I have, believe it or not, actually seen lawns owned by ardent golf enthusiasts who, after watching golf programs (and perhaps consuming too much pretzels and beer), went out and cut their lawns down to the ground because they wanted "their turf" to look like a beautiful golf course. It can't be done, not with ordinary grass. Later on we'll discuss a grass that you can mow low, but I don't recommend it for home lawns. It's too difficult to maintain.

Having short grass on shaded lawns is much more difficult than having home lawn turf grass on a level surface with lots of sunlight and special dwarf varieties of Kentucky bluegrass. In the shaded lawn, the short mowing problem is usually compounded by knobby roots, trunks, bumps, depressions, heaving in the spring, and, of course, inadequate sunlight. My recommendation is a minimum of 2½ inches for sunny yards (see the chapter on mowing for some exceptions, e.g., new dwarf grass varieties), and 3 inches for shaded lawns (especially as you move southward). Here are my reasons. First, remember that the more leaf the grass plant has, the better the process of photosynthesis* works, which gives you more and stronger leaves, deep root penetration, and richer, fuller growth. Secondly, mowing too low is asking for other troubles. Here is what happens. Your poor mower is cutting so low at 1½

---

* Photosynthesis: the combining of carbon dioxide and water to form sugar and oxygen in the green plant when it is exposed to sunlight.

inches (especially when the ground is soft) that the blades hit every root, bump, and low spot. They also scalp the peaked grass mounds that are sometimes found around tree trunks. This is ridiculous. Not only does low mowing damage the shade grass, but on uneven ground it dulls your mower blades and rattles and disturbs the whole machine. It could also prove very dangerous to you, if suddenly the mower blades slammed into something hard and the mower rebounded off a root towards you. Or God forbid that a young child should be mowing the lawn, which is frequently allowed by careless or lazy adults. (I don't recommend children under 14 years of age mowing lawns, because I have seen too many accidents.) So why take chances with your mower, your grass, and your limbs? Mow at 3 inches and I'll tell you what you'll get: the surprise of your life. Your family, especially the kids, will be delighted. The change will transform a scalped and unsightly yard into a shade lawn of flowing verdant green and healthy grass. Raise your mower to 3 inches.

Q.—My Kentucky bluegrass lawn withstands a short cutting of 1½ inches in the front yard, where I have full sun, but the fully shaded backyard lawn looks like the dickens cut at the same height. Am I mowing the backyard too low? What shall I do?

A.— Raise the mower to a higher setting for the front yard and then try this higher setting on the backyard. Your letter comes from Minnesota, and fescue can usually tolerate a lower mowing in the northern states than in the South. But 1½ inches is too low. Go higher. An alternative is for you to get another mower just for the backyard. But set it at 3 inches.

Q.—What kind of mower do you recommend for a shady lawn? Reel or rotary?

A.—I recommend a reel mower for lawns that will receive top-notch maintenance throughout the growing season from home-owners who are interested in having the best (and who do not go around with mowers carelessly running into trees, roots, walks, flower beds, dogs or neighbors' cars.) Otherwise, get a rotary. Keep it at a high cut with the blade very, very sharp. (See chapter 6.)

Q.—How many times a year should I fertilize my red fescue shade lawn, and can I do it in July or August, when it usually turns off-color?

A.—My recommendation for fertilizing a shade lawn is twice a year, spring and fall. Never do it in warmer weather, especially in hot months like July and August, because if you do, you and the fescue lawn will soon part company. Fescues respond best to fertilizer in the cool months of the growing season. So be careful. Remember also that fescues decline when they are overfed. Let me also make clear that I am against any homeowner fertilizing any type of grass in the hot stress months of July and August. You risk burning the lawn, as well as setting the stage for disease, and you are reducing heat and drought tolerance.

Q.—My shade lawn looks fine except around the trees, where it is thin and spindly. What should I do to make it thicker?

A.—Double-fertilize around your trees when you normally fertilize your whole shade lawn as recommended, in spring and fall. Simply go a second time around the trees, preferably with a cyclone spreader. (Be sure to water carefully under the trees where you double-fertilized; otherwise fertilizer injury might occur to the grass.) This will help force turf growth in an area that has high competition from tree roots. Also double-fertilize next to heavy shrubbery, where the turf is usually a little sparse. Keep in mind, though, that because of restricted light, there are fewer carbohydrates for root growth and tillering in deep shade. Therefore, the carrying capacity of that environment is not adequate for a dense turf, and extra fertilization is not the answer for this plant species in *extreme shade.* Another ground cover instead of grass should be planted.

Q.—What about rolling a lawn? Is it beneficial, and what time of year is best? Spring?

A.—This often-asked question is here for a good reason. I don't recommend rolling any dense, uniform lawn. It doesn't do a bit of good. The real time to roll a lawn smooth and get all the undulations out by careful grading is *before* seeding or laying new sod, not after the grass has matured and taken good root. To level any bumps or mounds after the grass has spent a couple of seasons growing, a homeowner would need a power roller the size that contractors use for rolling asphalt or building highways, not the puny little hand roller that you buy from a store and fill with water. That type of roller is acceptable for rolling seed or sod just after it's been planted, but not for a good mature stand of grass. I am advising you not to waste time by rolling sunny lawns after they have developed. However, *I do recommend* rolling shady lawns—but only in early spring, and even then the weather has to be right. Roll when the ground in your shade lawn is almost dried out, never when it is wet and soggy.

Why roll only a shade lawn? Because there is a difference. In shade lawns and in areas around trees and sometimes shrubs, the ground stays wet and waterlogged longest. (It is also usually the barest.) This wet condition is further aggravated by more heaving of the ground there than occurs in treeless areas, and this condition gets worse where roots are particularly close to the surface. As a result, shady lawns in spring are usually bumpy and uneven, with the grass loosely heaved up and split open in clumps and bunches, sometimes with the roots exposed.

In many areas there are grassless spots. Owing to the muddy condition of the ground, mowing is almost impossible for homeowners who set their mowers too low. My recommendation is to wait patiently until the ground becomes reasonably dry and friable. Then fill up your roller and get to work, taking wide turns so as not to damage the lawn further with sharp, cutting turns. After rolling is usually a good time to fertilize. If you have a place that *never* dries, don't fill your roller with too much water. Use a roller just heavy enough to push down the grass, but not so heavy it forms a crustlike compaction.

There is one other tip I might suggest before you roll. If the ground is loose and friable (sometimes with long cracks), throw some fine fescue seed on the dry spots or in the cracks. Then roll your lawn and press the seed down. (No raking is necessary.) If you do this and also fertilize your shady lawn, as I have suggested, you will be rewarded. You will trigger an excellent growing reaction with only one possible drawback. If you do all this too early in the spring, you will be wasting seed. But what the heck! Take a chance. Even if there is doubt in your mind about the weather, remember that you are only spot seeding and anything wasted won't amount to much. On the other hand, if your timing is right, you'll hit a green jackpot.

Q.—We are seeding a brand-new shady yard that is high and dry. What seed do you recommend, and how much?

A.—I suggest a good creeping red fescue for your well-drained and shaded property. Use 4 pounds of fescue per 1,000 square feet. This is twice as much as I recommend for Kentucky bluegrass lawns, but there is over three times more seed per pound in Kentucky bluegrass than there is in a pound of fine-leaved fescue. So go heavier.

GRASSES FOR LAWN AND SPOT RENOVATION

There are many reasons why home lawns get shabby and finally deteriorate. And the homeowner is not always to blame. Mother Nature has her unpredictable idiosyncrasies. Flooding rains, extremely cold winters, tropical storms, unusually long spells of hot, humid weather, and abrupt changes in the seasons all contribute to endanger outdoor plant life. But we have almost no control over these things. When bad weather comes, we try to remedy any damage we can and hope for the best. But our concern here is with lawns whose poor condition is the fault of the homeowner.

A run-down home lawn with bare spots all over it is like a person who hasn't been taking care of himself—no pep, no vigor, listlessness, and perhaps going downhill fast. The difference, of course, between a deteriorating person and deteriorating grass plants is that once the sick person begins to realize that there is something physically the matter with him, he can remedy his condition with medication, rest, balanced diet, and vitamins, or by going on the wagon. But when the grass in your yard gets into such a dismal condition, its recovery and survival depend on someone else. And that someone is you, the homeowner.

Of course if we just left the grass alone and let it grow to its normal natural height (up to 2 feet or so), it would be perfectly fine. At this hay-field height, the root and leaf systems are vigorous enough to derive all needed nutrition and moisture from *one spot,* and the wild grass seeds falling at harvest time would take care of any open spots. But we don't want a hay-field lawn. We have cultivated and domesticated certain grass species until we have turf types to suit our needs—grass that will grow low, thick, tight, and lush. Instead of hay fields, we try to have attractive showplaces in our yards. Lawn grass (especially the new cultivars) can't possibly be very attractive unless the homeowner carries out a management program of good grooming and care. Anything less will result in a lawn of poor quality. It is also well to remember that grass, shrubs, flowers, and other plant life start to deteriorate (and depreciate) as soon as they begin to grow. As time goes by, the only living things that contribute to the investment of your property are the trees. Trees alone of all plant life can be virtually left alone if properly situated and planted, and they will keep looking more beautiful and stronger as long as you live. But even trees need attention once in a while.

Over the years I have discovered there are three types of people who, more than anybody else, allow lawns to run down. Number one is the homeowner who gets spring fever a couple of times a year. He works enthusiastically in his yard in the spring; impulsively buys lawn and garden books, seed catalogs, and garden equipment; and then unexplainably stops and lets the lawn decline—until the next time he is possessed. He also switches turf product brands frequently.

The second type consists of the "mod group," the young homeowners who move into new homes in new communities and who lack any knowledge, comprehension, or sense of horticulture. These nice young couples often think that if the lawn is beautifully green when it is first installed (a sodded, or "instant," lawn, the most common type today in new communities), then by golly it should remain that way for the rest of its life if it is given a sprinkle and maybe some wishful thinking now and then. They haven't learned that nothing beats a little common sense and hard work. The lawn might look great the first year, but after that it starts going to pot because the young owners don't have the know-how to get it looking attractive again. They would be better off seeding a lawn. At least it's cheaper and they would learn more about grass. Another type of new homeowner is the one who is wildly enthusiastic and has a keen interest for about two years, but then finds better things to do with his time, like golf or a new wife.

The third type (most numerous of all) honestly doesn't give a damn. A yard to them is just a place in which to work and play. They are probably the happiest and least frustrated of all homeowners. Their children run all over the brown lawn with their friends, digging holes, playing tag or hide-and-seek, or tossing a ball to their dog or to each other. Mom and Dad and the kids *use* their lawn; they see it as a property for family traffic and not a hands-off, feet-off, regal showpiece which many turf experts and commercial companies have psyched us into thinking it should be. Basically, a lawn is to be used by a homeowner. For all those conscientious homeowners who try to have handsome lawns and also use them, I am happy to report that the homeowner who "doesn't give a damn" is sometimes a paradox who shows sudden concern for improving his lawn. Then watch out, because when this fellow finally notices his worn-out brown lawn, he becomes a working demon, energetically starting to repair his disgustingly sick grass and frequently yelling at the kids and dogs to hightail it. Can't they see he's working? What the hell is this? White Sox Ball Park? And Mabel, where is my beer? I guess this chapter is really for this typical American individual and his family. Along with the other two groups, they need just a little guidance to help them put their shoddy lawns into respectable shape again.

In the previous chapter, we discussed Kentucky bluegrass lawns for sunny locations, and at the beginning of this chapter, we covered the prominent desirable grasses for shade lawns. Now we start a third category—grasses for spot-seeding and for complete lawn renovation. And I recommend the *perennial ryegrasses*.

I am sure this will come as a surprise to many homeowners, especially the old-timers, who have always renovated with Kentucky bluegrass, not the ryegrasses. But don't be unduly upset. This method is better and will make the job of lawn renovation much easier, because there are superior turf grasses tailored now for practically every need. In my opinion, the new perennial ryegrasses are best for lawn renovation.

Ryegrasses in the past have been used mostly as "nurse" grasses or for instant cover. In other words, ryegrasses historically have demonstrated an ability to cover rapidly a piece of ground with something usually not permanently desirable. But good news is in store for the homeowner. During the past few years some outstanding varieties of perennial ryegrasses have been discovered. And while at this writing I still don't recommend the ryegrasses for your permanent lawn, no matter how improved they are, I do recommend them wholeheartedly for old lawn and spot renovation. I have several reasons for this recommendation. The improved varieties have a darker color than the apple green hue of the old ryegrasses, so they blend much better with the permanent Kentucky bluegrasses. The new strains also have a longer life expectancy, durability, and a much finer leaf blade. And they don't require much maintenance. Turf scientists are working to build into them an even better winter hardiness. The new strains are easier to mow, which is certainly good news, because the perennial ryegrasses we have known have always been tough to mow and leave a ragged appearance. However, I suggest using a sharp reel mower, not a rotary machine, on all ryegrasses.

Put these outstanding advantages together with the ability of ryegrasses to germinate and grow faster than other northern turf grasses and you have a remarkable grass to spot-seed in your deteriorating home lawn. Groundkeepers have been doing this for years in athletic stadiums. I can assure you that these fine new strains of ryegrasses mix so well with other grasses that no one will know you put anything but the best in your old spotty lawn. Permanent grasses like Kentucky bluegrass and red fescue are much harder to establish in an old lawn.

It's been my observation that most homeowners with spring fever overseed their lawns. No amount of instruction will ever make them believe that this is a fruitless waste of time, which often introduces weedy perennial grasses into the lawn. Seed germinates slowly in cold temperatures, especially in ground just thawed out after a cold winter. Sad to say, some commercial seed companies actually encourage this practice. If you're determined to do it, try seeding with a new variety of ryegrass. Your chances with it are much better for germination than with other grasses, especially if you can catch a warm spell or two.

Best of all, I like the vigorous and thick primary root system of the new varieties, which spear boldly into compacted ground and take good root even when other grasses are present. In other words, the perennial ryegrasses are not afraid of a little competition, especially in a weak lawn that needs repair. I recommend seeding the ryegrasses in late April and the other perennial grasses, like the fine fescues and bluegrasses (if you still insist on using them for renovation), in early May.

Some of the perennial improved ryegrasses are Manhattan, Pennfine, Norlea, NK-100, NK-200, and Pelo. (I use Manhattan on my golf course with great results.)

But enough palaver. Let's have some questions and answers.

Q.—How fast will the perennial ryegrasses germinate?

A.—Under ideal conditions, which means temperatures consistently over 65 degreees, the seedlings will be out in four or five days.

Q.—How fast is the germination of other perennial grasses, such as Kentucky bluegrass varieties, fescues, and *Poa trivialis*?

A.—Fourteen to twenty-eight days for Kentucky bluegrass (depending on conditions), less for the others.

Q.—How do you suggest that I renovate bare spots on my lawn? Every time I try, nothing comes up, or if it does, the grass soon shrivels and dies.

A.—I think bare spots in the lawn dismay and frustrate more homeowners than anything else. They try and try to reseed and renovate their tired lawns, but year after year it's the same old story—little survives. So here's the solution to the stigma of bare spots, once and for all. We will use the improved varieties of perennial ryegrasses instead of whatever the homeowner has been using. First, let me warn you, never try any lawn renovation, large or small, in mid-season when the weather is hot. Instead, spot-renovate in spring or fall (fall preferably, because this is Mother Nature's time). This advice applies to the renovation of a complete lawn, also. In hot weather the soft, weak seedlings will come up, but then falter and die. In spring or fall, their chance of survival is considerably greater, especially if you follow these instructions. Take a small metal rake or hoe and scratch up the spots. If there are noticeable depressions, fill them with pulverized soil taken from a bump or hump in your yard (some area you have been scalping in the past) or with loose soil from a flower bed or garden. If your yard is level, get a half cubic yard or several bushels of good top-dressing soil from your local soil and stone man. (Consult the yellow pages or ask your county extension agent or golf course superintendent who handles quality soil and fill in the area.) Now sprinkle by hand a little complete fertilizer (see chapter 1) on the worked-up soil. Rake it in and then seed with one of the new perennial ryegrasses I have recommended. Tap or press down the seed with your feet; don't rake it in. Most homeowners rake the seed in too deeply, and when it doesn't come up, they wonder what happened to it. Just step on it firmly. The ryegrass will come up even if the seed is visible after the tamping or stamping, so don't worry. The next step is to cover the seeded spot with about a quarter of an inch of cheap peat moss. Then water gently but thoroughly, and sit back and wait for it to grow. (Keep the spots moist.) Mow *over* the seedlings when they come up. But don't let heavy clippings lie on the new young grass, because the seedlings might suffocate. Remember, if your mower is set at 2½ inches, it won't be cutting into seedlings until the new grass reaches that height, which is my recommended height for the first mowing of your young grass. Be sure to use a sharp mower. (As I said before, I prefer a reel mower to a rotary, especially with ryegrass.) Homeowners can't always afford the best type of mower, but they can afford a good sharpening. Also, don't worry about the difference in color between seedlings and your permanent old grass of mixed varieties, which most likely is of many hues. After the seedlings mature, their color will blend so well with your potpourri of Kentucky bluegrass or other mixtures of grasses that even the community "expert" won't notice. If you follow this advice in spring or fall, before there's any really hot weather, you will seldom need to water the spots. Bare spots that I seed on my golf course rough always fill in without a sprinkle from me.

Q.—Is there another way of repairing open spots, except with seed? What about sod? How do I go about laying it down?

A.—Very good question. Sod is a good, quick way to patch bare spots in your yard. (I prefer, though, to use sod on extra-large spots or on large, unturfed, open areas of a yard rather than on small spots.) First work up the soil and get it ready the way you would for seeding small bare spots. But don't fertilize. You might put on too much and burn the severed roots. It comes to mind that first you had better find out whether you are near a sod nursery or a reputable lawn and garden store that can get you a few strips. Many times lawn and garden stores have sod piled in front at very reasonable prices for quick sale. Be sure to measure the quantity you will need to lay over your prepared bare spot areas. When laying down and fitting the patching sod, make sure it is no higher than adjacent turf; otherwise, scalping will occur. After laying the sod, roll it and then water it very thoroughly. Three days later, repeat the rolling and watering. Do this four times during the next twelve days or so. After that, top-dress it a couple of times to improve smoothness, fertilize the entire area (it is too easy to burn sod by spot-fertilizing), and then start normal lawn maintenance. *Note:* Another good tip, and a money saver, is to cut strips or plugs from lawn turf adjacent to the vegetable or flower gardens and use this sod for plugging bare spots.

Q.—My lawn is in deplorable shape. The grass that is left is full of weeds in the open spots, and the turf is thin and spindly. How can I bring back the lawn to what it was before the kids and my lack of success with grass got at it? P.S. I've tried everything.

A.—Don't blame the kids. It's the degree of knowledgeable lawn care that usually makes the difference between success and failure. It's difficult to suggest easy-to-follow magic rules or to give blanket recommendations and be right all the time, but try this method and *be sure to follow all the steps.*

First, find out what types of weeds you have in your lawn and carefully eliminate them with a weed killer that's easy to obtain at any lawn and garden store. (You must identify the weeds correctly, so that the proper chemical is used.) After the weeds begin to succumb to the weed killer in about a week or so, inspect the vegetation that is left and see what grass you have. If your *total lawn crop,* after the weeds are killed, looks more than 50-percent shot, don't fool with it. You'll be wasting time and money. At this point there is no use kidding yourself about your lawn. No matter what you do to it, the lawn will always be an embarrassing eyesore. My unequivocal advice is to start all over and rebuild from scratch. Plow it under and either reseed completely or do the yard in sod. Believe me, it's the only way.

If, however, after the weeds have all died (or almost died) and you estimate (ask a neighbor to help) that over 50 percent of what's left is thriving grass, then you should renovate and try hard for a 100-percent comeback. Follow these important steps. Rake the whole lawn from one end to the other, thoroughly scratching up everything, especially the open spots and voids. (Rental power rakes, thinners, and sweepers are permissible if you know how to use them, but this is drastic action and extreme care must be taken.) Rake out all the thatch, old clippings, and debris, including any loose grass that may pull up. Have no qualms about pulling up the loose turf; if it comes up easily, you don't want it. It's weak and apparently has no root system, so rake it out, because it will never amount to anything. *Note:* After this severe action it might be advisable to look again carefully at the skimpy lawn. The hard raking could have reduced the overall grass to below the 50-percent level. If not, proceed with the next step, which is to overseed with a perennial ryegrass such as Manhattan or Pennfine. (Mix with the better bluegrass varieties if you wish.) My recommendation for overseeding, per 1,000 square feet, is somewhat similiar to the common sense method used in the South, although the quantity will be less. Some homeowners in the South overseed their Bermuda lawns each winter, usually with a common ryegrass for winter color (see chapter 3), using up to 20 pounds per 1,000 square feet. Golf courses take much more; in the southern states the Bermuda greens are overseeded with sometimes as much as 50 pounds per 1,000 square feet. My recommendation for renovating cool-region lawns is to use 6 to 8 pounds of perennial ryegrass per 1,000 square feet. This is why. The perennial ryegrass seed ratio, compared with other cool-region grasses such as red fescue and Kentucky bluegrass, is considerably less per pound. Also, it's worth noting that some of the ryegrass will not come up, owing to an unfavorable rooting condition, and also some will be inhibited or wasted because of competition from the existing thriving grasses. So, if you have been throwing a pound or two of seed of other fine-textured grasses, remember that they have many more seeds per pound than perennial rye has. And since, judging by the desperate tone of your letter, you didn't get satisfactory results with those grasses, whatever the seeding ratio was, then I suggest you now try my grass and my seeding rate recommendation, which is up to 8 pounds per 1,000 of perennial ryegrass. Okay? Now let's go ahead.

Pour the perennial ryegrass into a small seeder hopper or spreader (be sure the opening is closed), and then seed twice in opposite (perpendicular) directions, being careful to calibrate the hopper to use between 3 and 4 pounds per 1,000 square feet: that means 3 or 4 pounds of seed per 1,000 square feet one way and 3 or 4 pounds per 1,000 square feet the opposite way. In this way the total seed rate per 1,000 square feet will come to approximately 6 to 8 pounds.

You don't have to do it this way, of course. Seeding by hand is one possible alternative. Another is the stop-and-go broadcast hopper method, which is dropping the seed wherever there is a bare area and then shutting off the seeds in places where the old grass is thriving. But these methods, unless you're extremely careful, don't always distribute the seed evenly, and you'll find that they frequently result in "misses" all over the yard. These missed, bare spots will be very apparent after the other seedlings come up. So it's much better to accurately calibrate the seed spreader and go over the lawn in opposite directions. In this way, it is almost impossible to fail.

After seeding the whole lawn, mow it short, about 1½ inches, without the grass catcher. Let the clippings fall onto the bare areas of your lawn. Don't worry—they will act as mulch, which is helpful nutrition. This single low mowing will give your yard at least ten days of precious time to allow the young seedlings to come up without a mower going over it. So cut it low, *once*. We want neither traffic ruts nor mower damage on your renovated grass for at least ten days—and keep your pets and kids off the lawn. Give the existing old grass a chance to spring back, and give the new seedling grass a chance to grab a strong foothold in the soil.

After you have mowed the grass low and rolled the whole lawn in two different directions, fertilize the whole yard with a complete fertilizer (see chapter 5). The old adage "Fertilizer makes the grass multiply itself" is most important in renovation. Then water and keep the seedlings moist until they mature. At this time slack off the watering to once a week or so. But in the early stage, be careful. Don't allow the grass to shrivel and die, especially when the weather suddenly becomes hot. Also, don't mow again below 2½ inches. Set your mower high and maintain your renovated lawn at a high cutting. Believe me, the lawn will be much healthier at this height, will last longer, and will look very attractive if you or your wife cut it more than once a week during the growing season. (Change off with Mabel; it's good exercise.)

I also suggest that you fertilize again with a complete fertilizer right after Labor Day, and perhaps once more in October, depending on where you live, this time at half the rate of the September application. In the middle of June, spread an organic fertilizer—one pound of actual nitrogen per 1,000 square feet. This fertilizing program will adequately nourish your young grass, and at the same time help thicken and stimulate the sparse and spindly turf that you have been growing up to now. *Caution:* Don't be tempted into using more weed chemicals until one entire year has passed. Forget about verticutting, power raking, and top-dressing unless you're an expert. We will discuss these machines and top-dressing later on.

I will close with two final suggestions. After seeding, if you want to, protect the seedlings in spotted open areas by spreading inexpensive peat moss over them to keep the ground from drying out and to keep the seed sheltered from possible disturbances. My second suggestion is to get a qualified soil test (see your county agent), which will show whether your soil needs lime, phosphorus, potassium, or trace elements.

SEED BARGAINS AND SEED MIXTURES

Q.—How good is bargain seed? I am moving into a new home with an open yard and grass exposed to full sun. I want to seed the lawn. Please advise if a mixture of Kentucky bluegrass, red fescue, and ryegrass is okay. The house and moving have been very expensive, and I can't afford an expensive grass seed at this time.

A.—What makes you think that you will be able to afford a better lawn in the future, when it will cost you twice as much? Are you suddenly going to get rich? It so happens, though, you can't afford not to get the very best quality seed the first time.

Let me state very clearly now that if you're going to seed your lawn, especially for the first time (and it should be the only time), then, my friend, go with the best seed. You'll never get a better chance than now, when the ground is freshly prepared for seed. Believe me, the most expensive way, when it comes to seed, is the "bargain" way. In the long run, you can't afford it. Remember the adage, "You only get what you pay for." I can tell you that if you go out one less time for dinner this year or have fewer cocktails at lunch, you'll be able to afford a good turf grass seed and a lawn that you, your family, and community will be proud of.

However if you persist in buying "bargain" mixtures instead of a pure Kentucky bluegrass blend that will cost more, here's what will happen. First, since you apparently have no shade, the money for the fescue will be wasted. You don't need it in the mixture unless you live in a sandy, droughty area or intend to give your lawn minimum care. Secondly, the ryegrasses will shoot up fast in a few days and smother the slower-starting Kentucky bluegrass, which is still the best grass to have in a cool-region climate. Oh, sure, some bluegrass will come up eventually, but ryegrasses grow many times faster than Kentucky bluegrass. Ryegrasses are also harder to mow, though the new improved varieties of perennial rye are getting easier to mow—but with sharp reel mowers, not with rotaries. Sure, the old image of perennial ryegrass has changed with the improved varieties, and even newer and better varieties are on their way. But Kentucky bluegrass in a pure stand can't be beat—not in my book, anyway.

Now back to your letter. You weren't very specific, nor did you mention whether the bargain seed formula consists of annual or perennial ryegrass. If it's the former, you're even worse off. Annual ryegrass is coarse and acts as a nurse crop, then fades away in a year or so. Another hitch is that when it is not properly mixed with other species (the same goes for the perennial ryegrass), the ryegrass seed will bunch and form clumps. It can also separate in a seed hopper or spreader. The fine-textured seed and the coarse seed will not come out at the proper seed ratio required for an even distribution of seed. My sincere advice is, don't futz around with nursery grasses in a Kentucky bluegrass mixture. Stay with the more expensive bluegrass blends. You'll never regret it and they're cheaper—honest; and besides, the lawn should last, with proper care, as long as the house, and there is no shortcut to quality.

Q.—What is tall fescue? And should it be included in a seed package? A friend of mine is moving away and wants to give me some for nothing. What do you think?

A.—Oh boy! I think you should look for another friend. What

did you do to him? Tall fescue is the most objectionable grass that can be found in a bluegrass lawn. It sticks out like a sore thumb, and in a luxury turf brand is considered a noxious weed.

Tall fescue is a very low-maintenance lawn grass with a deep root system and coarse wide blades. It grows well in the South but is especially well adapted to the "twilight zone" where the North meets the South. Tall fescue grows in clumps unless heavily seeded and is particularly noticeable if the seed is badly out of proportion in a seed mixture. It becomes an obviously undesirable weed in a good cool-season lawn, and is almost impossible to get rid of.

Years ago, cheap housing developers used it without thought or discretion. Park Forest, Illinois, where I first lived when I got married, was covered with tall fescue. The cheap and hardy stuff suited developers, and the pasturelike lawns provided a good lesson for us renters, because when we moved away to our own homes, we knew for sure what grass *not* to plant—tall fescue. A lawyer friend of mine in a Chicago suburb once moved because he had tall fescue growing profusely in his front yard and couldn't get rid of it. I know, because I helped him try to get rid of it, but all in vain. Finally after a while, he took my advice and moved to a new house. There he successfully put in a beautiful Merion Kentucky bluegrass lawn, which is still doing great. Of course it would have been cheaper to have a sodcutter and put in a new lawn, but I think he also wanted a new home.

Tall fescue grows well in shade, sun, and drought, and takes heavy traffic. It is of value for athletic fields and highways (it is the most widely used grass in Illinois for stabilizing highway road banks), though recent tests show that Manhattan perennial rye takes abuse almost as well. But more about athletic fields later on. As I mentioned before, tall fescue is used down south quite extensively and is also popular in the transitional zone. It will surprise you to know that one famous lawn uses it (see chapter 3).

Well, we have covered all the cool-region grasses, except one, which we won't cover—creeping bentgrasses. I don't recommend creeping bent lawns for homeowners. This beautiful, high-quality, low-mowing grass is best suited for golf courses, where it can be meticulously maintained by experienced professionals who have the special and expensive equipment it needs. (If you doubt my word, drop in on your local golf course and look at the vast array of equipment. Most of it is used for creeping bentgrass.)

Oh, I know a few striving homeowners have creeping bent in their yard, and I realize that more than a few homeowners are curious about it, especially after playing golf on a well-kept course or after watching TV golf. But frankly there just aren't enough pages in any book to clearly explain to homeowners the exceptionally high upkeep and stringent grooming needed by bentgrass, the finest-quality turf grass available. Creeping bentgrass requires almost perfect drainage, top-dressing, vertical mowing, and, of course, knowledgeable disease control measures. (Bent gets hit by more diseases than any other type of grass.) It requires besides weed and insect control, frequent mowing (golf greens are mowed daily), fertilizing, and watering—all magnified to a higher degree because creeping bentgrass needs more stringent care than other grass species in the cool-region climate. The average homeowner just can't cope with all the attention that creeping bent requires, and his pocketbook will give out long before his patience will.

To those of you who are successfully growing creeping bentgrass on the home lawn, I take my hat off. You don't need my advice. To those of you who are contemplating a creeping bentgrass lawn, after watching Gary Player, Jack Nicklaus, or "Old Arn" sink a long putt, my advice is—don't. If you still don't believe me, just talk to the local golf course superintendent (or spend a few weekends working for him). You'll soon learn how difficult it is to keep bentgrass in a meticulous condition.

The only homeowner who should get himself involved with the stringent upkeep of a creeping bentgrass lawn is the homeowner who is very much a man of means—that is, he must be rich enough to afford the painstaking care of professional lawn maintenance. For the upkeep of creeping bent lawns, a company should be reputable, of course, and equipped with the best equipment, and thoroughly experienced in servicing this very beautiful, low-growing, luxury water grass. Nothing less will do—with one exception, and that is if you are a turf expert. And a tireless worker, to boot. To keep a creeping bentgrass lawn in top-notch condition takes so much expert care that such lawns are almost a thing of the past, of the days of the very rich and yachts and servants. Now it's mostly grown on golf courses and expertly groomed by golf course superintendents with high maintenance and labor budgets.

During the romantic era of F. Scott Fitzgerald, these magnificent natural carpets on large estates were meticulously clipped and groomed by hardworking, knowledgeable gardeners. Their labor was still cheap in these days when creeping bentgrass lawns were so popular in wealthy, cool-region America—in suburbs like Shaker Heights in Cleveland, Grosse Point in Detroit, Lake Forest and Winnetka on the North Shore of Chicago, and the posh places on Long Island. To be sure, there still are some of these beautiful lawns around the country, but not many, because the upkeep is too steep—too expensive even for some golf courses. That period and its life-style are gone, never to return. Going, too, are the creeping bentgrass lawns as our social and economic patterns change.

During this change the brilliant discovery was made by a "greenkeeper" (a once-suitable title, now changed to golf course superintendent) of an improved variety of Kentucky bluegrass that was named Merion bluegrass. I call this a brilliant discovery because this grand old man recognized the future value of a strain of grass that has become the king of grasses. The discovery of Merion was the big reason for the start of the changeover from creeping bentgrass to the higher-mowed, improved varieties of Kentucky bluegrass. Today's homeowners, who are moving into the wealthy old suburbs of America, have almost to a man changed over to the dark green, improved strains of Kentucky bluegrass. These varieties are much easier and cheaper to maintain, and they are just as beautiful.

3

Southern Grasses and the Transitional Zones

The PROMINENCE of the Bermuda family in the warm regions of the United States parallels that of the Kentucky bluegrass family in the cool regions. Other warm-region grasses besides Bermuda also grow well in the South, but they are not planted as extensively. Some of these species are St. Augustine grass, Zoysia, centipede grass, and Bahia grass. Tall fescue, though very unpopular in the luxury lawns of the North, is a convenient grass in some southern areas, especially in transition areas where sometimes nothing does well. Annual ryegrass is still the most popular grass in the South for winter overseeding, although the new perennial ryegrass and fescues are also used with success.

Before we start our question-and-answer format, let's sit back leisurely in our favorite armchair and visit some of the southern states. We'll observe the lawn grasses that thrive best in these lovely Southland states where beautiful magnolia trees bloom in May and June and the summer is hot and humid. But first, let's make ourselves a southern mint julep to sip as we meander. What! You don't know how to make a mint julep? Well, don't worry; here is my favorite recipe, which you won't find in bar books.

We'll make it together and then begin our meanderings in the home state of the great baseball star who broke Babe Ruth's home run record, Hank Aaron.

Here is my creation for the finest summer drink in the world. Let's take our time and follow the instructions. Good mint juleps are never rushed and take considerable time to prepare. A word of caution to my Yankee friends who are reading this: use the best bourbon; don't use inferior brands. Never stir a julep, and never, ever drink it with a straw. Stick your nose into the drink to get the full benefit of this wonderful, fragrant southern delicacy. There have been debates, disputes, disturbances, kneeknockings, bloodshed, even duels going on for two hundred years about how to make a proper mint julep; and the battle will probably go on for as long as mint julep enthusiasts exist in the world. Which whiskey to use? Bourbon or rye? Do you crush the mint or bruise it? And then, of course, there's the argument about whether to garnish the drink, or to leave out the extra ingredients and keep the drink basic, or to make a fruit salad of it.

When Colonel Irvin S. Cobb, a man who had a cigar, a bridge, a hotel, and a mint julep named for him, heard that his friend H. L. Mencken not only crushed the mint but poured Baltimore rye into his julep cup as well, he declared that such a barbarity was equal to putting scorpions in a baby's bed.

Anyway, try my favorite mint julep recipe. Put aside yours, for the moment, and please don't be tetchy. I don't want a duel.

Southern Mint Julep

1½ teaspoons superfine or confectioners' sugar	*1 to 1½ cups shaved ice*
6 to 8 sprigs fresh mint	*3 to 4 ounces bourbon (I like it strong)*
dash of cold water	*¼ teaspoon confectioners' sugar*

Place 1½ teaspoons of sugar, 5 or 6 sprigs of the fresh mint, and a dash of cold water in a highball glass. Use a muddler or similar tool to dissolve the sugar and to crush the mint until it is well bruised. Fill the glass almost to the top with shaved ice, packing it down firmly. Pour in the bourbon and with a long-handled bar spoon use a chopping motion to mix it with the ice. Dry the outside of the glass with paper towels and place the glass in the refrigerator for at least an hour or in the freezer for half an hour. The glass should be thoroughly frosted and the ice almost solid.

Remove the glass, touching the outside as little as possible with the bare hand so it remains frosted. Plant the remaining 2 or 3 bushy sprigs of mint in the ice and sprinkle the mint with ¼ teaspoon sugar.

For variation you can garnish the drink with slices of lemon and add 2 or 3 drops of brandy on top. However, a true southern mint julep rarely has any other trimmings besides the mint, so this last option is up to you.

Now let's bury our noses deeply into this chapter for information and into our glasses to get the full aroma of our southern creation. (Yankees: don't swallow the mint; it's intended for scent rather than taste.)

THE LAWN GRASSES OF ALABAMA

St. Augustine grass is a broad, dark green grass with flat stems and has a coarser texture than either Bermuda grass or Zoysia grass. Like almost all of the southern grasses, it is planted vegetatively and spreads by stolons. It is important to remember that St. Augustine is adapted only to the southern half of Alabama and is sometimes severely damaged by low temperatures in the northern part of the state. St. Augustine is used extensively on home lawns in the Gulf Coast area. Like most outstanding lawn grasses, it does best on sandy loam soils. It loves mists, fogs, drizzles, and rains, and the hot, sunny, humid weather of all coastal regions. St. Augustine grass will also do well in shade. Weeds are not a serious problem in a St. Augustine sod because its vigorous growth holds them back, but chinch bugs are a big problem.

The best time to sod or sprig St. Augustine in Alabama is late winter through early summer. Be sure that any topsoil brought in is free of hard-to-kill weeds like nut grass and common Bermuda. Apply 10-10-10 fertilizer (or 8-8-8 or 10-6-4) at a rate of 10 pounds per 1,000 square feet every March, May, July, and September. This will give your soil 1 pound of actual nitrogen, phosphorus, and potash each time you fertilize with 10-10-10, and this is adequate for a good St. Augustine lawn in Alabama. Mow your St. Augustine grass frequently at 2 inches and use a grass catcher to prevent a buildup of thatch. Right afterwards, water this grass deeply. I always like to water after a mowing if the lawn needs moisture. It freshens and stands up the grass.

Centipede grass. Centipede also is popular grass for home lawns in the Deep South. For homeowners who don't have much time for outdoor work and maintenance, it's a good grass. Centipede is widely used in church grounds, cemeteries, and industrial areas; but it can't take heavy traffic and doesn't perform well in athletic fields and playgrounds.

Centipede grass loves the sun but tolerates a little bit of shade. It also is fairly tolerant to cold in the South and will grow in all sections of Alabama. Centipede can be established either by seed or sprigging.

It doesn't like an excessive use of fertilizer, especially those that are high in phosphorus (which, although it sounds wild, sometimes causes iron deficiency). Apply about a half a pound of actual nitrogen every spring and summer, and that's all—unless soil tests indicate more is needed. Although other warm-season grasses like the Bermudas and St. Augustine and Zoysia like lots of fertilizer, centipede grass is just the opposite. Very little fertilizer should be applied to centipede grass, because heavy fertilization will eventually kill it. It takes months, years sometimes, to decline, but it does finally succumb to an abundant diet. Novice homeowners trying to get growth and color similar to that of hybrid Bermudas, Zoysia, or St. Augustine grass, unknowingly overfertilize their centipede lawn, and when it dies they wonder what happened.

Many times the appearance of decline in vigor of this southern grass is really from overfertilization; but the symptoms are just the opposite and very much resemble those in a lawn that is under-fertilized or damaged by disease or insects. Therefore, a good rule of thumb is to use 1 pound of actual nitrogen per 1,000 square feet *per season.*

Keep in mind that if it's a dark green color you want, don't try to get it by fertilizing centipede grass. Instead, switch to Bermuda grass, St. Augustine, or Zoysia. These grasses require high fertilization and produce a dark green color.

Homeowners also are often "sedated" by the persuasions of commercial lawn care companies and cannot associate heavy fertilization with growth difficulties in centipede grass. And no one tells them. Centipede grass loves acidy soil (4.5 to 5.7 pH). Therefore, lime should be kept off unless definitely indicated by qualified soil tests. This is very important for homeowners to remember. I can't emphasize this point enough: NO LIME—unless indicated by soil tests. Mow this grass about 2 inches or so, and water deeply whenever the ground needs it.

Zoysia grasses can be grown favorably in all sections of Alabama, and varieties like Matrella, Emerald, and Meyer do well. Matrella grows in light shade and is an outstanding turf grass under most Alabama conditions. Meyer is a little more tolerant to cold than the other two; therefore, it keeps its color longer than Matrella or Emerald. Meyer grows faster than the other two, so less time is required for it to cover the soil surface. One thing to remember about Zoysia is that once this grass is damaged by excessive wear or by mowing machinery, it is very slow to recover. A frost turns it the color of straw and puts it out of commission until warm spring growth begins. Fertilize the Zoysia grasses every two months with a complete fertilizer. Mow the grass no higher than 1 inch; if it is in shade, though, raise the mower to 1½ inches. Use a very sharp mower for Zoysia (check for sharpness several times a year) and use a grass catcher to help prevent thatch buildup. Zoysia can be planted by plugging, sprigging, sodding, strip sodding, or shredding; these methods will be explained more thoroughly in this chapter when we get into questions and answers.

Bermuda grasses. This grass is adaptable to all turf grass areas of the South—lawns, athletic fields, cemeteries, parks, and especially golf courses. All Bermuda grasses love fertilizer, and each year they should be fertilized from spring through late summer a minimum of four times with a complete fertilizer. They should be mowed frequently at 1 inch, preferably lower for best appearance. Use a sharp mower with catcher to help prevent thatch buildup; and believe me, this grass thatches like the dickens. Infrequent mowing causes scalping and unsightliness. Though there are elegant selections and hybrid Bermuda grasses available, like Tif-

green, Tifway, Tiflawn (very good for home lawns), Tifdwarf, and
Sunturf—nevertheless, old common Bermuda grass, which can be
started from seed, is still the most popular Bermuda with Alabama homeowners.

Most lawns in Alabama, as well as other states in the South,
become dormant in the winter and are not overseeded for winter
color. (I guess sooner or later we all get tired of mowing the
grass, and winter is a good time to quit.) However, I have noticed
that overseeding is becoming a little more popular as interest in
home lawns spreads through the South as a result of excellent information available to the homeowner through state universities
and their cooperative extension services.

GEORGIA'S GRASSES

Now to the Peach Blossom State, Georgia, where my favorite golf
tournament, the Masters, is played every April at Augusta. According to the turf experts in Georgia, they have a somewhat
unique situation in that both cool-season grasses (fertilized in the
fall and winter) and warm-season grasses (fertilized in the spring
and summer) are used for home lawns. Let's examine this a little
more closely to find out what grasses do best where.

Bermuda, a warm-season grass, is the major lawn grass used
throughout the state, and centipede and Zoysia are found in the
southern half. Centipede was becoming very popular in the southern part of Georgia, but has been losing popularity because of the
disease called centipede decline. St. Augustine is used at the very
southern tip. Carpet grass is used very little.

Now let's see where cool-season grasses are used. (Cool-season
grasses? This is hard to believe!) Sure enough, in the very northern mountain region of Georgia, Kentucky bluegrasses do exist on
home lawns. Another grass, K-31, which originated in 1940, is a
tall fescue and does well in the northern third of the state. While
I don't care for tall fescue (other varieties are alta fescue, released in 1940; Goar, released in 1946; Kenmont, released in
1963; and Kenwell, released in 1965) in the north-region climates,
it does very well in transitional zones and in a few of the southern
states, including Georgia. The whole secret of planting tall fescue

is to seed it 10 to 15 pounds per 1,000 square feet. This grass, which comes up sporadically in clumps if seeded lightly, grows to a profuse, even dense, stand if seeded at very high rates and fertilized with a good starter fertilizer, which usually means one with lots of phosphorus. However, some of the soils in Georgia are extremely high in phosphorus, so sometimes you don't need a high-phosphorus-content fertilizer. Though many of us turf experts have been knocking tall fescue's coarse, wide-leaf profile, and even calling it a weed in the North, I am beginning to think that this grass, because of its tremendous root power, is a grass for all seasons, although it is not nearly as attractive as, say, Bermuda or Kentucky bluegrass.

In other words, my respect is increasing for this pasture grass in hard-to-maintain areas. If it covers the ground where everything else fails for homeowners, then I believe it should have a little more respect, especially if its low maintenance saves money for homeowners. After all, beauty is in the eye of the beholder—and tall fescue could become increasingly beautiful in the eyes of the frugal homeowner who doesn't care much for the appearance of his lawn, only its durability, especially as seed prices and upkeep costs soar. I would like to see more experimentation on this pasture grass by turf scientists. *Note:* Just before this book went to press, I was delighted to discover that the Southern Regional Turf Research Group, which is comprised of state and federal turf workers from Arizona to North Carolina, is working to improve *Festuca Arundinócea* Schreb solely for turf purposes. This group of turf experts are selecting, breeding, and testing many cultivars of tall fescue for one reason. They have been alerted to the fact that people want this grass, probably because of the initial ease of making a lawn of it and the other reasons I mentioned. It would be interesting as well as monetarily desirable for homeowners if tall fescue could be made a little more attractive, a little more refined. If this could be accomplished, tall fescue with its tremendous root system, which enables it to survive in the hottest of weather and in impoverished soils, couldn't miss for cheaper lawns in the North and South. But until this refinement comes about, tall fescue grass still looks like hell.

Brown patch, dollar spot, and pythium blight (see chapter 10) are the major diseases in home lawns here, and are much more prevalent than in the North. For spring dead spot, a dreaded new disease on Bermuda grass in the spring, especially in the northern sections, there is no effective control to date and, what's worse, its cause is unknown. Spring dead spot (SDS) usually appears the third year after establishment and is found more often in heavier soils than in soils that are high in organic matter. There has been a little evidence that gypsum helps reduce SDS, but don't get your hopes up. Tests are still being conducted with gypsum as well as with a number of fungicides, but progress is slow and the true cause of SDS has so far eluded the scientists. Centipede decline, which strikes only this grass, is another disease whose cause is not known. Symptoms are failure to come out of dormancy in spring and death in the heat of summer. Through diligent cultural practices, a homeowner usually can keep centipede decline from occurring.

Most warm-season grasses in Georgia go dormant in the winter months, except in the southern tip of the state facing Florida. Very few homeowners overseed with ryegrass to achieve winter color; and as the price of seed rises higher and higher, it is likely that fewer still will do so. Tall fescue, a perennial cool-season bunch grass wherever it is used in the southern and transitional zones, stays green the year round. It grows very little during periods of extreme hot or cold weather, and many times is mixed with other northern grasses, for example, in Anaheim, California. In my observation of southern lawn grasses, only affluent homes and industries growing a warm-season grass downtown in public view continue year after year to overseed their dormant warm-season lawns. The majority of southern homeowners are practical; they still don't overseed much. My advice to southern homeowners who have weed problems is to see their county agent for information on controlling lawn weeds, as well as insects and disease. The grassy weeds are harder to get rid of than other types of weeds, such as the broadleafs. With the southern seeded lawn grasses (centipede, common Bermuda, tall fescue), precaution must be taken not to apply herbicides when the seedlings first come up. (The same precaution goes for north-region seedings.) Wait until the grass is well established and more mature before applying any weed chemicals.

However, it is permitted in newly vegetatively sprigged lawns of Zoysia, hybrid Bermuda, and centipede to carefully apply a pre-emergence treatment. But apply the preemergence herbicide at *one half* the rate recommended for established grasses, and be careful —even this half-rate sometimes will considerably slow the rate of sprig growth. Some chemicals shouldn't be used even on vegetatively planted new lawns. Check with your county weed advisor to be on the safe side.

THE STATE OF VIRGINIA

In old Virginia, as almost everywhere else in the South, modern life is conducive to outdoor living. Good turf for home lawns and other areas has acquired an importance never known before. The basic lawn grasses in Virginia are Kentucky bluegrasses, except in southern Virginia and the tidewater area, where warm-season grasses like Bermuda grass (Tufcote, U-3, and Arizona common) and Zoysia (Meyer and Emerald) are grown. Both genera are, of course, established vegetatively (except common Bermuda) and care must be exercised in obtaining fresh material that is not contaminated with weeds. The best insurance is to purchase only material that bears the certified or approved label. Before it can bear these labels, sod sold in Virginia has to be inspected by the Virginia Crop Improvement Association (the same applies to all other states) to ensure overall high quality and freedom from weeds. Seed bought by homeowners should be certified. If this is not possible, then buy variety names, e.g., Merion Kentucky bluegrass, Pennlawn creeping red fescue, or Manhattan ryegrass. This is not as foolproof as certified grass seed, but it is an indication that the percentage of seed claimed is of the variety marked on the package. If you buy only by genera and species, e.g., Kentucky bluegrass, creeping red fescue, or ryegrass, you have absolutely no assurance that the species the package contains has all of the expected qualities of a desirable grass required for a good home lawn.

Virginia's geographic location and climatic conditions make turf management difficult. Virginia is located in a transition zone (where some species of both cool-season and warm-season grasses grow, but where neither is well adapted) and maybe that's where I should have put it—under transitional zones. Certain varieties of Kentucky bluegrass perform satisfactorily in northern and western Virginia, but as yet there are no registered varieties that can live satisfactorily through the southeastern Virginia summers. The warm grasses, like Bermuda grass and Zoysia, survive with difficulty the severe winters in the coastal plains and southern Piedmont of Virginia.

So why did I put a state in the transitional zone in the southern grasses section? Well, I spent the first twenty-five years of my life in Saskatoon, Saskatchewan, where winters get to 50 below zero, and all my life there I thought of Virginia as a hot southern state, especially after visiting it once as a young man. So I'll be darned, just because some Yankee grasses survive well there, if I'll put good old Virginia with its many glories under the transitional zone heading. Or, for that matter, anyplace else in this book except in the Deep South. Virginia, to me, will always be a 100-percent southern state, even if it freezes once in a while.

The best seeding dates, as recommended by the extension division of Virginia Polytechnic Institute State University, are:

"In the Northern Piedmont area and in the areas west of the Blue Ridge, the recommended seeding dates are mid-August to mid-September, or during March and early April.

"The best seeding dates in the Southern Piedmont area and Eastern Virginia are between the first of September and mid-October or during February and March.

"Improved strains of warm season grasses such as Bermuda grass and the Zoysia grass, which are normally sprigged or plugged, should be established during May after the soil is warm. They may be planted as late as July. May and June plantings give the best turf. Late summer plantings are not recommended because there is not time for them to get established properly before cold weather.

"Common Bermuda grass is frequently established from seed, and may be seeded in winter or late spring, depending on whether hulled or unhulled seed is used. Plant hulled seed in late April or May, or unhulled seed in late fall or winter. (*Note:* The observation has been that common Bermuda seed germination is not satisfactory until night time temperatures reach 70°F.)

"Sod of Kentucky bluegrass and fescue can be installed during most of the year except in midwinter when little or no growth is taking place. Sod should not be cut or installed when either the turf or the ground is frozen. When extreme heat and droughty conditions exist in summer, sodding operations should be delayed. If done under these conditions, the turf must be kept moist and cool, the soil should be watered enough to cool it prior to installation, and thorough watering should be done as the sod is layed."

In Virginia, hardly any lawns are overseeded for winter color.

THE AMERICAN SOUTHWEST

Now let's move to the great Southwest of the United States. There are wilderness areas left here, they say, where covered wagon tracks are still visible. But if this is true, then only a few people know about it. Perhaps prospectors and Indians came across them. Most signs of the pioneer trek into the Southwest, such as the tumbleweeds and the old forlorn campfire songs, are gone forever with the desert wind. And nothing much remains of the great past of the Apaches, the Navajos, and other Indian tribes of the Southwest, except what comes to us in the shameful distortions of Hollywood.

We will visit Arizona first, where "streaking" has been done for hundreds of years by a very interesting bird called the roadrunner. If you ever go out in the desert or a national park for a walk, you'll have to keep an open eye. The roadrunner (a great hunter) streaks past so fast that you think your old eyes are playing tricks on you.

Turf grasses used for home lawns in Arizona are chiefly Bermudas, though northwards in the state and in higher elevations, Kentucky bluegrass also thrives. In Arizona, like everywhere else, poor home lawns result from improper construction, mowing too closely, improper fertilization, lack of water, incorrect species of grass, and poor soil conditions. All soils in Arizona should be analyzed for pH and total soluble salts before any amendments are added. The local county agricultural agent will help you in taking the soil sample and will send it to the University of Arizona soil-testing laboratory. The southwestern county agent is also the best man to help interpret the soil analysis report for you when it comes back. The great plus factor of southern states is that when you are seeding either a new home lawn or a golf course, the grass is established and available for use so much more quickly than in the North because of the warm climate. A homeowner gets to enjoy his turf investment much sooner here. Of course there is not much difference in immediate availability with sodding—except that the southern homeowner gets the good of his investment about five months longer each year.

In the southern part of Arizona, sprigging of southern grasses is less expensive than sodding. Warm-season sprigged grasses require about three months before they are ready for hard use. Homeowners in northern Arizona should use the cool-season grasses, such as the Kentucky bluegrass varieties, which are most adaptable to that region. In southern Arizona, warm-season grasses are of course the logical choice. Seeding with northern grasses in Arizona should be done in early fall (early spring is the second-best time). Bermudas should be mowed at ½ to 1 inch high. Elite Bermudas, because of their ability to withstand low mowing heights and their rapid rate of growth, need mowing more often than cool-season grasses. Vertical mowing (verticutting) once or twice per season helps keep to a minimum the thatch accumulation and long stolon growth. Bermuda grasses are heavy nitrogen feeders and require between 6 to 8 pounds of actual nitrogen per 1,000 square feet each year. (And you Yankees think you have it tough with 2 pounds of actual nitrogen per 1,000 square feet each year.)

Now let's take a look at Nevada home lawns. In the famous gambling resort town of Las Vegas, more business places have Bermuda grass lawns (casinos on the Strip, especially) and are overseeded to common annual rye for winter color than anywhere I've been. Some turf areas are even dyed. The reason is obvious— to attract the public. Las Vegas, as you know, attracts millions of tourists. Here casinos compete for suckers' gambling dollars with their ornate luxuries, their terrific stage shows, and their variety of vices. Outside, the casinos spend lots of money keeping the landscape attractive. The majority of customers in this city, however, don't give a tinker's dam how anything looks outside, or whether the grass is brown, green, or turquoise.

Before we discuss Las Vegas home lawns in detail, let me tell you a story about the biggest commotion I ever saw there, over a loss. Not a gambling loss, mind you; this loss concerns a steak and what I will always remember fondly as "the great cowboy steak fistfight."

A few years ago, a friend of mine and I kept driving past a well-known casino with a large billboard sign beside the highway stating: "Try our 24 ounce Cowboy Steak—only $3.95." So after driving past this sign for a few days, I said to my friend one evening, "Voody, what the hell is a cowboy steak? Is the steak for real, or what?" My slim, Nevada-born, desert friend explained that a cowboy steak is a ranch-style steak dinner, which consists of homemade bread, pinto beans, lots of fried potatoes, coffee, and, of course, a huge steak—but oddly enough (to me anyway) no salad. I guess cowboys don't go much for greens. "Well," I said, "let's try this cowboy brand steak tonight. The price sounds right."

That night we ordered the cowboy steak and it came, sure enough, with all the trimmings that Voody had mentioned: pinto beans, homemade bread, coffee, and fried potatoes (no salad). Everything was delicious and plentiful, except for one perplexing doubt in my mind, which had to do with the size of the main item. The cowboy steak didn't look like 24 ounces—in fact, mine didn't even look like 12 ounces. My companion and blackjack expert made questioning references to the size of his steak, also. But what the hell, we really weren't seriously complaining—not with all the other food heaped so high on our plates. It seemed like an okay deal for $3.95—to us, anyway. But just as we were about to leave after the cowboy dinner, we heard a loud commotion behind us. Somebody was banging on the table and yelling words that sounded like "Now I've got you cheating bastards, now I've got you. Look here everybody, look here!" We, along with other surprised diners, looked toward the shouting and, much to our amazement, saw a well-nourished, small man whose head was bald except for a thin fringe of hair, which gave him a kind of a dignity. He was red in the face and standing at a table that was surrounded with people who looked like conventioneers (all more than a wee bit intoxicated). The little man was yelling through his heavy moustache and pointing (so help me) to one of those small-sized

Way-Rite scales that are used for weighing heavy letters and small packages. Except this scale didn't have a letter on it. This scale had a greasy steak draped over it. He was yelling and complaining that his steak was only 10 ounces, "same as last night," and he wasn't going to be cheated any more. Tonight he had brought a scale to prove the restaurant's slight miscalculation. No, he didn't want his money back—he wanted "a 24 ounce cowboy steak." He threatened to call the police, the Better Business Bureau, the mayor, the FBI, and even Frank Sinatra and Earl Butz. Well, by now everybody was looking at his own undersized steak and muttering about being shortchanged too. Sure enough, they started to voice opinions about their undersized cowboy steaks, first quietly, then louder and louder. The waitresses and the hostess came running, and finally two managers rushed out. One of them was foreign-speaking and rather hard to understand. He was waving his arms a lot, and it seemed to me he made a "finger sign" to one of the fat man's friends, who kept tugging at his black jacket and repeating over and over: "That's right—George is right! That's right—George is right!" By now, everyone (including Voody and I) started to complain loudly about his own steak. To make things worse, people started to come in from the casino to see what all the racket was about. It was really comical except for the fact that everybody was so damn mad, especially those who had had the most to drink. Things were fast getting out of order, and pushing began. To top the whole incident off, a waitress carrying one of those large, flat, oval trays of food turned around to see the action and hit a man with shoulder-length hair right in the forehead. Everything on the tray spilled over onto the poor man's head and shoulders and onto another table of "gracious living" diners. Well, swearing began immediately. Right away, someone complained about the language in front of his wife. There were a few pushes, more swearing, and a fist was thrown. The great cowboy steak fistfight had begun in earnest. It was the zaniest thing I ever saw, better than any casino show. Steaks and pinto beans were flying around, and our table was rewarded with an extra loaf of home-made bread, which bounced off Voody's head. Women were screaming and men were puffing and wheezing and trying to look, swing, and sound like fighters. It didn't last long. Nobody was really hurt. (How can you fight with pinto beans all over your face and hair?) There was only one casualty, a man who had got hit in the nose. He was having a bad nosebleed, and a gorgeous waitress, almost topless, was leaning over him administering first aid with ice and cold cloths and cooing in his ear. His wife was also trying to soothe him, but he just kept looking wide-eyed at the waitress and her two endowments. A quick-thinking manager quieted everyone down with promises of two-pound cowboy steaks for everyone in the room on the house and dry cleaning bills paid for, plus California wines. I don't remember what else. Just like that, the situation turned around, and now everyone was laughing and talking to each other, having a very nice time anticipating a second steak, with just a few mutterings heard now and then of "It better damn well be 24 ounces." But they soon clammed up, and gracious dining was restored in the casino restaurant. Of course Voody and I also had a second steak and left the happy dining room waving good-bye to everyone, full to the brim of steak and wine.

Now let's get back to talking about grasses. And how not to get shortchanged in this department (in Nevada or anyplace else). Most homeowners in Las Vegas and Nevada grow home lawns of common Bermuda, which, under the average homeowner's care, is still the best variety. Some homeowners also plant Alta fescue (tall fescue). But the winning bet in this region is common Bermuda seeded at about 1 pound or less per 1,000 square feet. It takes hulled Bermuda seed between 8 and 10 days to come up, and unhulled seed about 15 days. The seeding time usually is in early April. Temperatures at night have to be consistently between 65 and 70 degrees for good Bermuda bed germination. The starter fertilizer, mixed in the soil, should be something like a 16-20-0, 10-10-5 with iron and sulphur added to help get best color and growth. Mature stands of Bermuda should be fertilized every fourth week until the first frost in September.

The one big mistake made by Nevada homeowners is that they cut their Bermuda lawns too high (and their Kentucky bluegrass lawns too low). The recommended mowing should be 1 inch or below every week. Homeowners who mow less frequently will run into big trouble with thatch later, especially if they use rotaries which can be set higher than 1 inch. Some rotary mowers now are made to go below 1 inch. With hybrids like Tifgreen or Tifdwarf, rotaries are not the answer and a "putting green," reel-type mower, such as is used on a golf course, should be considered. In September when nights are cooling off and autumn is approaching, Bermuda grass will start to turn brown and go dormant. Homeowners should then set their mowers as low as possible. Don't worry if it scalps—that's what you want. Let it scalp and turn brown; this drastic low mowing action won't kill the grass. The reader must understand that whenever I refer to turf grass dormancy in this chapter, I am talking specifically about completely dormant turf and not turf in semidormant stages. The difference is significant, especially when I am explaining about overseeding. In Nevada, Georgia, Alabama, etc., homeowners frequently get a browning off of Bermuda grass due to frosts which just affects the leaves. If this occurs early enough in the winter season, the stems are not completely killed off and in fact some respiration continues, but at a reduced rate. Also, photosynthesis may continue to produce carbohydrates. Scalping with a mower at this time, when the turf grass is just in semidormant condition, will lead to winterkill. Mower scalping should be done for overseeding only when the whole top portion (leaves and stem) is actually dormant. Never before. This is preparation for the overseeding with common annual rye—about 10 to 15 pounds per 1,000 square feet. The rye will take about 6 days to germinate. If you wish, rake the scalped clippings in windrows first; then rake the windrows lightly over the seed. Spread over the new seed; the scalped clippings will act as mulch. This idea of using the clippings as mulch was brought to my attention by one of the best golf superintendents in Vegas, so don't hesitate to use them. Most homeowners pick up the scalped clippings with the mower catcher and throw them away. Power rakes (vertical knives) can also be used to renovate a thatched lawn or to prepare the lawn successfully for winter ryegrass. Power rakes can be rented quite reasonably. Some bluegrass (Newport and Windsor) is coming into Vegas. Merion doesn't do well. Humidity and disease are always the big dangers to bluegrass in this desert area. Residents of Vegas and scientists have noted an ever-increasing accumulation of humidity due to the growth of population and industry. With any bluegrass lawn here, the homeowner should spray fungicides for disease control, but of course he never does. Bluegrass shouldn't be cut lower than 2½ inches. The problem in extremely transient centers like Las Vegas is that the homeowner doesn't know what variety of grass is growing and doesn't take time to find out how to best cultivate it, so soon he is in trouble.

In this area there is no such thing as good black soil. It's either silt or blow-sand. The local soil is alkaline (salty) and home-owners have to depend more and more on fertilizer that contains both iron and sulphur. This is very important for lawns and shrubbery. You can tell alkali (salt) because it always rises to the top. The more you water, the more it comes up. It is whitish in appearance. The poor transient homeowner just moving in doesn't always know what is happening and sometimes finds out only when it's too late.

In May, help old Mother Nature bring Bermuda out of its dormancy with 21-0-0 or 38-0-0 urea-form fertilizer. Remember to give the Bermuda some iron to keep its color in June, July, and August (when Bermuda starts to fade out). Hybrid Bermudas, like all vegetative grasses, are sprigged (stolons), plugged, or sodded. A hint for the homeowner (I'll get shot for this) is that he can sometimes economize when planting a lawn by going to the local golf course when they are verticutting and dethatching the fairway grass, and asking the superintendent for the hybrid verticut stolons. These accumulate in piles like haystacks on every fairway, and I am sure any superintendent would be willing to give the homeowner a few bushels. However, it's best to ask the busy superintendent far ahead of time. The verticutting of hybrid Bermuda is usually done in June.

Let's leave Vegas now; it's not a good idea to stay too long—unless you don't gamble. However, if you like blackjack like I do, I'll give you one good hint. Don't gamble on weekends. End your play by 6:00 P.M. on Fridays. Monday through Friday afternoon is best (for me anyway). Why? I really can't explain, but I know your chances are better during weekdays. The dealers, when the weekend crowds come (especially from L.A.), all of a sudden get ridiculously better, to such an extent that though I have won time and time again on weekdays, I have never had the slightest sliver of luck on weekends. I consider myself a good blackjack player who frequently gets lucky (two or three times winning or tying ten hands in a row), but on weekends forget it. Lady Luck leaves me faster than Secretariat ever came out of the "big three" racing gates.

Two of our largest states, Texas and California, are so vast that their climates vary from one border to the other. So do their home lawns. Though both are considered southern states, the northern grasses thrive in their cooler areas as well as in the shade of their high altitudes. (Yes, Kentucky bluegrass planted in the South in dense shade is sometimes able to survive the hot summer. It has also been noted by turf scientists that in the South, with the possible exception of Florida, many natural Kentucky bluegrass clones persist all around. Some of these clones are found thriving in the open sun. Careful selections are being made from these natural Kentucky bluegrass stands along with the recent bluegrass cultivars that have been released by experimental stations and seed companies to see whether or not they can be of use to the homeowner and the golf course superintendent in the South.)

However, the major turf grasses for home lawns in Texas are St. Augustine grass in the southern half and Bermuda grass in the northern and western parts. For St. Augustine to do well, it must be treated by the homeowner for brown patch disease and for chinch bugs. I recommend spring and fall application of a complete fertilizer. Put on up to 2 pounds of nitrogen per 1,000 square feet. St. Augustine thrives best in Houston, Waco, Galveston, Baytown, Texas City, and La Porte. In these areas, the winter climate is much warmer than anywhere else in the state. Here, many of the homeowners overseed with common rye for winter color, but most Texas homeowners let their lawns remain dormant for three to five months, depending on whether they live in southern or northern Texas. The warm-grass transition zone (or dividing line) between St. Augustine and Bermuda grass is Abilene. Everything north of this region is mostly common Bermuda U-3. U-3 Bermuda grass is allegedly the most cold-tolerant of all the vegetatively planted Bermudas here, and is used in the Texas Panhandle with a fair degree of success. But hulled common Bermuda (introduced from Africa) is by far the most extensively used grass in the northwestern region. It is the only turf variety that can be established from seed. Texas homeowners in this area usually don't overseed in the winter, so the Bermuda lawn is left dormant. Any Kentucky bluegrass planted in this area is common and comes under the simple brand name Kentucky bluegrass.

Buffalo grass, though you can buy it at a store, is a natural prairie grass and comes up in rough country lawns and pastures like crazy through its own seed. The homeowner in Texas should be encouraged to purchase only turf grass that is certified, whether he buys it as vegetative material or in seed form. This is his assurance that he is getting genetic purity and a minimum of weed content. Noncertified planting material from unknown sources may result not only in the wrong variety but in a yard full of weeds, such as nutsedge, Dallis grass, and carpet burrweed. There are many improved hybrid Bermudas available to the Texas homeowner, including Sunturf, Tifdwarf, and Tifway. I encourage homeowners to use these better selections, but to make sure first which variety does best in his particular area. To do this, he should get in touch with the College of Agriculture, Department of Soil and Crop Science, College Station, Texas 77843. Local county extension advisors and golf course superintendents are your two nearest turf experts.

It is well to remember that Bermuda grass varieties differ in nitrogen requirements, and that the fine-textured varieties generally need to be maintained at a higher level of nitrogen than the common Bermuda grass. Whether you live north, south, east, or west, a homeowner who desires a dark green, dense turf will have to spend more money on fertilizer and an improved variety of Bermuda grass or Kentucky bluegrass. How much you spend on your grass depends on the kind of turf you have, the length of your growing season, the soil type, and most of all, how much you care about your lawn. It's no use buying a Cadillac if you're going to be driving over rough, bumpy country roads full of potholes; You'd be better off with a four-wheel-drive jeep. It's the same with grasses. It's no use buying an elite strain for a tough-upkeep area, where something less expensive but more durable will do better.

And now on to sunny California, where we will end our easy-chair journey of the southern states and then go on to questions and answers. It's too bad that turf specialists don't publish enough advice for the southern homeowner and his lawn. Most advice in books and magazine articles is aimed at the northern states, or so it seems to me, and is written by northern writers.

A whole book could be written on California home lawns. There are so many different climatic areas and soils in California, and even different water qualities, that one set of recommendations doesn't begin to cover everything.

The University of California divides home lawns in this state into two broad zones—the temperate zone (where cool-season grasses grow) and the subtropical zone (where warm-season grasses thrive). Actually, there is also the "twilight zone," a transitional area where either cool or warm grass species can be maintained by careful management and know-how. Homeowners who are smart enough to learn how to manage one of the adapted species in their particular area will have verdant yards for most of the season and save money, as against trying to maintain poorly adapted grasses. The homeowner in California has a more difficult time selecting the proper grass species than, say, a Minnesota homeowner whose choice is basically one Kentucky bluegrass. So the California homeowner has to be smarter.

The subtropical species in California are Bermuda grass, St. Augustine grass, Zoysia grass, and an extremely attractive ground cover called dichondra, a low-spreading, broad-leaved plant with small kidney-shaped leaves that spreads by stems or runners, needs very little mowing, and seldom grows higher than 2½ inches.

The temperate zone grasses are Kentucky bluegrass, perennial ryegrass, tall fescue, and bentgrasses.

Bermuda lawns, common or hybrid, and St. Augustine grass can be overseeded with 12 to 15 pounds per 1,000 square feet of common annual ryegrass. The whole secret of winter overseeding is to make sure that the annual rye reaches the soil before it germinates; you're wasting seed and time if it stays on top in the thatch. Rotary mowers are considered wrong machines for some areas because they tend to build up thatch with their high settings. Cutting dichondra with rotaries is never recommended. Rotaries cut more like "karate" chops than scissor cuts. The dichondra plant is an extremely fragile "grass." Dichondra can be easily bruised or damaged and browned off at the top if rotary mowers are used. Another disadvantage is that rotaries take dichondra seeds by rotary vacuum action into the bag, rather than dropping them on the ground as reel mowers do. This makes dichondra lawns thin out in a few years. Otherwise, new crops of seedlings come up each year to keep the dichondra lawns full and dense.

In southern California a majority of lawns are dichondra, and they are called "grass" by the homeowners. Many professional maintenance companies and gardeners service only 100-percent dichondra lawns. Professional gardeners are very big in California and are top-quality. Gardeners of Japanese descent are numerous. There are many damn good Mexican-American gardeners, too.

Bagging is an extremely important factor in California. In an area where there is only one season (rather than four), clippings lying on the ground tend to rot and cause disease problems. So most Californians are very conscientious about bagging.

Homeowners who want their yards to stay green all the time (in the Walt Disney area of Orange County, for example) mostly use mixtures of northern grasses that include everything under the sun—Kentucky bluegrass, Chewings fescues, *Poa trivialis,* creeping red fescue, bentgrass, and, naturally, tall fescue. (Tall fescue is the only cool-season grass that acts as a true perennial throughout the South.) The contents of a package on a store shelf might read like this:

Alta tall fescue	29.10%
Kentucky bluegrass (common)	19.00
Newport Kentucky bluegrass	19.00
Chewings fescue	14.00
Creeping red fescue	7.76
Highland Colonial bent	6.79
Crop	.08
Weed	.01

A finer-textured grass lawn would consist of the following species of grasses in the package offered to the homeowner:

Newport Kentucky bluegrass	39.00%
C1 Kentucky bluegrass	31.00
Chewings fescue	9.80
Pennlawn creeping red fescue	9.80
Fylking bluegrass	7.82

A shade lawn in this area usually consists of *Poa trivialis* (55.20%), creeping red fescue (24), and highland creeping bent (14).

As I said, this type of lawn stays green all year and can certainly be mowed with a rotary. And if that makes a California homeowner happy, it's all right with me.

Interestingly enough, on the shelf next to these "Heinz 57" mixtures of grass species, there can be sitting unobtrusively over to the side and looking very lonely, a seed package marked "unhulled Bermuda grass" with a purity of 98 percent.

If you are buying tall fescue for places where a year-round permanent turf is more important than summer quality and appearance, a high rate of seeding is necessary. Tall fescue is a bunch-type grass, and seeding with less than 8 to 10 pounds per 1,000 square feet will result in a clumpy lawn. So in a lawn grass mixture, tall fescue should always constitute 70 percent of the mixture. For example:

Tall fescue	72.00%
Chewings fescue	9.70
Kentucky bluegrass	9.70
Highland Colonial bluegrass	5.60

Some lawn maintenance companies in Orange County recommend that homeowners stick with two types, a mixture of Newport Kentucky bluegrass and Manhattan perennial ryegrass, rather than use the conglomeration of grasses mentioned earlier. In recent tests in Michigan, Manhattan did better under wear and tear than even tall fescue. This mixture of Newport Kentucky and Manhattan is a wise purchase. It does quite well at 2½ inches in the heat of summer and at a lower height during the winter months. The mixture will come up usually in from 3 to 5 days, and in 14 days a homeowner should be happily mowing his new grass. This mixture also does quite well in some of the more northern areas, and I would like to see homeowners in northern California try several of the improved Kentucky bluegrass varieties recently discovered. However, check with your county extension service before you buy tons of a new bluegrass variety for your lawn. Let them advise you as to how well it will do in your particular area. Usually the desirable characteristics of such regal varieties as Merion, Nugget, Fylking, and Pennstar, as well as their advantages over common Kentucky bluegrass in the North, are of little importance when these grasses are planted in the South. It's best to stick with a "home brew" common Kentucky bluegrass produced in Kentucky or some other southern state, and not use seed grown in northern states.

For those homeowners who live close to the ocean or in the higher temperature zones of California, hybrid Bermuda or St. Augustine grass should be used. Nothing beats these two fine grasses for hot temperatures in the South.

The question most often asked about southern lawns (especially by Northerners moving south) is how best to overseed a dormant Bermuda grass lawn for winter color. Before I answer, let me first explain the difference between *reseeding* and *overseeding,* two terms often confused in garden books. Reseeding means duplicating with the same seed; for example, Kentucky bluegrass seeded over a Kentucky bluegrass lawn. Overseeding, on the other hand, is seeding with a species other than the grass originally established in your yard; for example, a Bermuda grass lawn or St. Augustine yard overseeded with ryegrass for winter color. I hope this clears up the confusion for homeowners (and garden writers).

I will answer the question about overseeding a dormant winter lawn by advising southern homeowners that the paramount concern is timing. You can do it anytime from September through November. The day, week, or month depends on your location in the South. But wherever, *never* overseed until the warm-season grass that is established in your yard has become *fully dormant.* (See page 60.)

Now I am going to give you three ways to overseed a dormant grass for winter use and appearance, and you can take your pick.

I rate them as fair, good, and super. Your choice will depend on your ambition and wallet. Actually, the majority of independent southern homeowners have a fourth way (perhaps the most practical considering how seed prices are rising)—and that is to leave their dormant lawns alone and do nothing.

Method one is to set your mower as low as possible and intentionally scalp the lawn when it reaches the fully dormant stage. Don't worry, you won't kill it. (Remember, I advocate these methods only for healthy lawns that have been brought to this stage in time in the proper way. Drastically scalping a weak lawn that isn't healthy for winter overseeding can result in turf loss over the winter and spring, depending on the severity of the winter.) This only cuts off a lot of grass and growth-hindering thatch. It will enable the new ryegrass seed to drop more readily into the turf and make contact with the soil. Overseed with about 10 to 15 pounds of annual ryegrass per 1,000 square feet. It's best to divide this amount in equal parts and spread the seed in two opposite directions. Now fertilize with a good starter fertilizer and water the fertilizer and ryegrass seed.

The second-best overseeding method is a little more drastic, a little more expensive, but also more effective. Before overseeding, dethatch your Bermuda grass lawn mechanically with a special power rake (available at rental agencies) that has vertical knives or blades to thin out the matted grass and dead thatch. Verticut in two directions prior to seeding. Rake off and remove all the thatch, then seed 10 to 15 pounds per 1,000 square feet of annual ryegrass. Dethatching a lawn not only prepares your Bermuda grass yard for overseeding, but also gets rid of restrictive thatch that robs your lawn of air, water, and a good root system. Thatch is a barrier of dead matter that doesn't allow penetration of water and nutrients and doesn't allow exchange of O_2 and CO_2 (aeration). It is particularly severe on Bermuda grass lawns. We'll talk about thatch later on. For now, set the cutting height of your lawn mower down from the summer mowing height and cut your lawn with no catcher in two directions. Let the clippings from the lawn mower cover the seed and act as a mulch. Fertilize with a starter fertilizer. Keep the grass watered until the seeds come up, and then water accordingly.

The third method of overseeding is the most drastic and the most effective, if done properly. Let's do it in steps. Step one: verticut the lawn in two different directions, then rake off and remove the clippings. Step two: get a second power machine called an aerifier (it also can be rented) and aerify the lawn. For best results do it in two directions before seeding. This will not only open up the thatch but also will relieve possible compaction of your lawn. Seed the same amount of ryegrass per 1,000 square feet as in methods one and two. Now lower your mower from the regular summer height and mow the lawn in two different directions. Leave the catcher off. The mower will break up the aerifying plugs and knock the seed down. Drag mat the lawn if you wish. Now fertilize and give your lawn a really deep watering. From here on keep the lawn wet with subsequent light waterings. Depending on how much moisture is lost to evaporation and transpiration, water just enough to keep the soil bed from losing moisture and the ryegrass seeds from drying up. Don't let up. Frequent light watering is very important during overseeding and makes the difference between success and possible failure. The ryegrass usually comes up in 5 or 6 days.

Any of these overseeding methods can be supplemented by lightly top-dressing with a good quality soil or by spreading no more than a quarter-inch layer of weed-free steer manure (generally available at southern lawn and garden centers). Besides giving organic strength to the grass, steer manure produces heat and fermentation, which keeps the seed warm and causes rapid germination. Another plus of this organic material is that it acts as a sponge and keeps seed moist; the ryegrass seeds draw moisture from it. Lastly, the steer manure forces the seed into the ground and starts germination—and that is the whole secret of a successfully overseeded lawn. Oh yes, steer manure also offers some nutrient value to your grass. Try it, you'll like it. Buy it from a store where it's packaged, dried, and weed-free. Your neighbors and wife might object if you get it from a fresher source.

One final word on overseeding. There are turf experts who recommend improved varieties of perennial ryegrass for overseeding; still others recommend creeping red fescue and even Kentucky bluegrass. In my opinion, these species are best left to the experienced golf course superintendent. The southern homeowner needs nothing more than common annual ryegrass for overseeding his dormant grasses—provided, of course, that he does it right. The price of this annual grass is still cheap, and it always disappears more quickly from your Bermuda or St. Augustine lawns than the perennials at that very important growing time when Mother Nature brings the warm-season grasses out of winter dormancy and into spring awakening. The other grasses sometimes linger on and on and on. Therefore, I doubt whether the higher-quality, much more expensive perennial cool-season grasses are any better than the old standby—annual ryegrass.

Q.—What is the best way to bring a warm-season lawn out of winter dormancy? Do we let Mother Nature take her own time, or is there a way we can help with the rebirth of the brown grass? And please tell us when dethatching is best—in spring or fall?

A.—The transition during spring of an annual ryegrass from winter back to a permanent warm-season grass can be helped by lowering the cut from wintertime ryegrass mowing (so that the Bermuda will not be shaded out) and delaying application of nitrogen until ryegrass starts to die out and the Bermuda grass breaks winter dormancy as temperatures rise. When this occurs, fertilize with a straight nitrogen to bring out the Bermuda. But don't be in too much of a hurry. Be sure the Bermuda grass is emerging from dormancy before you rush in with the fertilizer, otherwise you might be prolonging the life of the annual ryegrass or the northern grass you have overseeded with.

Now for your question on when is dethatching best for warm-season grasses. Dethatching, *if you are not overseeding,* is usually recommended during spring. If you do it earlier during dormancy, it will usually take weeks and weeks for it to come back, and the retarded, opened-up Bermuda grass most likely will have an increased weed population. But if you do it in February or March (depending on your location), when the grass is coming out of dormancy, it starts to green up. Fertilizing and watering right after dethatching is very important in order to end up with a tight, healthy turf for the summer. If you overseeded your grass for winter color with an annual ryegrass, and used my second or third overseeding method, dethatching will not be necessary in spring;

simply lower your mowing heights when the warm-season grass breaks dormancy so that you are mowing at the recommended height for your particular warm-season grass (never higher) and catch clippings all summer long. Then next fall, repeat: either renovate and overseed for winter or dethatch in the spring.

Q.—What is thatch and what problems does it cause if we don't dethatch our Bermuda grass lawn every year?

A.—We will answer for both the southern and northern homeowners. In fact, the reason we are putting this question here is that, in the South, Bermuda grass lawns have a tendency toward greater and more rapid thatching than any other grass, including any existing creeping bent cool-region lawns. Tests have proven that. Therefore, a southern homeowner has to worry much more about his thatching problem than one managing a northern lawn, which consists predominantly of Kentucky bluegrass turf.

Thatch is a buildup of intermingled, undecomposed leaf blades (clippings), roots, and stems of grass that lie below the living soil layer (green vegetation) and above the mineral soil layer—in other words, a barrier of dead material at the surface of the soil. Living material growing on top is referred to as the *mat of grass,* and the dead material is called *thatch.* Thatch buildup creates a spongy layer that acts as a shield between the living plant and the soil. This unhealthy situation inhibits vital water and air drainage and also keeps nutrients from entering the soil.

Thatch buildup results in a poor lawn in which a number of problems usually occur. The lawns has less tolerance to drought and cold; localized dry spots appear in it with scalping; and browning and severe wilting occur after lawn mowing. Thatch also encourages an increase in the insect population and provides an excellent incubation area for organisms of disease to live and thrive on. Most of all, a lawn with thatch has a poor and restricted root system that can never penetrate into the soil for a healthy root rhizome growth. As a result, prolonged extremes of heat, drought, or cold usually are fatal to an overly thatched lawn—whether it is located in the North or in the South.

Q.—Please tell me what causes thatch. And how does it occur?

A.—Thatch occurs when dead organic matter accumulates on the soil surface at a faster rate than it can be decomposed by microorganisms in the soil. Thatch is the result of poor turf culture practices by the homeowner: overfertilization, overwatering, improper mowing techniques (such as high and infrequent mowing of southern grasses), and failure to pick up the clippings in a catcher. In the North, mowing Kentucky bluegrass infrequently at too low a cut and not picking up the clippings contributes to thatch. Picking up clippings in the North is necessary only in spring, when heavy growth occurs, or if you mow less than once weekly. Compaction of soil and lack of mechanical aerifying also will contribute to thatch, especially in the North.

Q.—I heard that earthworms in the soil help keep lawns from becoming too thatched. Could you please explain this?

A.—You heard right. Earthworms help reduce thatch by their natural aerifying action, plus the fact that their miniscule mounds or castings of pure topsoil mix with dead matter at the surface and start an organic reaction, which hastens the decomposition of thatch.

This is what composting is all about. However, in lawns, let the earthworms do it. A long time ago I noticed this significant natural phenomenon: whenever lawns, gardens, or golf courses had an abundant earthworm population, the turf had a strong root system and much less thatch, and was extremely healthy-looking even when undernourished. On the golf course, earthworms have to be kept to a minimum with chemical control. Their sticky castings are a hindrance to golf play on fairways, particularly on greens. Also, the extremely low mowing done in the early dew of the morning can make quite a mess of the castings on the grass and play havoc with the reel blades. However, a homeowner cuts his lawn much higher—above the mounds and castings (especially in the North) —and he can mow in the evening when the grass is dry, so there is no valid reason for him to poison his worms. Believe me, no machines can duplicate the natural aerification process caused by Mother Nature's snaky little creatures. And wherever earthworms exist abundantly, there is a prominent lack of serious pests, particularly grub worms. Furthermore, I have never seen localized dry spots, fairy rings, or compaction problems where these wonderful friends of the soil are numerous. A homeowner who unwisely listens to contrary advice and eradicates the lowly earthworm is opening a Pandora's box of lawn problems. Besides, what would your little boy with his fishing pole say, or a hungry robin?

This is as good a place as any to begin stating my views on organic food and on the faddists who peddle much unadulterated nonsense. They can quit worrying about homeowners, at least a tremendous majority of them, because no matter what *chemicals* they are using in their landscape management, they must be using them wisely and carefully to have earthworms thriving in their yards. Their very presence indicates proper use of chemicals, and to me a healthy population of earthworms in the soil means gardening of the highest order, whether organic or chemical.

Q.—Please explain to me vegetative lawn planting in the South. What do such terms as sprigging, plugging, stolonizing, and strip sodding mean?

A.—Vegetative planting is the method by which most southern grasses are planted in lawns. It means replanting living grass.

The most expensive way to install grass in a southern yard is by *sodding*. Total sodding of any area in the South is recommended only where steep grades exist and erosion is a major problem. (Or if you're very rich.) Bermuda and Zoysia vegetative material should be planted in full sun.

Vegetative stands of turf rather than seed have to be established in the southern lawns because the hybrid Bermudas, St. Augustine, and Zoysia cannot be grown successfully from seed and still be of the same variety. They won't produce a true-to-type plant or hybrid.* Actually all grasses can be propagated vegetatively but this planting method works best with grasses that have a stoloniferous growth (runner-type growth like a strawberry plant).

Sprigging is done in spring in straight, furrowed trenches or rows. (It is similar to planting radishes and other vegetable crops, only much deeper.) The closer the rows, the quicker the lawn will form. Always presoak the seedbed when you plant sprigs. One square yard of good sod broken into individual sprigs (stolons, runners) will supply enough material for close to 1,000 square feet of lawn. It all depends on how healthy the sod is. A sprig or

*Hybrid: the result of crossbreeding between two selective individuals or species. Selection is picking the best of the lot and propagating that type.

stolon is capable of putting out roots or shoots when planted from its nodes or joints. Plant the sprigs vertically (like any other plant) in the parallel trenches 2 or 3 inches deep and 8 to 10 inches apart. Cover the sprigs well with soil, but never completely cover their foliage. Sprigged hybrid Bermuda should cover the yard in 3 months; Zoysia is much slower to establish and takes up to 12 months (if you're lucky) and usually much longer. Good planting and good soil-culture management, like proper fertilization and watering at the time of planting and later, will make the difference between a well-established lawn and a poor one. Sprigging is a satisfactory and inexpensive way to establish a new lawn vegetatively.

Stolonizing is the planting of chopped or shredded stem growth by broadcasting the material as lightly and uniformly as possible over a prepared seed bed. Right afterwards, the stolonized yard should be rolled, top-dressed, and kept wet until the stolons take root. With stolons (as with sprigging or plugging) it's important that you don't get too far ahead in planting and forget to keep moist what you have already planted. I usually do a third of an average green or lawn, then stop to roll, top-dress, and water that portion. Homeowners who don't take this precaution might very well lose some of their vegetative material to drying out. Never let the soil become dry until there is a union (rooting) between the vegetative material and the soil, and the grass is well established. Frequent light watering of sprigged or stolonized lawns is essential. Heavier and more thorough soaking is needed for plugged, strip-sodded, or sodded lawns. Stolons are sold by the bushel in sacks. And 3 to 5 bushels of broadcast stolons will cover 1,000 square feet. The stolons will all turn brown and look like straw before they turn green. Don't be alarmed by this condition; some of the stolons will die, but the majority will make contact with their nodes and joints and start to root, and in a week you'll see a transformation from brown to green. (Roll hard for stolons to make contact with the soil.)

One final bit of advice to southern homeowners. With all methods of vegetative plantings, it is very important to prepare a proper seedbed and to make certain the vegetative material receives adequate fertilizer to get started. Inexperienced homeowners should check with turf experts in the area about the special fertilizer needs of the specific grass they are planting and the soil they are growing it in. By turf experts, I mean the people at the community nursery where you bought the material or county area advisors or golf course superintendents, not the cheap pamphlet advice offered by far too many commercial companies with their advertising offices in New York.

Plugging is more expensive, and in my opinion should be considered only by homeowners whose desire is to introduce a new variety of grass, such as a new hybrid of Bermuda or Zoysia, into an old and established lawn that isn't doing well. Plugging is also recommended for the planting of bare spots in established lawns. The method is to plant small pieces of sod 2 to 3 inches in diameter every 6 inches or so in rows that are 8 to 12 inches apart in a prepared seedbed. Use larger plugs when plugging into an established lawn or into bare spots. The closer the spacing, the faster the coverage. Plugging is usually done with a special hand tool called a plugger. The plugs should be fitted tightly into prepared holes and tamped firmly into place. However, there are excellent machines now that are made especially for plugging and sprigging large areas.

Strip-sodding consists of transplanting lengths of sod and leaving space in between the lengths, where the grass will spread across and fill in. Strip-sodding is more expensive than either sprigging or plugging, but it establishes faster because more sod is initially transplanted into the yard. Strip-sodding is advised for steep slopes, inclines, or terracing. Although expensive, plugging, strip-sodding, and sodding all occasion little fatality, because each starts with a root system, which enables it to survive conditions that might kill sprigs or stolons.

Q.—Everybody around me is using common Bermuda grass. I will soon be moving into a new house and someone at the office suggested I try a hybrid Bermuda. Please tell me something about hybrid Bermudas and the varieties available to the homeowner.

A.—The hybridizer, long acclaimed in the garden and flower world for great success in developing outstanding vegetables and flowers, has in the past few years turned to the development of superior varieties of grasses. The hybridizing of grasses is somewhat unusual, because two varieties must be placed in an isolated crossing cage to ensure that no pollen from other grasses is introduced. Also, the hybridizer must cross certain grass varieties only during the predawn hours when the grass blossoms and will accept fertilization.

The advantage of most hybrids over common Bermuda is that they usually have more resistance to disease. They also keep weeds out better, attain greater sod density, have fewer seed heads, and gain a finer texture with better color. They also have a higher tolerance to salinity and close mowing and recover more rapidly from injury. The paramount thing to remember about hybrids is they wouldn't be developed if they were not an improvement over the common type. Amen. Otherwise, why advertise and sell them? Their disadvantage (like north-region elegant bluegrass varieties) is that they require a greater degree of management. Example: the hybrid Bermuda needs more nitrogen, accumulates more thatch, and therefore requires conscientious thatch removal annually by the homeowner. An economic analysis would show that hybrid Bermuda grass costs much more to maintain than common Bermuda—twice as much or more.

U-3 Bermuda is the oldest selected variety in existence. U-3 (sounds like a submarine) has some tolerance to frost and low temperatures. It is a coarser variety than the (new blood) hybrids. Durable U-3 spreads rapidly and produces a tough, quality turf that has excellent resistance to wear. It is suitable for use on lawns, fields, and park areas.

Tifgreen. This hybrid is my kind of grass, because it never sheds pollen. Let me explain. I am allergic to soil molds, tree pollen, and—you guessed it—grasses. Tifgreen is one grass I don't have to worry about. It's completely sterile. Tifgreen thrives in the humid South, and it is great for putting greens and top-quality home lawns where beauty is the paramount objective. Keep in mind that a homeowner is interested primarily in appearance and ease of maintenance, while a golfer must have a particular type of surface for putting. Tifgreen is very dark and has good disease resistance and sod density (all "musts" for fine putting greens). It should not be used where lawn management is less than tops. In lawns having good management, Tifgreen will grow in the light shade of high-branched trees (except pines) better than some of the other varieties. In areas of high pollution, Tifgreen discolors severely.

Tifdwarf. This is apparently a vegetative mutant of Tifgreen. It grows low and becomes very dense. Its tiny leaves closely hug the ground. Cut Tifdwarf low and mow it frequently. People sometimes mistakenly believe that Tifdwarf needs no mowing. They are wrong. Tifdwarf has good spring recovery and in some areas has gained popularity over Tifgreen on the golf courses. It has a dark green color that turns purplish when temperatures drop. It's a coincidence that the old Washington creeping bent strain that I have on my putting greens at Briarwood has the same color characteristics as Tifdwarf when the weather gets cold. Washington creeping bent becomes a beautiful green in the summer, but as soon as temperatures drop below 50, it begins to turn almost purple black, especially at the first touch of frost.

Ormond. This selection provides a dark green lawn that retains its color late into autumn. It has few seed heads, but more than the latest hybrid discoveries have. This tough grass is vigorous and aggressive and heals quickly when damaged. It has fairly good disease-resistance.

Tiflawn. This is a hybrid that survives traffic damage superbly; it is great for heavily trafficked home lawns, athletic parks, and industrial areas in the South. However, the best grass for a playground is not always the most attractive. Nevertheless, if you have a large family, it sometimes is practical to go with a turf that takes abuse, but whose appearance isn't all that important.

Tifway. This chance hybrid mixes well with Tiflawn for a good home lawn turf. (The reason most of these hybrid Bermudas that I've mentioned start with *Tif* is because they were introduced by the excellent coastal plain experiment station in Tifton, Georgia.) Tifway also has fairly good disease-resistance. The stiff leaf of Tifway gives this hybrid grass a more upright growth. It has only fair frost-resistance, but provides color for the homeowner earlier in the spring and later in the fall than most other hybrid Bermudas. In other words, Tifway is our "early bird." Like most hybrid Bermudas, it doesn't like pollution, which turns its tips orange.

Santa Ana. Although developed specifically for California's conditions, it does acceptably well in most southern states. Santa Ana has excellent wear-resistance and recovers rapidly from abuse.

There are other good hybrid Bermudas that do well in certain areas of the South, but those I've named are the outstanding varieties. Many more are in the experimental stage. Check with the turf experts in your area before planting a new hybrid Bermuda variety. They will be happy to advise you if it's adaptable to your local environment. If it isn't, don't try it.

Before we discuss the touchy transitional zones of the United States, I would like to comment on the insect, disease, and weed problems in the South. The majority of lawn weeds plaguing southern homeowners are pretty well the same types that give trouble in the North; clover, chickweed, dandelions, and crabgrass are common to both. Basically, the pesticide controls given in chapter 5 should take care of such problems—with perhaps some slight variations in central calibration and application for the South. The pesticide safety guide in that chapter applies to all homeowners, no matter where they live. *Be careful!!*

Weeds indigenous to the South, such as nutgrass, Dallis grass, Kikuyu grass, geranium cut leaf, and various types of sandburs, can best be controlled or exterminated through measures advised by experts in your local area or at the county extension office. They can also help you control such insects as the infamous chinch bug, billbug larvae, flea beetles, scales, and the ferocious fire ant (it's very dangerous to people), which is steadily advancing northward. Fire ants are no laughing matter and are so ferocious that they leave an infection with every sting. They can inflict a couple of hundred bites in just a few seconds, and medical cases have been recorded where people actually lost limbs after being stung by these awful creatures. A chemical preparation that kills them consists of ground-up corn cobs soaked in soybean oil and a tiny bit of insecticide called mirex. Apparently, next to people and animals, they love soybean oil best.

Southern homeowners are having increasing troubles with parasitic animals called nematodes, which are tiny worms best identified by an expert with a microscope. A handful of contaminated garden soil might contain thousands of nematodes. It is impossible for any homeowner to positively identify nematode damage without help from a specialist.* As a rule, though, the infected lawn shows a general loss of vigor and vitality, a thinning of the grass, and what seems to be a lack of fertilizer (similar to a description of centipede grass decline). If you suspect nematode damage, call your nearest university and ask advice from its entomology and plant pathology departments.

Most diseases in the South are similar to those in the cool region (see chapter 5), except they are more prevalent. The reason is obvious—warm temperatures and longer seasons. The hotter and more humid the climate, the greater the problems with fungus and disease. And of course, the longer the duration of stress, the worse the disease when it breaks out. As a result, the tougher the cure or control must be. So vigilant controls for disease are needed, along with top-level management of lawns by the southern homeowner. The homeowner in the short growing season of North Dakota certainly has less headaches over turf disease than the homeowner in Georgia. But then again, sometimes, just sometimes, "it ain't necessarily so." In the long run (of time and seasonal change), perhaps everything evens out in Mother Nature's old book of turf ailments—in all areas except one, that is. And that area is our next subject.

The transition zone. This "twilight zone" is the most difficult turf-growing area for homeowners, because neither a northern grass nor a southern grass does well in it. The reason is that this devilish zone, which is best described as moving along the line of the central states, is too far north for warm-region grasses and too far south for cool-region grasses. Therefore, none of the grasses feels at home in the long shadow of the so-called "twilight zone." No grass is adaptable here throughout the season. In some parts of the transition zone a warm-region grass will do better; in

---

* Throughout this book, I frequently suggest that the reader check with turf experts in his area. This is not a cop-out. It is the soundest advice I can give if you have serious lawn problems. Even where I prescribe a solution, it is still best to double-check with someplace like the university extension office in your county that has qualified experts who are more familiar with your conditions than some author from Illinois. If that's a cop-out, then I plead guilty.

others a cool-region grass is better suited. And sometimes both types (species) do well.

The transition zone starts in Kansas City, Kansas. To the south is Oklahoma, where lawns are predominantly solid Bermuda grass and homeowners don't have problems growing these "AC-DC" grasses. In Kansas City, Meyer Zoysia lawns are becoming very popular and have made quite a hit with homeowners, so much, in fact, that Zoysia sod sometimes is difficult to obtain. Homeowners are putting in Meyer Zoysia where once they would have tried growing a bluegrass lawn. However, most transition zone homeowners don't like Zoysia's major disadvantage, which is its extremely slow establishment. The homeowner who can afford it buys Zoysia in sod form, but it's expensive. In the early 1960s, U-3 Bermuda was the first elite Bermuda grass selection to hit the market, and extensive plantings were done on golf courses and home lawns. Although heralded as a panacea, bad results occurred with U-3 due to winterkill and spring dead spot, for which there still is no effective cure or protection. But homeowners never really went into the elite Bermudas with hybrid sprigs or plugs. They used Kentucky and ryegrass with poor results, and although common Bermuda still prevails with fairly good results here and there in Kansas, Meyer Zoysia has established itself as the best up-and-coming grass for the 1970s.

Let's leave Kansas now and move down the central line to St. Louis, Missouri, where Zoysia is blooming also. Here, many shopping centers and industrial areas are completely sodding their grounds, especially the noticeable entrances. I should make clear that they are sodding with the successful new grass types. The largest percentage of Missouri home lawns, parks, and cemeteries contain Kentucky bluegrass mixed with a lot of red fescue, tall fescue, and perennial ryes, and homeowners still use this mixture. In the South and in the transition zone, however, the perennial ryegrasses usually tend to act like annual ryes. It is very hard for them to make it through the summer, and the perennial ryes usually last only one year (although some of the perennial ryegrasses recently discovered last longer).

Homeowners in Springfield, Missouri, are learning that a pure seeding of Kentucky 31 tall fescue does very well. They don't mind its coarse appearance as long as it grows. To get away as much as possible from the tall fescue's growth habit of clumping, seed very heavily, as much as 10 to 20 pounds per 1,000 square feet. This is important, because a heavy seeding of tall fescue makes a thicker, denser, and more upright growth—and this will make you Missouri homeowners much happier. In situations that are especially hard to maintain, pure strains of a tough tall fescue (like the K-31 variety) do very well.

A few "wild type" Bermuda grass lawns are scattered throughout the state. These do all right, but locally. Overseeding for winter color is not common, although some industrial areas and a few homeowners do apply colorants for the winter season.

Now the line of the twilight zone passes through Evansville, Indiana; Columbus, Ohio; Louisville, Kentucky; and includes Cincinnati on the other side of the polluted Ohio River. The great Ohio is formed by the Allegheny and Monongahela rivers joining west of the Allegheny mountain range. When we come to the Alleghenies and the mountain climate of Kentucky, the elevation rises and even at a jump of only a hundred feet, you won't find any warm-season grasses. Kentucky bluegrass grows well here, naturally. But then, as you pass through the mountain range and drop down to old Highway 50 (Virginia) and then into Washington, D.C., you are back to lawn problems, particularly in Washington, D.C., where it's difficult to grow either a warm-season grass or a cool-season grass. Here, Kentucky bluegrasses are used by homeowners, and some seeded Bermuda lawns are successful but a lot of it winterkills. Zoysia is very slowly starting to catch on. Once we get about 100 miles north, we are out of the transition zone and in the Wilmington, Delaware, area where it's mostly Kentucky bluegrass. On the other hand, 100 miles south of our Capital, in the Richmond, Virginia, area, the basic lawn grasses are predominantly Bermudas!

Now let's take one specific metropolitan area in the transition zone and talk turf. Let's pick Kentucky and the great old derby town of Louisville. The average American homeowner may wonder why anybody would have trouble raising a lawn in Kentucky. Isn't that where the famous name originated for the major cool-region grass—Kentucky bluegrass? So let's take a closer look.

Some people have the idea that Kentucky is a state with a blue green carpet of grass, where everyone runs around in bib overalls, with feet bare and a felt hat that has a bite out of the brim, and a squirrel rifle on one shoulder and a jug of "corn squeezins" on the other. Nothing could be farther from the truth as far as the dress of the local citizens is concerned. As far as Kentucky bluegrass is concerned, it does beautifully here in the horse country of the Lexington/Versailles/Paris area, where thoroughbreds behind white board fences wander through it knee high, which is the way Mother Nature intended it to be. Where horses and other domestic animals can reach down and with one bite get their green nourishment.

But it's a whole new ball game in the Ohio Valley area alongside Kentucky, especially the Louisville region, which borders the Ohio River. (They blame part of the river's pollution on Cincinnati's poor sewage treatment. Lexington is just across the river from Cincinnati.) Once you drop down into the "valley area," the elevation is only about 500 feet above sea level, with a prominent southwesterly wind that brings a flow of moist air from the Gulf of Mexico and gives the Ohio Valley's citizens a summertime humidity of over 90 percent on many days and rarely if ever below 65 percent. Combine this with daytime temperatures in the high 80s and low 90s and nighttime temperatures that rarely get below 70 during the 100 days of June, July, and August, and you find yourself in a pressure cooker. When this condition exists, the Louisville area is not unlike Rod Serling's *Twilight Zone*. The combination of the cool and wet springs and cool and dry autumns is great for cool-region grasses, while the hot and humid summers are great for the warm-region grasses. Now I think you can see the problem: this particular area is too far south for good cool-season turf grass and too far north for good warm-season turf grass. Hence, the twilight zone.

For years all you saw in the Louisville area were poor-to-fair stands of assorted Kentucky bluegrass, mostly of the common variety. Lack of lawn management know-how as much as anything else allowed these springtime carpets of green to turn brown in the hot summer. Then, about fifteen years ago, an invasion of the wondrous Bermuda grass began. This was going to be the promise

—the breakthrough that transition-zone homeowners had been waiting for. But Bermuda was not a cure-all. The cold winters and late springs soon disheartened most homeowners, except for the brave few who had some natural strains that stayed green about 100 days during the active growing season. Then, about ten years ago, Meyer Zoysia was introduced and everybody jumped on that green wagon. Zoysia was a slow grower, it had to be plugged, and it turned brown in the winter (which is *not desirable* if you want it green by the first week of May to impress your Derby guests). It did do well with little management, fertilizer, and water, however, and it provided a dense turf for the neighborhood kids and their dogs to run on. But, alas, even the strongest grasses fall to the whims of nature and Zoysia has been no exception to the rule. Spring leaf spot was working on virtually all stands of Zoysia in this area. The disease is devastating, to say the least. The plant turns yellow, and about 80 percent of the leaves fall off, not to return to a green condition until the middle of June. Thereby exit Zoysia.

So where does this leave the homeowner? Mother Nature knows. Back to bluegrass again—but this time with proper lawn management and away from the "hardware store" common Kentucky bluegrass to improved varieties bred especially to adapt to the climate. Some of them have some disease resistance; however, the infestation of *fusarium roseum* ("frog eye") has taken a heavy toll of all bluegrasses. The "Wonder Contract Chemical Lawn Services" (each one sometimes promoting a different grass), which now abound throughout the Ohio Valley, don't know what *fusarium roseum* is and therefore don't use the proper fungicides to control it. The confused homeowner, who has laid out good money to these lawn service companies, should make damn sure that they know how to treat a *fusarium roseum*-infested lawn. With proper chemical treatment, a diseased lawn can be restored or, better still, treated for *fusarium roseum* and hopefully with good preventive maintenance that will keep the disease from "hitting" the grass.

The grass today for home lawns in the Ohio Valley most certainly leans to a mixture of Kentucky bluegrass varieties. A blend of three or more of the patented varieties mowed at a high cut is certainly the best direction to take. Often people cringe at the price of these better varieties, but it is money well spent and the result is a much better grade of turf and a high resistance to both leaf spot and *fusarium roseum*. There still are a few people trying to grow Bermuda and Zoysia—and crabgrass—but Kentucky remains the bluegrass state, even, with proper management, in the hard-to-grow grass areas like the Ohio Valley. Amen.

Before we answer a few more questions, let me again emphasize the importance of dealing with the turf experts in your area when it comes to sound information and direction, especially you homeowners who are living in the transition zone. If you made a mistake, it's a disaster, and there is no second chance. In this area you usually have to start your lawn all over, *or* put up with a weak-looking lawn for the season. My firm suggestion would be to seek the advice of an experienced golf course superintendent who has been in your area for a long time. These superintendents in the transition areas go through hell trying to keep their many acres meticulously manicured and green at the extremely low desired mowing heights for golf play throughout the summer. They eat, drink, and sleep grass management, and have the latest, the best, and the most up-to-date methods for keeping their golf course healthy and verdant.

Even if there's a fee for a consultation, it's worth every cent.

Q.—Please tell me the different varieties of Zoysia available to me in the transition zone. We are located near Evansville, Indiana. Which one is best? How good is Zoysia?

A.—Meyer's Zoysia is strong in the Evansville area of Indiana and is best in my opinion. It's comforting to note that a golf course in Evansville was the first to put in all-Zoysia fairways.

Zoysia may very well be the up-and-coming superior grass in hard-to-grow areas this decade. Zoysia came to North America from Asia in 1905 and sometimes is still called Korean or Japanese grass. It has a terrific root system, once it's established, and forms a very tight and dense sod. Zoysia spreads and intertwines by rhizomes and stolons in the same way that Bermuda does. Zoysia requires very little moisture and lots of sun (it stops when it hits shade). Its dense growth, I am happy to say, crowds out weeds better than any other grass. But weeds are a definite problem during the one to two years it takes Zoysia to establish in a seed-bed and become a good lawn. The major disadvantages of Zoysia are that it is very slow to establish a solid sod (also up to two years) and, because of its slow spreading habit, it recovers slowly after excessive damage. But it does take wear and abuse extremely well. The homeowner putting in Zoysia by vegetative transplanting (plugging is the most popular method) should be very careful during the first crucial weeks after planting it in his yard. A crucial time for Zoysia is during transplanting, *no matter what the Zoysia ads say.* Zoysia is also one of the toughest bladed grasses to mow. Make sure you have a sharp, good power mower. A hand mower won't do—unless you're Samson.

I like Zoysia and think it is a panacea for certain areas in the transition zone. But don't try it unless you give it some thoughtful study. The Northern homeowner should leave it alone unless he wants to plant a patch of it on a berm or hill facing full sun. You'll have it green from late May to September or thereabouts, but it will look like an odd patch on your kid's jeans the rest of the time. It stays brown for a long, long time, and it's a fire hazard when brown (so is Bermuda). Don't fall for the misleading advertising if you're in the cool-region climate. A lot of people do, and end up with sad results on their lawns. If you're curious and want to experiment, try a few plugs and see for yourself what happens to Zoysia sod in the northern lawn, but don't go overboard.

Here are the four predominant Zoysia grasses.

Meyer Z-52. Named after Frank N. Meyer, who worked for the USDA and brought this unusual plant grass material from Korea, Meyer Z-52 has medium leaf width and a dark green color. It has proven to be more winter-hardy than the others in the transition zone. Meyer Zoysia's ancestors survived some pretty cold temperatures in Asia, but the selection doesn't act that way here. In Indiana, Zoysia leaves will turn brown in October and it won't green up until the middle of May. Meyer is the best grass for the twilight zone, which is also referred to as the "crabgrass belt" of the United States. In color and texture, Meyer somewhat resembles Merion bluegrass.

Midwest. This is another Zoysia that grows in the transitional zone in the Midwest. It is a vigorous Zoysia with medium green color. Midwest's leaves are wider than Meyer's, but according to the USDA it is faster spreading than Meyer.

Emerald Zoysia. Here is a hybrid Zoysia that is finer-textured and of a better quality than Meyer. It is comparable to the finest Bermudas. Emerald is not recommended for the transition zone because of its winterkill. It is an old favorite in the Deep South, especially in Georgia, and is also recommended for the California area, where it needs to be mowed only once every two weeks. Both Emerald and Matrella (see below) winterkill severely, but both are more drought-resistant than Meyer and Midwest. Because of very thick growth, Emerald does not take very well to overseeding with common ryegrass. Emerald is more shade- and frost-tolerant than Bermuda.

Matrella. It's an Emerald look-alike, but Emerald is supposed to be the classier of the two. A friend of mine in Georgia has had a Matrella lawn for fifteen years. It is beautiful and never has been pampered.

Remember, this discussion is about the Zoysias, and good, careful, and persistent management is very important for their establishment as a lawn. Without a good maintenance program by the homeowner, several years may be required to establish it. That's too long to wait for any lawn to establish, no matter how wonderful the grass might look eventually.

Q.—Why not overseed a Bermuda lawn in the transition zone?

A.—Overseeding Bermudas in a transition zone for winter color by opening them up with power machines increases the severity of winterkill. Remember that in the "AC-DC" zone the winters are colder than in the warm-region zone. Another disadvantage of winter overseeding is that the grass used for overseeding usually stays longer in the spring than is desired, and therefore contaminates the Bermuda lawn. It's best to leave a Bermuda grass lawn that is growing in this zone alone in the winter. Keep it long for the winter, and one half inch to three quarters of an inch in the summer.

Q.—Is it true the White House lawn is in the "Twilight Zone"? (No pun intended.) Of what grass is the White House lawn really comprised?

A.—I would say that the White House is in the twilight zone alright, as far as grasses are concerned. Remember that surprise I mentioned back in chapter 2? I was going to tell you about a very famous lawn containing tall fescue. Well, act surprised now. The White House lawn is almost completely K-31 tall fescue. The reason given by the United States Department of the Interior is that it "can tolerate the hot weather in the hot months and is capable of withstanding heavy use." And that's exactly what tall fescue's great forte is wherever it's planted—the ability to withstand drought, hot temperatures, and cold winters, as well as heavy traffic, poor soils, and difficult terrains. Besides that, it's great for pastures and sheep and cattle grazing. It keeps the farm animals fat and happy. Herefords show enthusiasm for it and enjoy it as you and I enjoy ice cream. But the White House Lawn? In the time of the Kennedy administration, I wrote in my first lawn book how the White House Merion lawn was lost to the dreaded disease of stripe smut, and how a sad President Kennedy was observed standing in his office window unhappily watching the demise of his once beautiful green. Well, a lot of things have gone to hell since then, not just the White House lawn of pure Merion Kentucky bluegrass. But glamor isn't everything, and that goes for some of the elite, regal grasses that are great performers at first and show terrific promise for the future, but suddenly, when the stress comes and the going gets tougher, collapse and don't finish off their highly advertised "term" of performance. So nix on them. On the other hand, using tall fescue is the sensible solution arrived at by the head professional turf employees, who maintain the White House lawn and who put in a tough grass to do a "man's job." Others should "get the hell out of the kitchen." Appearances, here as in many other areas of the transition zone, are second to performance.

My respect for tall fescue increases every day. Even the White House rose garden, where much traffic exists, is K-31 tall fescue, but fertilized at higher rates. They tried Zoysia in the spring and a top quality bluegrass in the fall, but K-31 did and does best of all (a good slogan for K-31 tall fescue if you like grass poetry).

The private, small east lawn of the White House is Warren's A-34. It does not get much traffic and is doing well. This lawn is mowed at 1½ inches and is fertilized with 3 to 4 pounds of actual

nitrogen per 1,000 square feet annually. The major weed bothering the White House lawns is nut sedge; however, the control
chemical DSMA that gets rid of it has been put on the pesticide
restricted list by the government. Nut sedge is considered by experts to be the most detested weed in the world—it's a real Public
Enemy No. 1 in some parts of the United States.

My somewhat astounding realization in this chapter is that the
shining knight in rough clothing, the one that succeeds again and
again for homeowners in areas where grass is tough to grow, is
tall fescue. Like a character in a novel, tall fescue appears at first
as a suspicious and villainous character (a real rogue, for north-
region homeowners anyway), but then in the end, when he finds
the right job (area) and the right people (homeowners in tough-
to-grow-grass areas), he saves them (one hot summer) and
emerges as a hero. And so it is with tall fescue.

Anyway, if tall fescue is good enough for the White House, it
should be good enough for your over-taxed little acreage until
something better comes along, something that (to use my son's
favorite expression when he is watching *his* hero, Evil Knevil)
doesn't "wipe out" during the stress of summer.

The USDA announced on September 1, 1974, that "Alta" and
"Kentucky 31" will be recognized and designated as separate dis-
tinguishable varieties in enforcing federal seed-labeling regulations.
The USDA and many other people had previously considered
"Alta" and "K-31" to be single varieties, and their names were
thus often used interchangeably. Research recently has indicated
that there is a fair amount of difference between the two, as far
as origin, growth, resistance to rust, and ability to withstand close
mowing in lawns are concerned. Perhaps, hopefully, with more research and development in the future, this "ugly duckling" of a
grass (by northern standards anyway) will eventually turn into a
beautiful swan. For the sake of all homeowners living in the hard-
to-grow areas, I hope this occurs. I know of one major seed company that is already trying to make it happen.

4

The Preparation and Installation of a New Home Lawn

PREPARING A SEED or sod bed for a new lawn is an important basic step that has to be carefully carried out by the homeowner if he is doing the job, or carefully supervised by him if somebody else is doing it, because no other step goes further to ensure a successful lawn for the future. The soil base for the new lawn must have adequate drainage, proper grading, and a topsoil of good quality before the lawn can be seeded or sodded. Without these time-proven construction basics, a homeowner will later face major turf problems with all aspects of his landscape, and not just with the grass cover. Anything he does afterwards will be undermined by his failure to first provide a proper soil base for his new turf.

The purpose of this chapter will be to keep the homeowner from making any mistakes at this basic stage. I will show you how to put in a soil base successfully so a strong healthy lawn will grow in the yard now and in the future, regardless of whether it's a brand-new lawn or an old lawn being completely rebuilt. (If it's the latter, it's probably because it wasn't constructed properly the first time.)

Q.—We are a young couple who soon will be moving into a

new home that has no lawn. In fact, there is nothing in the yard except piles of mud, dirt, and debris strewn over the construction base. How do we go about preparing a proper seedbed for our new grass? We have no experience and need lots of guidance.

A.—You're not the only couple who have never put in a new lawn. Many homeowners in America are in the same boat. The problem need not be difficult, but some diligence is needed in following my basic steps. Let me say first that I will describe how the lawn bed should be constructed, *whether* you do it yourself, or hire landscape contractors, or have it done by the building firm that put up your house. Who does the basic groundwork matters less than that the work be done properly, and that the steps I recommend be followed carefully. Okay?

Before beginning actual construction of a new house, the building contractor should move all available native topsoil to one side and stockpile it while the house is being built. When the house is finished, make sure that all building debris—boards, bricks, beer cans, discarded roofing paper, stumps, wire cables, and other junk —is completely cleared away. As time goes on, this debris has a curious way of moving up gradually through the turf until you damage your mower or your toe on it. Sometimes it decomposes and makes potholes in your yard. So get rid of this junk before rough-grading (subgrading) the lawn area.

After rough-grading the subsoil to a desired contour, making sure to pitch the gradient of the yard away from the house, move the topsoil back over the subbase. Redistribute the topsoil uniformly, and smooth and grade the slope gently away from the house down to the street curbing below. It's always best to have the grade level with the sidewalks, driveways, or other landscape paths so that when the seed grows up, or when the new sod is laid, the grass will stand slightly higher than the concrete. If the grass is much below the cement, as it often is, the lawn mower hits the concrete edges, makes sparks fly, and dulls your mower blades. Some settling will always occur, so be sure that the grade level to be is packed level with the top of the concrete or asphalt. Next check the yard carefully for signs of standing water, which will cause chronic wet spots later on. Chronic wet spots cause major headaches, because they eventually kill the turf and look unsightly.

Sometimes, for one reason or another, the topography can't be graded or easily changed to permit water to run to the street. In this case, subsurface drainage must be installed—and installed before you seed or sod. It will be much cheaper then, because you can still grade out the muddy mess that results from the trench digging. (This also goes for the installation of automatic sprinklers, as well as water, gas, sewer, telephone, and electric lines and all other modern conveniences. Have them installed now. Trench lines should be packed and allowed to settle well before you start any type of lawn. Otherwise, depressions will occur.) If the tiling job is small and you decide to do it *yourself,* get professional advice before you start. In fact, weigh carefully whether it might not be best to have the job done by professionals who are familiar with local soil conditions. Tile must be laid correctly to work properly.

The best source of tiling information I know comes under the heading of Building Materials in the yellow pages of the telephone book. These firms stock tile, which is made of concrete, clay, or perforated plastic. Modern plastic tile comes in varying lengths and is very easy to use. I have used it successfully all over my golf course. The building material people usually have access to good topsoil or fill, which you probably also will need. (In my experience, a yard never has enough good-quality soil.) The experts at the building material firms will be happy to help you with your particular tile problem, if you live in the community. They never disappoint me. However, if you find that extensive tiling must be done on your new property and the building contractor has already left and taken all his equipment to another developing site far away (believe me, this happens often), then ask your local golf course superintendent or the building material people to refer you to a qualified tiling contractor. They know who is the best, but it's financially prudent to get three estimates. Sure, it costs money for tiling, but if the house contractor leaves you in this bind, or if you are rebuilding a poorly drained old yard, you have no choice. Get the tile job done before you put in grass. It will be less messy and cheaper, believe me. Then have your lawyer send the bill with a strong letter to the building contractor.

It should be apparent by now that it's wise to meet frequently with the builder before he moves away to another job. Check everything he's doing. Ask a lot of questions. Don't worry about sounding stupid; better a few questions now than a lot of grief later on. Make sure you and the builder understand and agree about who is to be responsible for what, and keep reading your contract. If the specifications state that he is responsible for the final grading of your yard, then don't let him get away until this is carried out and your property is drained and graded to your complete satisfaction. There is a difference between rough-grading and smooth-grading. Be sure you know the difference and how each should look. (Discussions of these come later in this chapter.)

Most new yards need additional topsoil for their new lawns. Unfortunately, most homeowners hesitate to purchase extra soil, mistakenly figuring that the original topsoil that was put back over the subbase is sufficient. Frequently it isn't. Often it isn't even topsoil, but just looks like it and is actually heavy, dark clay loam. Once for all, please remember that 1 inch of good soil is not sufficient to top a lawn bed. I recommend at least 3 inches for a seed lawn and even more for a sodded lawn. I am quite puzzled that so many homeowners will spend money liberally on new furniture, kitchen appliances, and household gadgets that they often don't need (like a TV in every room), but when it comes to providing adequate topsoil for their yard, they skimp worse than old Scrooge ever did at Christmas. Believe me, this is not a wise road to follow. Don't skimp. Reliable dirt suppliers will help you estimate the quantity and correct mixtures of extra topsoil you will need for your new lawn. Remember that in this day and age there is no such thing as cheap black topsoil (incidentally, it doesn't have to be black; in some areas it's red topsoil and just as good as black), and there hasn't been since your dad was a boy.

Quality topsoil is expensive, but it's worth every cent you invest. A soil of good quality should have a 2-1-1 ratio; that is, a mixture of two parts soil, one part sand, and one part humus. Its structure should be a sandy loam—loose and crumbly—and it should not become a "plastic" mud ball when you squeeze it tight in your hand. When you squeeze and drop it, it should be of a texture so friable that it falls apart when it hits the ground. Have a minimum of 3 inches of this good topsoil on your lawn if you are seeding. Measure the depth at several locations in your lawn with an old school ruler, particularly if someone else is putting in the lawn. The next step is to pulverize, level, and smooth-grade the topsoil with a landscape rake attached behind a tractor. Go over and over the lawn area, working the soil until the grade is sufficiently pitched for drainage. Rake out all depressions and high spots until there is a uniform surface. I can't emphasize enough the need for careful attention to final grading. As far as future effort and expense are concerned, it will make the big difference in the maintenance of your lawn.

Be very careful with the power grading rake not to push soil high up the tree trunks (or hit the sidewalks). A few inches around a tree won't matter, but if too much soil is deposited around the tree's base, the tree (especially if it's an oak) will die of root suffocation. Oak trees are very susceptible to dirt piling or any other disturbance of the soil surface around them. The death of a tree is not immediate; it sometimes takes years, but the tree eventually dies. I've seen it so often that it makes me sick to see a careless operator pile up dirt around trees. I feel much better if I talk to the superintendent in charge of the project and explain to him the possible fatal consequences to the trees if the operator continues his carelessness. Sure, it's none of my business, especially if it's a private construction project (and the soil disturbance in any construction project is fantastic), but I do it anyway. It makes me feel better—and it makes my tall friends the trees feel better, also.

Tree bark will not adapt itself below the piled soil surface. Around the base, build shallow wells, or short walls with bricks or stone. And possibly provide further ample drainage with drain tile under the base for air circulation and water drainage. Don't take chances with your trees. They are the only living things that will increase the value of your property in your lifetime. That's right. Grass deteriorates with time, shrubs get old and woody, and flowers die out, but the trees get better and lovelier as they grow older. So take good care of them. There is one important precaution to take to protect your trees, especially if contractors are doing the job. This is to prevent the base of the trees from being hit, and sometimes fatally damaged, by construction equipment. Wire a shield of boards (use 2 x 4's, 2 x 6's, 2 x 8's and 2 x 10's) around the tree trunk so they extend vertically about 10 feet above the ground base. You won't regret the effort.

Finally, after the topsoil is graded, fine-rake it by hand in opposite, or cross, directions until the surface becomes perfectly level. Remove all stones, lumps, and bumps.

Q.—When is the best time to seed cool-region lawns? In spring or fall?

A.—I prefer that any seeding be done in late summer, approximately one week before Labor Day, for the Chicago area and the Midwest states, and up to the third week of September for the southern portions of the Midwest. If you live in the northern tier of states or Canada, seed earlier, which can be any time after August first. The reason I like this time best for the seeding of cool-region lawns, rather than springtime seeding, is that more horticultural and natural breaks come your way during the waning days of summer; after the hot summer, the soil is more receptive to grass seed, and weed growth declines, which makes less competition for the new lawn during its critical establishment period. Damping-off, the prime enemy of young seedlings, especially in the spring, is not a serious disease threat during the late summer and fall planting days in the cool-region climates.

The days become shorter, there is less light, and the nights are longer and cooler. Leaves begin to turn color, and a few dry ones fall to the ground. The lights go on earlier in our homes and young mothers squint through the autumn haze calling their children home from play. During this period there is less need for frequent watering, the chance of heavy rains and subsequent erosion diminishes, and also people are more patient. Take advantage of it. Any annual weeds that come up will be killed by the frost, and the cold winter will take care of the hardier ones. Therefore, the following spring your new grass has a good head start (especially if you have followed my recommendation of fertilizer for new grass) on the fresh weeds coming up.

The advantages of fall seeding are so great that I have seeded lawns with good success even after the recommended fall seeding period, rather than face the problems of springtime seeding. I have dormant-seeded (sometimes called winter seeding) cool-region winter lawns, also, but this should be left to the professional turf man, because timing is of major importance.

Sometimes, however, because of continuous fall rains or late completion of a home, homeowners must wait till spring to seed their lawns. People usually have more energy at this time (it's called spring fever), but they get more impatient too, which is a mixed blessing for their lawns. Expect the soil to be muddy (especially in shade areas) for a long time; it might be well into May (when the days get longer and there is more light for drying) before you can prepare a satisfactory seedbed. But that's all right, as far as I am concerned, because I don't like seeding lawns too early. Germination in colder weather is extremely slow; so if you seed grass too early, you'll be looking at bare ground for a long time before anything comes up except weeds, especially crabgrass, and you can expect washouts from heavy spring rains and sometimes snow. I suggest using a mulch (marsh hay or peat, even straw) to reduce chances of seed washout and hold down damage to soil structure and seedbed. Expect more erosion on slopes, no matter how gentle.

Selective preemergence application of a crabgrass control herbicide, such as Siduron, should be carefully measured and put down in conjunction with the seeding of Kentucky bluegrass lawns. (Don't use it on Bermuda grass.) Calcium and lead arsenates also can be used, but they are messy and not immediately effective, so they should not be used by inexperienced people. The advantage of calcium and lead arsenates is that they stay in the soil a long time and therefore have a prolonged and lasting effect, which results in fewer applications of crabgrass control herbicides. However, because of this residual characteristic, they are not favored by environmentalists and in fact might be banned. But professionally applied, they are absolutely harmless, except to crabgrass and harmful white grubs. If you use any of the above herbicides, don't apply them to shade areas. You'll be wasting the crabgrass control material. Crabgrass, you see, doesn't grow in shade.

With spring lawns you will probably have more bare spots, and therefore will need to do some reseeding here and there. So always be sure to save a few pounds of your original seed, whether you are seeding in spring or fall. And always duplicate with the original seed. Don't use something different.

Probably the best tip I can give you to assure success with spring-seeded lawns is to have patience. Wait until the ground is dry and the soil friable enough to be worked before seeding your grass. Don't try constructing a seedbed when the ground is wet. Another good tip with spring-seeded lawns is to keep the young tender grass nice and long throughout the summer. Don't mow under 2½ inches.

One final factor in favor of spring lawns is this: a homeowner should never wait until fall just to have the advantages of ideal fall seeding weather. If your new house is completed in spring and you are ready to move into it, seed your new lawn. Don't wait. Why put up with mud all spring and dust all summer? Better still, if you can afford it, sod. However, a homeowner who intends to completely renovate a poorly lawn can certainly wait to do the job till late summer, when his chances for success are greatly improved.

Q.—How do you suggest we go about modifying our soil before we put in a new lawn? Our area is mostly of clay loam and the physical structure of even the topsoil seems to be on the clay side. Are there soil conditioners or soil amendments that we can use to mix in with our poor topsoil?

A.—There are many soil additives on the market, such as lime, sawdust, mica, calcined clay, peat, and sand, that can improve a lawn by working into the surface of the existing soil. However, they are usually expensive and are unnecessary if top-quality soil is used. The number one reason for purchasing top-grade soil from a reliable dirt dealer is to eliminate the necessity for buying expensive soil supplements. If you buy good soil, then fertilizer high in phosphorus is all your soil will need. Why add all that junk? Keep in mind that beautiful lawns were built many years before the advent of soil amendments, which now are heralded as panaceas for poor soil. The old lawns were good because only top-quality soil was used in them. Go forth and do likewise, my friend; besides, you have no idea how much it would cost (lots) to modify properly and expertly a poor soil with soil conditioner. Suffice it to say, you'll be paying five times as much for soil conditioners as you would for a good-quality soil (sandy loam) purchased from a local supplier.

Q.—We are moving into a brand-new home. Our agreement with the contractor specifies that he is responsible for the final grading and preparation of the yard for seeding. But it's up to us to put in the grass. We have decided to seed the lawn with a quality Kentucky bluegrass blend. Please describe how to seed properly. We want to know the important steps to take, and how to go about carrying them out properly. It's important for us to be successful with our grass seeding the first try because our budget can't afford a second try—or problems later on.

A.—A new lawn can be a once-in-a-lifetime investment if done properly. In planting a new lawn, all construction and seeding steps are important, and careful attention should be given to all details. Here is what you must do to ensure a trouble-free green yard for many years to come.

Once the ground has been smooth-graded to your satisfaction, seed your yard immediately, while the ground is porous and freshly raked. This is where good communication between the homeowner and the contractor comes in very handy. The contractor can be of enormous help to you at this point. Seed as soon as he completes final smooth-grading. He should give you advance notice as to when this will happen in order for you to be prepared to seed. If signals are crossed at this stage of the game and there is a lapse of a week or so between the seedbed preparation and the actual seeding, the ground can become crusted or eroded or compacted by sudden storms or continued rain. When this occurs, the homeowner nearly always has to start over, and very likely he will have the necessary extra expense of working up the compacted yard again to make it receptive for seed and fertilizer. Don't be naive and think the developer is going to come back and redo your whole yard; no way, once he fulfills his contract. So it's to your advantage to jump in immediately.

Here is what you must do. Apply a "starter" fertilizer, which is a fertilizer with a high phosphorus content. It usually comes in 50-pound bags marked 5-10-5, 18-24-6, 6-24-24, 8-40-16, 10-10-10, 8-32-16, or 5-20-20. The first number depicts the content of nitrogen, the second phosphate, and the third potash. (Read chapter 5 first, then carefully follow the directions on the fertilizer bag.) You'll be getting two to four times as much phosphorus as nitrogen and this will really give your grass a good start. At this point we are interested in phosphorus (the second number), which is responsible for fast root development. The main diet now for seedling grass is not what is usually recommended for mature stands of turf later on—nitrogen primarily—but rather the nutrient phosphorus. Phosphorus is essential to help your young grass develop fast. Once established, turf tolerates less phosphorus and requires more of the other two important turf builders, nitrogen and potassium. Remember that the other complete fertilizers (such as 16-8-8, 10-6-4, 10-8-6, and 12-8-8), with less phosphorus and more nitrogen, are still sufficient in phosphorus and potash to be incorporated into the soil of your yard. But apply these fertilizers at a double rate and your grass will love you.

Spread the nutrients in opposite directions (east-west, then north-south), and thoroughly rake the fertilizer into the top 2 inches of soil. Get a good spreader, because you will also use it for future seeding, more fertilizing, and, most likely, applications of pesticides. The whole secret of planting a good lawn is to use enough fertilizer in combination with the grass seed. A lawn seeded without fertilizer, especially phosphorus, will never amount to much.

Okay, now get your seed, divide it into equal parts, and sow it as uniformly as possible in opposite directions, as you did with the fertilizer. Don't seed on a windy day and be sure to change the setting for seeding. Make very sure that no portion of the seedbed is overlooked. Though I generally recommend the use of chemicals at slightly less than the recommended dosage, I do the opposite with grass seed and recommend that the homeowner use half again as much to allow for seed lost or buried too deeply. For example, if the recommended seeding rate on the package is 2 pounds per 1,000 square feet, I advise you to sow 3 pounds for the same area (even more when seeding with a common Kentucky bluegrass). However, if you know what you're doing, then don't waste the expensive seed. Apply the recommended rate. Usually 2 pounds is the high limit and 1 pound is enough for a professional seeding rate. After the seed is sown, rake very lightly so it just settles in the loose soil. The precaution here is not to push the seeds together with the rake, or worse still, bury them below a quarter of an inch.

More goes wrong at this stage than at any other time. The homeowner will either miss sowing or fertilizing part of the lawn —that's why we do it crisscross—or bury the seeds. So if you're heavy-handed or a little shaky from the party the night before, don't rake at all; just roll your lawn in several directions until the soil is firm. I like a heavy roller—the heavier the better. Get a neighbor to help you pull the roller. Some seed will stick to the roller, but don't worry; there are 2 to 3 million seeds in each pound of Kentucky bluegrass. So if you're sowing this grass and a few thousand stick to your roller, it won't shortchange your lawn one bit. Also, don't worry about compacting the soil. Seed will nearly always germinate, unless you have buried it too deeply. How many times have you seen grass come through almost invisible cracks in cement or asphalt and marveled at the seed's strength? So don't worry about compaction when rolling your newly seeded lawn. Your chances that the seed will burst through the soil with vigor and vitality are pretty good. The several rollings will also help to further level the lawn surface.

Q.—Is there a mulch that you can recommend to cover a newly seeded lawn to conserve the moisture? Also, what material do you recommend to reduce erosion on slopes?

A.—The best mulch to help keep the seedbed moist and warm is marsh hay. It is fairly weed-free and doesn't blow away, as straw does. Marsh hay clings to the soil surface. Straw will eventually blow away because it is hollow; it also has more weeds. Marsh hay hastens germination, and when the crop comes up, the hay mulch protects the seedlings from winds and hot sun. To a certain degree, marsh hay mulch will prevent erosion during heavy rains. Best of all, after seeding, the hay will keep the bed moist and stop soil crusting. After a while the marsh hay breaks down and dissolves. Any hay that doesn't disintegrate can be gently removed with a bamboo rake. Marsh hay comes in bales 2 feet by 2 feet by 4 feet long. It's inexpensive.

Another excellent mulch is peat, although more expensive. It's absolutely weed-free. I often use this product at my golf course when I "spot seed." I place about a quarter-inch of peat material over the seed bed and then water it down. Peat clings well to the soil and acts eventually as a soil amendment, because it goes back into the ground.

For sloped or terraced areas, I recommend burlap, which usually comes in rolls 3 feet by 50 feet. It's something like the old potato sacks your dad used to rip open and place over hard-to-start areas like slopes. However, burlap rolls are cleaner and more airy. The burlap is "ironed" and doesn't have the tight weave of old potato sacks, which shut out sunlight and smothered the young seedlings with their weight. However, even the special landscape burlap that you buy has to be taken off once the seedlings come up; otherwise the grass will turn yellow and smother. Hold down the burlap sheets with bricks or peg them down at the corners with clothespins. Sometimes erosion nets (woven netting) are available at lawn garden centers. Buy them if you can find them, but usually they're available only to commercial landscapers.

For very steep slopes, banks, and terraces (avoid steep inclines, if possible), I recommend that you sod them rather than use seed. Ditto for problem areas like drain spots. They are much easier to sod and in the long run not that expensive. I will cover this topic in the discussion on sodding later on. Another good method of covering high slopes or banks is with a nongrass groundcover, like myrtle, pachysandra, winter creeper, creeping juniper, English ivy, or periwinkle. The state of California makes beautiful use of southern groundcovers along high banks.

Q.—How do you water a new lawn? What shall I use? When is the best time?

A.—This is perhaps one of the most difficult questions in the book to answer properly, because knowing how to water a new lawn usually comes after much experience (which includes mishaps like overwatering, underwatering, and washouts). I can only tell you to keep the soil *moist* all the time, until the grass is at least 1 inch high. Cover all the spots lightly (as close to a mist as you can) with a wide-type spray rather than with a pointed nozzle spray. Hand spraying is best. Try not to wash away the seed. Use boards or planks to walk on while watering to avoid foot ponds. Get all the corners. Be sure the new seedbed never dries out or develops cracks. Never saturate, puddle, or flood. Fast or heavy rains that suddenly fall can't be helped, and this is the only time that I recommend light, frequent irrigation (see chapter 7).

Consider wind velocity, temperatures, and most important, the type of soil you are watering. If the soil type is sand, it will need more irrigation and frequent nutrition. If the soil in your yard is clay, it will need less moisture. But watch out for crusting. A hot windy day is the worst danger to a newly planted lawn, so a careful watch and frequent waterings are necessary to compensate for the faster evaporation of water from the ground surface. Cautious irrigation on slopes and banks will reduce the likelihood of erosion.

When the grass is about 1 inch high or so, taper off your watering by hand spraying. At this point the lawn will need less water, so it's permissible now to use an oscillating sprinkler that goes back and forth. However, stay on your toes; too much water will erode those young seedlings. Conversely, if you underwater the young seedlings, they will shrivel up on you and die. A lawn can grow without any water except rain, but this is too chancy for the homeowner. A lawn will become established much faster with a good watering program. Reach a happy medium with the watering so your seedbed becomes neither washed out nor dry and cracked.

Q.—When should the first mowing on your grass begin? And how will my wife know when to mow?

A.—The first mowing should be done when the new grass reaches about 3 inches. Mow it before it grows any taller. Set your mower to cut 2½ inches high, and definitely not any lower for Kentucky bluegrass or any of the other cool-region grasses (except, of course, creeping bentgrass). For homeowners who seed their lawns, I recommend only one height—2½ inches, both for starting lawns and for later on when the lawns become mature. Don't go up and down with your mower settings, as some homeowners do and as some turf experts advise. Establish a long-term limit between the leaf blades and the root system and leave it there.

Your first mowing will also whisk off all kinds of weeds. Don't worry about them at this point. With frequent mowings, the grass will become dense and uniform and some of the weeds will disappear. What happens if the young grass is mowed too short? Such short mowing weakens the grass and makes it even more susceptible to disease, drought, and temperature extremes. Short grass will also encourage a further weed invasion. Mowing the grass too short or taking off too much grass at any mowing (this goes for mature lawns also) will shock the grass severely and brown it off.

I would like to see a new homeowner use a reel mower for young grass. Buy a reel mower if you are just starting out with a new house, new wife, and new lawn. You see, rotary blades chop at the grass, whereas reel mowers scissor the grass (see chapter 6.) However, if you have already purchased a rotary machine, then always be sure the rotary blade is very sharp. There is nothing worse than a rotary mower with a dull blade, especially for seedling grass. Rotary machines also pull up weak soft grass with their vacuum action. Remember, the purpose of mowing is to cut the grass cleanly without mashing it or pulling it up. It is better, too, if the young lawn is dry when you mow. Don't cut in the dew of morning or in the heat of the afternoon. The best time *always* is just after work (early evening). Water the new lawn after mowing to keep it from drying out. The water will also keep the dust down, lessen the shock of the first mowing, and make any soft young grass flattened by feet or the mower spring right up again.

Clippings don't have to be removed unless there is an extremely heavy growth that might result in clumps of grass bunched all over, smothering the young turf. If you mow frequently, grass clippings never have to be removed. They will disappear in the ground and disintegrate, and release essential nutrients and humus material back into the soil. I have a Japanese friend I play poker with during the winter months. He informs me that Japanese gardeners mow almost every day when grass is growing heavily. As a result, their lawns never have a thatch problem. He is absolutely right. When grass is frequently mowed, the tiny green leaf cuttings shift easily down to the soil and quickly disintegrate upon making contact with mother earth.

Q.—Please explain to us the correct way to fertilize a new lawn during the first year. And what brand of fertilizer do you suggest that we use?

A.—The only fertilizer that I recommend for a first-year lawn is organic-type fertilizer. I have nothing against other fertilizers— they are all good if properly and carefully applied—but I recommend organic fertilizers the first year if only to prevent any mishap by a homeowner. With "hot" fertilizers, there is always the possibility of burning the young lawn. Too many good new lawns that started in great shape have been killed or damaged by novices using too much inorganic chemical fertilizer. With an organic fertilizer, even if you make a mistake and put on too much of it, the new lawn won't burn out. But always *be careful* with any fertilizer, no matter how innocent it seems. An overdose of any of them will make recovery difficult, not only from burning or browning off, but also from disease if too lush a growth is carelessly promoted. Very soft and lush grass also has a hard time withstanding hot weather and winds. So be careful—but use organic. Your chance of mishap with this fertilizer is diminished.

The fertilizer rates for the new lawn, if planted in the fall, should be 2 pounds actual organic nitrogen per 1,000 square feet in the spring of the next year (preferably in the first week of May), then 1 pound per 1,000 square feet in the third week of June, and then, sometime after Labor Day, 2 pounds per 1,000 square feet. However, if you have planted a new lawn in the spring, apply 1 pound of actual organic nitrogen in the latter part of June and then go with 2 pounds of actual organic nitrogen right after Labor Day. Keep in mind that you have a very good application of a complete fertilizer already mixed in the soil. The "starter" fertilizer will keep your grass growing for a long time, so don't be in too much of a hurry to spread more fertilizer as soon as your seedlings pop up. On the other hand, don't expect the "starter" fertilizer to keep the young grass growing all year either. Wait a while and then, after a first mowing or two, apply a little organic food. This is not any endorsement of organic fertilizer. I would prefer using a complete fertilizer. It's just that at this stage of your young lawn, organic fertilizers are the safest to use for the average homeowner.

Q.—What shall I do about the heavy growth of weeds on my new lawn?

A.—Don't worry about weeds in the first year, when the grass is still young and tender. Herbicides should not be used while the grass is establishing (especially 2-4-D), and later on only if necessary. If crabgrass is a problem in your area (and it will be), there are crabgrass control chemicals like Tupersan (use them only if seeding in spring) that can be used safely at the time of seeding. But carefully check with any controller before buying to make sure that the product is definitely recommended for your particular seed. Otherwise you might wait and wait and wait for your expensive seed to come up, if a wrong, preseeding, crabgrass control chemical was put down. Lots of weeds will come up at first, but don't worry. Most of them will die when you start mowing the young lawn. The majority of weeds that come up rapidly in a new lawn can't stand a low mowing; these include mustard weed, thistle, sheep sorrel, curley dock, lamb quarters, and pigweed. Other nuisances, like dandelion, spurge, ground ivy, chickweed, and knotweed, can be easily killed off after the new lawn grass becomes more mature. Safe herbicide chemicals are now readily available at lawn and garden centers (see chapter 8).

Keep in mind when planting lawns that spring-seeded lawns will have more weeds than autumn lawns. Frost and winter freeze will kill most of the fall weeds, especially the annual ones, of course. Meanwhile, if you've got ants in your pants, pull the weeds out by hand. Weeds in a soft young lawn come out easily, and it's great exercise for your chubby wife, while you supervise with a beer in your hand. But remember if the weeds come out easily, then so will the young seedling grass—in chunks and clumps, leaving holes in the lawn. I have found that some of the "overnight" weeds are good shade for the new seed sprouts. Wait a year or a season to let the turf become more mature before applying the herbicides.

Q.—Are there any precautions I should take with seeded grass?

A.—Yes. Permit no traffic during the first winter that would tear up or compact the grass and weaken its root system. Keep children, sleds, toboggans, and in-laws off the lawn. Make no shortcut paths across the lawn. The roots of still immature grass are easily harmed by any traffic during the winter months. Something else also frequently happens in the wintertime: snowmold likes to start in footprints and other depressions.

During the first season of growth, especially if you start in spring rather than fall, keep everybody off the lawn as much as possible. This precaution should be strictly adhered to when the grass is coming up and everything is wet and muddy. Let the family try out the new lawn after about the second cutting. Buy some cheap laths at the lumberyard and make stakes out of them to set around your lawn. Then use binder twine to rope off your seeded yard. Spray the top of the stakes on the outside with red paint from an aerosol can. Then put up some "Keep Off the Grass" signs in your yard—but not the kind that once were mistakenly put up on mine.

Owing to five children and their trillions of friends who play on it, my small lawn (all greenkeepers have small lawns) lost most of its life last year. So I renovated the lawn, using the chapter 2 renovation method. When the seeding was completed, I asked one of my green crew, who understood little English, to bring a few "Ground Under Repair" signs from the golf maintenance building to my home and set them out in my lawn. I was sure he understood what I meant. Well, when I came home that night, I saw a most interesting sight (so, of course, did everyone else in the community). There were signs, all right, sporadically stuck all over the yard facing the sidewalk, but they were the wrong kind; instead of what I had requested, the signs posted by my worker were the red and black signs used to communicate some of the needs of the golf course: "Carts in Rough Only," "Course Closed Today," "Rake Sand Traps," and "Out of Bounds" (a good one). The kids and neighbors thought they were hilarious, and I was too tired to take them off that evening. Besides, in a way they told the story better than the old "Keep Off the Grass" or "Ground Under Repair" signs. So I left them. And much to my surprise, no one stepped on my lawn. Maybe they were laughing too much. This year one of the neighbors, who was renovating his old lawn, asked me if he could use the signs. So you, too, might want to try this effective, friendly way of keeping traffic off. By the way, the most interesting lawn sign I ever saw was on a university campus. It read: "Please Keep Off the Grass—It May Grow Up To Be a Good Smoke."

Q.—What shall we do about open spots and bare areas that grass hasn't filled in a new lawn? Do we have to reseed or what?

A.—Why don't you wait until the next seeding season,* duplicate with the same seed, and seed all open and bare spots? In other words, if you seeded a new lawn in the spring, then touch it up in the fall. If you seeded in the fall, then touch up in the spring. Here's why. Give your lawn every chance between seasons to spread and get thick. Have patience. Mother Nature doesn't work by buttons or switches. Give her time and you'll be pleasantly sur-

---

* Though grass in the cool region can be grown anytime between spring and fall, the seeding seasons for the homeowner are spring and fall.

prised to see how many of those bare areas that you are worried about will become grass-covered. But, of course, if after say a summer period of growth, the area is still grassless and bare (but weedy), then touch up in the fall. Please use the original seed.

Q.—Should I take soil tests before or after the planting of a new lawn?

A.—Though most turf specialists advise the homeowner to make a soil test during any seedbed preparation, I recommend a soil test first only when seeding or sodding an old home lawn that is being replaced and regraded but not changed drastically with fresh additions of soil or dirt. Give yourself plenty of time before you decide to plow up your "east forty." The results don't always come in fast, and don't do it yourself. The accurate measurements needed for your soil should be done by experts.

Why don't I recommend the same thing for *new lawns*—testing before planting? Time is essential, with the homeowner moving in and the developer trying to finish up and get out. The homeowner doesn't know exactly when to do it. And frankly, the experts don't know either. It's very frustrating, because exactness is very important. At what step are you supposed to obtain the samples for the test? Remember that the mixture of the overall soil should have the same constituency in your yard. So should the soil tests be taken when the topsoil is stockpiled at the side of your yard? When the additional soil is brought and dumped in your yard? When it's mixed with your original topsoil? Or should you do it at the time of rough-grading? Or perhaps after smooth-grading and raking?

Let me ask you a question (one more won't hurt). If the soil tests show that lime or some other element is required, will you have to spend time mixing it uniformly into the soil? Of course. But while you're waiting and waiting for the results of your soil tests, the perfect seeding days are flying by (the contractor has already said *au revoir*). Then when the tests arrive, so does the rain. And now you really have a messy headache. The building of a new lawn is a construction operation that has to be done smoothly, step by step, and without delay. You and your lawn are at the mercy of Mother Nature's idiosyncrasies. Her changes are frequent and each day lost puts you two days behind, especially if you're approaching hot summer or freezing weather. So forget soil tests for the time being, unless you are in one of those extremely acid or alkaline localities.

I recommend that you take soil tests after the ground has settled somewhat and your new grass crop has come up. (Fall is best.) If your seedbed was properly constructed in the beginning, and the top 3 or 4 inches of soil were uniformly mixed (not layered), the soil analysis will advise you as to whether you need to apply an additive like limestone to your soil. If your soil is found to be acid and you need to apply limestone, this can easily be done during the lawn's first year of growing. You'll have lots of time. Be sure to apply limestone evenly, and then water it to get the white dusty material off the blades. But I'll bet you a bag of seed that your soil analysis will show your yard doesn't require anything extra (or at most very little). That is why liming a yard without a soil test is so foolish. It's wasteful of time and money. And if you don't need it, then you're needlessly upsetting your soil balance. This can be damaging to your grass.

Lime and trace elements should be applied only after a professional soil test indicates it. Overliming must be avoided. Overliming causes nutrient deficiency, especially with trace elements. This is a good time to tell you what material is best to use if the soil tests indicate an acid soil. (A good example of an acid soil area is Ohio, where almost 80 percent of the cropland has a major problem with soil acidity.) Purchase dolomitic limestone. It is a good source of both magnesiums—carbonate and calcium carbonate. Most soils needing lime are usually deficient, to some degree, in both of these plant nutrients, magnesium and calcium. But be careful if the soil analysis shows that your lawn is extremely acid. When this condition exists, it is better to raise the pH in two or three applications, one year apart, than all at once in a single large application. Gypsum or calcium sulphate is used for alkali soils (soils high in sodium) such as are found in western United States. Gypsum has demonstrated in many areas of the Midwest an ability to bring about a flocculation* of impermeable clay soils resulting in a significant improvement in their air and

---

* A term applied to the coagulation of dispersed particles.

water percolation. Gypsum has no adverse reaction on *heavy clay lawns* when applied up to 100 pounds per 1,000 square feet per year. It is entirely safe and has an insignificant effect on the pH. The pH is a quantitative measure of the degree of soil acidity. Here is a chart that shows what I mean:

		pH
Extremely acid	Below	4.5
		to
Strongly acid	Below	5.5
		to
Medium acid	Below	6.0
		to
Slightly acid	Below	6.5
		to
Approximate Neutral Zone		7.0

Any soil having a pH higher than 7.5 has an alkaline problem. Sulphur and frequent applications of ammonium sulphate will tend to increase soil acidity. In large polluted cities, sulphur falls in rains whether you need it or not.

Q.—How do I go about getting a soil test, and where do I send the samples? Do I really need one?

A.—Every homeowner should get a soil test even if it's only for the satisfaction of being absolutely sure in his mind that he doesn't need lime or something else in his yard. That way, if he is having a lawn problem, he can at least eliminate the possibility that his lawn is short of this or that element and proceed confidently to look for other causes of the problem.

Now let me explain how to take a soil sample and where to send it. First, get a sampling soil probe from a lawn and garden center (or golf course supply company). However, if you can't find a place to buy a soil probe, use a clean table spoon, sharpen it, and dig in. At ground level (if it's old lawn, be sure it's not at thatch level), take a dozen plugs 2 to 2½ inches deep from different areas of your lawn. Take more if your lawn is larger than average, which would be 6,000 square feet. Samples should be taken to represent an even core of the surface soil. Uniformity is very important for an accurate reading. Since elements like phosphorus and potassium occur at different levels, a 2 to 2½ inch plug is specified to get suitable results. Dry the soil samples first and then mix them all together and send the composite to a soil-testing laboratory. However, samples of unlike soils in your yard should not be mixed together. Instead, put the plugs of the different soil areas in your yard intact in small paper bags (get them at a grocery store) and mark them clearly and individually for proper identification. The best way to find out where to send your soil samples is by consulting your local county agricultural advisor or your golf course superintendent, or by writing to the state university extension department. There are also commercial testing facilities. For your convenience, I list the addresses for each state in the back of this book.

A laboratory soil test is also the best means of estimating the existing supplies of available plant nutrients. Always write to the laboratory before you collect the samples in order to meet any special requirements of the laboratory. You see, the more precise the information about your plant growth that you furnish is, the better the analysis and recommendation you receive from the laboratory will be.

I don't recommend making soil tests with home kits. Vital information about your lawn or garden should be scientifically interpreted by qualified soil-testing laboratories. After the first soil test, do it again three years later. After that, one soil test every five years is enough.

Q.—This fall we are moving into a new home and we want to put sod on our new lawn. Please tell us how to go about it. Explain what we must do to have a successful lawn. Though we are on a tight budget, we don't want to cut corners.

A.—The most important step in sodding a lawn, which usually is never done by homeowners, is to make sure you have a minimum of at least 4 inches of good topsoil so that the short roots (cut off during the transplanting) of the newly laid sod and new roots developing from buds on rhizomes can grow down deeply into the soil and establish a desirable root system. If only a thin layer of good soil is spread over the subgrade, the chances for a good lawn are greatly diminished, though frankly, in the first year the sod will look healthy even if planted into poor soils, but then watch out during the next year. Even with good maintenance care, here is what will happen after the first year to sod growing on a thin soil base. Roots of the grass will grow down through the skimpy layer, reach the impenetrable hard subgrade, and stop, unable to break through this "concrete" layer. The results will be a thinning out of the grass, weeds, localized dry spots, and poor color. Deterioration will start during the first spell of hot weather, although decline will begin before this.

So, to have success with your new lawn, spread at least 4 inches of good-quality topsoil over the subgrade of your yard before sodding. Extra topsoil is an expenditure that you must make when sodding a lawn, if you don't already have enough topsoil on the site.

Sodding is good experience and isn't difficult to do. Once you decide to sod your lawn, try to observe a sodding job done by professional landscapers. There usually is a sodding job going on in a new community or development. Also, the place where you are buying the sod should be able to give you clear instructions on how to sod properly. The best suggestion that I can give you is to get some of your friends to help. Be sure you have first prepared a proper bed for the sod. The preparation is exactly the same as for the construction of a seedbed (see pages 89–93), except, as I said previously, I like additional topsoil for a sodded lawn. Be sure to roll the yard before sodding. Don't worry, if you have good friable soil; the sod roots will penetrate into it with no difficulty at all.

Sodding is like laying tile on the floor, except that you must stagger the sod pieces in much the same manner as a bricklayer does with bricks. (Look at the wall of a brick home.) Begin by laying a straight line of sod down the center of your ground bed. Now sod first on one side and then on the other. If you have help, then use teamwork with two people on one side and two people on the other side of the center sod line. Overlapping sod can be fitted by using a hand sod knife cutter that is available in all lawn garden centers and hardware stores. Remember to rake out any footprints as you go along. Snug or butt the pieces with the back of a garden rake—but keep lines straight. Don't leave cracks between the strips. Remember to stagger the pieces so they'll knit better. Keep in mind that if the ends are in a straight line, as in a tile floor, and a flooding rain occurs, the lines will spread apart and form runoff channels. This action will disturb the soil between the sod strips and also cause erosion underneath the sod. Erosion is quite prevalent on slopes, terraces, berms, and banks; sometimes it even causes the pieces of sod to move around.

That is why I strongly recommend laying sod on any prominent slope *across the face* of the incline, not up and down the slope, which is frequently done by novices. The homeowner will be wise to securely peg with small stakes the strips of sod (usually 18 inches wide by 6 feet long and ¾ to 1 inch thick) on a prominent incline. Lift the stakes out carefully only after the roots have made firm contact with the soil. This step will save a homeowner a big headache later on. Remember to leave lots of room for foundation shrubbery, or border shrubbery, and possible hedges along lot lines. There is no reason to install sod in areas that are to contain shrubbery and flower beds. It's money wasted.

After sodding has been completed to your satisfaction, don't leave it (especially if it's warm outside) and go in and have a beer with your working-bee company. First roll the dry lawn a few times and then immediately after you're finished rolling, start watering the planted strips of sod. (If you have a tamper, use it to tamp all the edges to ensure contact with the underlying soil.)

Don't wait; really wet the sod and the soil underneath. And don't be conservative with your water at this point. Irrigation must be done as soon as possible after sodding in order to avoid moisture stress. This is usually first indicated by a wilting appearance and then drying out (desiccation). So really soak it. The newly sodded yard has to be watered so thoroughly that when any corner of sod is lifted, it will be dripping wet and the soil underneath wet and muddy. Don't quit watering until you make this test in many places, such as at property line borders and along the sidewalks. These are where sod pieces dry out first. Use plywood boards or long boards to walk on so you won't sink in. Be sure to move the boards around every day to avoid causing a yellowing underneath. Soak the lawn again heavily on the second and third days. Don't let up. Let me repeat, this is not the time to economize on water. After the third day of watering, let up for a few days. Let the soil get good and firm, then roll it again several times to enhance further good contact with the soil. If you don't allow the soil to get dry before rolling, mud will ooze out between and over the strips of sod. You don't want this unsightliness and possible damage. After the rolling, water it well again. Then persist with watering every few days until the root system of the sod becomes well established. After that, use less water.

Play it by ear—rolling and watering the sod until it has knitted and you see that there is an appreciable foliage growth. Excessive top growth does not occur for quite a while after the transplanting. But when it does, set the mower down to no less than 2½ inches. Remember, the tender sod is still soft and a 2½-inch setting is really mowing at 2 inches. Even if the ground feels firm enough to support you and the mower (use a sharp reel mower), there is considerable sinkage under the weight. So if you unwisely mow at 2 inches, you'll really be cutting half an inch lower and possibly severely scalping the grass. Don't get in trouble with your new grass before you get a chance to use it. Take my advice and mow your sodded lawn at the sensible height that will make it thrive; don't brown it off and shock it with low mowing.

Occasionally lift gently an edge of a sod strip. If it's making good contact, you'll see many strong white roots. Dislodging the strip will be difficult. When this happens, fertilize your sodded lawn to get the sodded "strip seams" knitting together on top before weeds pop up in between the rows. I like to do it right after a mowing. Let's play safe and apply an organic fertilizer so you won't burn the new lawn. Organic fertilizers break down slowly (see chapter 5), are safe to use, and best of all, they don't stimulate a sudden lush top growth. We certainly don't want that to happen now. A lush top growth, without a strong root system, contributes to a lost cause in adverse weather. Go easy with excessive surface fertilizer the first year. Remember, the sod you purchased had already been properly fed with fertilizer, and you initially mixed a starter fertilizer into the top 2 inches of your topsoil (or should have if you followed my instructions on seed and sod bed preparation). The lawn has enough fertilizer for the time being. Don't add any more fertilizer until the next cool season, when the roots of your sod have started to penetrate deeply into the 4 inches of topsoil. At that time, use the fertilizer guides in chapter 5.

Q.—Is there anything else we should know about sodding a lawn?

A.—Yes. Be sure to measure your lawn correctly before buying sod. It's wiser to have a few pieces left over than to be short and have to go back for a few pieces. Be sure, also, that the sod comes from your locality. Never buy sod from far away. That sod is usually offered at cheaper prices than sod from your local area. Sometimes it's full of quack grass. Stick with a reputable sod firm nearby. Good sod also is certified with a guarantee (provided you don't mess up when laying it and looking after it) for many months.

Keep all traffic off your new lawn until the sod starts to root, which is about three weeks to a month. Not sooner. I realize that commercial sod companies sometimes advertise that with "instant sod" you can go right out and play on it, or at most wait only two weeks before using it. Don't believe this nonsense. Wait a month before allowing heavy traffic on the new sod.

Fit the sod next to sidewalks and driveways so that it is just a little higher than the concrete. Never have it so low that the mower will dip and hit the concrete. And never have it much higher, because this will cause scalping and result in thinning of your lawn. This is a very common error. The ideal way is to spend extra time on your edges so half the mower can safely run over the sod on a plateau so level that there is no raising or dipping at any point in your mowing. It's time well spent, believe me.

When ordering sod, be sure to arrange with the supplier that he will transport the sod from the field to your yard as quickly as possible. Sod that sits in storage for a long time, even when kept in refrigeration, is never as good as sod fresh from the field. Buy sod that is never cut higher than 1 inch. Sod mowed at three-quarters of an inch is even better. Sod cut thinly will knit to the underlying soil faster than thicker sod.

One last thing. Your sod company or landscaper is ready, willing, and able to assist you. If you have problems, contact him right away. Early attention will help bring prompt solutions. Don't wait. His reputation and your money are at stake.

Q.—When is the best time to sod?

A.—The best time is when growing conditions are most favorable for rooting. Though sod can be transported in cooling vans at almost any time and transplanted, I suggest the homeowner never sod his yard during hot weather. The best period to sod is from the middle of April to the last week in May, or during September to the middle of October. The conditions for moisture and temperature are best at these times in the cool-region areas of North America.

During the stress of summer, you're taking chances with the possibility of roots shriveling or at most making only a weak contact with the soil. As a result foliage growth yellows. Remember, the sod has been transplanted and the root zone has undergone "major surgery." Sod has been cut to 1 inch or less. Roots have been shorn severely by sod cutters. And the grass is in a state of shock during the transplanting from the nursery farm to your yard. Exposing sod to further stress in the hot weather is not recommended by me—unless, of course, you want to take chances with disaster.

The fact that sod can be stored in refrigerated buildings and transported in cooling vans helps us professionals in the business of growing grass. Sometimes, it's true, we buy sod and put it down at times other than those I mentioned as ideal. But we know what problems to expect from Mother Nature when sodding in summer, and we take extra precautions. The homeowner takes his sweet time when sodding and usually is not so well organized as professionals. Although sod may be stored for a few days in cool weather, it can be safely held for only a very short time in hot weather. If laid in late fall or winter, the sod doesn't "take" until the warming period of the following spring, which, though not an ideal situation, is still much safer than sodding in hot weather. Sod laid this late doesn't usually die off. It just lies dormant, achieving at most very little growth. The problem here is that if the homeowner doesn't keep traffic off all winter, the grass gets messed up, leaving it loose, disarranged, and full of potholes caused by shoes.

Q.—(By phone.) What if the sod arrives and the rain begins to fall for days and days? The yard is muddy and the rolled-up, stacked sod is starting to turn yellow. Please, what shall we do?

A.—This has happened a couple of times to me. Here is the way I solved it and it works beautifully. Buy a few sheets of three-layer plywood 8 feet by 4 feet. Then, instead of laying a straight sod line down the center of the yard (recommended for normal conditions), start instead at the street sidewalk and work up. After you lay the first few rows of sod (as far as you can reach forward while still standing on the sidewalk), place the plywood (or wide boards) over the rows that you have already sodded and proceed to sod as far as you can reach forward from the boards. Keep on doing this. Kneel and work forward, move the boards (flop them over), kneel and work forward, move the boards, and so on. As the job progresses, be sure to have long planks on hand to place behind the plywood and over the laid sod so the plank road will reach the sod stockpile on the driveway or sidewalk. This enables you to walk back and forth without sinking into the soft yard. What about rolling? No need. The weight of your body on the plywood boards presses the sod into the wet soil. As a result the sod makes such good contact with the soil that no rolling is necessary after the uncomfortable job is finished.

Q.—Which is better—sodding or seeding a lawn? (The universal question.)

A.—With a sodded lawn ("instant lawn") you have eliminated the problem of waiting for grass to grow. There is no worry about rain washing out the seed sprouts or weeds growing faster than the young grass. The yard becomes beautiful immediately—no mud, no dust, no unsightliness—and your family can use it in just a few weeks. In the long run, an instant lawn will cost less than a seeded lawn. Instant lawns are popular. Concerning erosion, I particularly like its advantage over a seeded lawn on slopes and steep banks. A quality turf cover rapidly provides control of erosion on inclines. So why should anyone prefer seeding a lawn over sodding a lawn, except for the initial high cost?

Well, I think I have one important reason, which comes from years and years of doing both sodding and seeding. Although I have no data on rooting depth to support this observation, lawns and other areas that are produced from seed develop a deeper and more profuse growth of roots in the soil. As a result of this key factor, the foliage on top is better and denser. This I attribute to a strong relationship between the roots and leaves from the very beginning, from the time the seed first sprouts, to the time months later when the grass becomes mature. And this relationship gets more firmly established as time goes on. Remember the "major surgery" I was talking about before? In any sodding operation the transplanted turf is shocked severely by its severance from its original root system. But most crippling of all is the former balance between root and leaf; it is lost forever when cutting of the sod occurs. (This happens with "transplants.") The turf never quite reaches that ideal natural relationship again. And in a sodded lawn of *dissimilar soil,* the development of foliage precedes development of roots. The weakened and severed root system is hard-pressed to support the foliage, especially if growth conditions are poor. Sure, with good soil underneath, and with careful watering, proper drainage, and excellent fertilizer practices, a reasonably close balance can be achieved between the root system and top foliage. But I am afraid it will never again be as good as it was prior to cutting, nor as long-lasting as it might have been.

Another factor to consider is that in most sodding transplants, the grass you buy is of one variety, and as I said in chapter 1, this sometimes is a disadvantage. Turf scientists are finding out that planting a blend of varieties is considerably better than planting just one pure variety in a lawn. (Reread chapter 1.) A minor point to consider is that seeded lawns green up visually faster in spring than sodded lawns. At least that has been my observation.

5
Fertilizing

ALL LIVING THINGS require food, air, and water—and that includes groundcover plants. A significant difference between animals and plants is that plants cannot move. Trees and grasses are anchored permanently for the duration of their leafy existence, and therefore cannot search for food and water. These plants must depend on an adequate root system for uptake of food. Their immediate microclimate must provide minerals and nutrients for their well-being and sustenance, or they will perish. Frankly, this situation would work out fine (especially in the case of lawn grass) if the grass were allowed to grow long naturally and develop a deep root system, as grasses on prairie land do. But of course we don't want this pasture-height appearance in our yard or, for that matter, anywhere near us. We proved this by allowing the destruction of almost all of our prairie land.

No, what we desire is a verdant pastoral paradise—a home lawn turf that can be groomed and manicured almost to perfection. And thanks to plant science and turf grass research, modern home lawns have improved tremendously since the days of ragged south-forty lawns with peekaboo wildflowers along their edges. Today, most homeowners strive to have green carpeted showplaces—in springtime, anyway.

During the stress months of summer, many lawns do not fare as well as they should. One big reason is usually a lack of adequate fertilization. A good fertilizing program is the key to good lawn quality. Since the grass plants are immobile, the homeowner must provide nutrition for their health, growth, and constant renewal, and the promotion of roots, buds, rhizomes, tillers, and leaves. Therefore, any good lawn management program that stimulates a vigorous growth of turf grass will demand increased fertilizer. And buck for buck, fertilization does more to improve lawns of poor quality and to maintain good quality than any other practice carried out by the homeowner. It is the basic cultural practice in lawn maintenance.

In this chapter, we will deal with the three paramount decisions a homeowner must make in order to develop a desirable fertilization program for his lawn: when to fertilize, how much fertilizer to apply, and what fertilizer to use. There are, of course, other necessary things to discuss, but more of those later. Let's start with the first decision.

Q.—When is the best time to apply fertilizer, and why? (Inquiry from Chicago.)

A.—The best time to fertilize in the cool region is during the first two weeks of May and then right after Labor Day. For the ultimate in color and density, top-quality lawns should be fertilized at approximately this time. I want you to know that I am using the Chicago area as home base for my fertilizing recommendation. If you reside quite far north, for example in the extreme northern states or western Canada, then be sure to move your initial fertilizing time to one or two weeks after my Chicago area recommendation (May 15.) By the same token, if you reside significantly south of Chicago, then just back off a couple of weeks or so and fertilize your lawns a little earlier. The importance of fertilizing during the first two weeks in May is simply the plain common sense of working with Mother Nature. This, of course, is contrary to the advertising of many name-brand fertilizer companies, which, as you know, are in a lucrative business and intend to get as many dollars as they can from you. You can't blame them for their hustle, but we don't have to listen to them. They have been misleading the homeowner now for many years with hornswoggling and half-truths. In fact, their sleek bafflegal tactics have been so effective that they have even clouded the judgment of some of our better agronomists and turf experts by advocating that the homeowner fertilize in April, March, and even February. This is foolish.

The ground in April is still cold and is kept this way by the long nights and short days and the angle of the sun. My recommendation is to wait until there are shorter nights and warmer and longer days. We must keep in mind that all plant life is influenced by temperatures and light. It is absurd to force the biological clocks of plants when Mother Nature isn't quite ready to promote sturdy root growth. If you fertilize too early, all you will get for your efforts is a profusely lush soft foliage growth. A desirable root system will not develop in cold soils with early fertilizer. Only top growth will result. A luxuriant top foliage without a balanced root system is for naught—especially in summer stress.

Something else happens to make your efforts useless during this period of cold temperatures and short days. Leaching and flooding may occur, owing to rain, hail, and even occasional snow, sometimes quite deep, washing your expensive fertilizer away or wasting it by depositing what remains in low spots where it suffocates, burns, or encourages disease when temperatures suddenly rise. Any fertilizer that remains on the lawn does nothing but nurture the weeds and make their top growth stand out even more obviously. (God forbid!)

Let's open our eyes to the fact that grass looks greenest in early spring. So why stimulate it further and waste expensive fertilizer? It's much wiser to wait until mid or even late May, when your lawn is starting to dwindle from the first surge of early spring growth and when it requires necessary nutrition for the summer months ahead. Fertilize in May, before the hot weather sets in. Then after the long summer, fertilize again in September, sometime after Labor Day. This will revive the lawn from its doldrums to greenness and prepare it for the onset of fall and winter.

Q.—Please explain the proper way to measure how much fertilizer to spread. I always seem to have problems with distributing fertilizer over my lawn because of improperly setting the spreader openings. I follow the directions on the spreader and set the dial as recommended, but I either apply too much or not enough. What am I doing wrong?

A.—Always make sure you have a good fertilizer spreader and that it works properly. Check it carefully each spring. Be sure it doesn't stick, isn't rusty, and isn't clogged with a solid mass of fertilizer left over from your last application many months ago. If it's clogged in this way, its soluble hot fertilizer salts are corroding the metal and ruining a good spreader. I have observed that more burn damage to lawns results from too-heavy fertilization caused by improper or careless calibration and distribution than from almost anything else. The only exception might be the stupid practice of some homeowners to apply chemical fertilizer or pesticides in hot weather.

Note: In the Deep South, attractive Bermuda grass lawns (the Bermudas have the highest fertilizer requirement of all warm-season grasses) require frequent fertilizer application, often of blended chemical fertilizers throughout the warm months. But be careful not to apply too much chemical fertilizer at one time, and apply it only when the grass leaves are dry. Then water immediately after applications to rinse the fertilizer off the leaf blades. Otherwise use the safer natural or synthetic organic fertilizers. In northern cool-region areas, a homeowner should never (nor need ever) apply "hot fertilizers" during the hot summer months.

If your old fertilizer spreader is grinding and creaking, and the shutter openings are jamming rather than smoothly sliding back and forth, why not invest in a cyclone or rotary-type spreader? I love these spreaders and prefer either one to the awkward, push-and-drop, buggy type. The cyclone spreader has a gear rotating a disc underneath the hopper to distribute the fertilizer approximately 3 to 4 feet on each side of the spreader. It is extremely efficient and easy to use. The cyclone's fertilizer distribution is very uniform, as far as overlapping is concerned, and most golf course superintendents use it for the delicate fertilizing jobs like greens and tees. So what if a little fertilizer gets in the flower beds? They probably need it. But caution. Fertilizers with weed killers are another matter. Be sure always to wash out your fertilizer spreader when you are through with it, especially if you're using chemical types. Then trickle a little oil on a rag and wipe it over all the moving parts. Remember, any fertilizer that remains will corrode metal. Discard the oily rag in the garbage can. Don't leave it in the garage, where it might become combustible.

Of course the old spreader is not always to blame. Putting on too little fertilizer, when you think you are putting on what the directions specify, will result in insufficient lawn feeding and starvation and loss of turf vigor. Also, in all my years of lawn and golf course work, I have yet to see a new fertilizer spreader that can be accurately used by the average homeowner. A test to measure the calibrated amount against your style of "spreading" is necessary, because we all walk at different speeds. Terrain can be different, too; for example, on a slope you're usually going slower uphill and faster downhill. Keep in mind also that different fertilizers have particles of different sizes. Of course some companies sell you spreaders that are calibrated specially for their fertilizer, but this is confusing and restrictive. Occasionally a spreader can be mechanically faulty in construction, which causes an inaccurate spreading. So it's always worth your while to first calibrate the correct setting before applying fertilizer to your hungry lawn.

Work out a proper setting in the following manner. First, accurately measure the total lawn. No, don't include the house, garage or kennel. Just the area of grass to be fertilized, please. Measure this area in square feet, because most instructions are based on rates per 1,000 square feet. The average home lawn's area is between 5,000 and 6,000 square feet, with some much larger ones in the suburbs.

Now find a convenient flat area and measure 500 square feet (10 x 50, 20 x 25, or 100 x 5). Use your driveway, street, or sidewalk, or even a park area where the ground cover is thin and sparse. In the park your test fertilizer won't be wasted. Don't worry about the street and sewerage becoming polluted with your fertilizer; you are experimenting with only a tiny amount. If while testing on the street or driveway, you accidentally dump a bit here and there, sweep it up and spread it by hand around your shrubbery. (Also sweep it up and use it if you go over the test area more than a couple of times.) Anyway, after measuring 500 square feet and marking the corners with four sticks, weigh the amount of fertilizer recommended on the bag for 1,000 square feet on your bathroom scales (don't guess) and pour it into the hopper. Set the dial to the setting recommended on the spreader or on the fertilizer bag. Now go over the 500-square-foot area at a steady gait, not too fast, not too slow. If you have the setting just right, you should have used half of the weighed fertilizer for the 500 square feet. For example, if the prescribed quantity was 10 pounds per 1,000 square feet, you now should have 5 pounds in the spreader. (Weigh it; don't guess.) If not, readjust the dial setting and try again until the desired amount has been applied. If you're having too much trouble getting a proper calibration, go back into the house, have some coffee, sober up, and try again—or let your wife handle this important job, and you cook the hamburgers. The results of guesswork or inaccurate setting of the spreader can be serious. Too much fertilizer can cause burn damage to the grass (especially if you are using chemical types), and not enough can result in a sickly weak lawn. Remember Goldilocks and the three bears; one bowl of porridge was too hot and one was too cold; only one bowl was just right. That is what testing is all about. Do likewise.

Once you have the ideal setting, record it along with the date and the name of the fertilizer and store this information in the folder containing other pertinent household records. Remember, similar fertilizers manufactured by various companies are not always the same, and many are different in size and composition. To ensure accuracy, the spreader should be calibrated for each different fertilizer used, and before each application. As the spreader ages, the holes get larger, so more fertilizer is deposited as time goes by.

Q.—Please tell me the various fertilizer types available for home lawns. There are so many different lawn fertilizers available now on the market that I am confused as to what they all contain and which are the best to use. What kind of fertilizer do you recommend for the cool-region home lawns?

A.—Lawn fertilizer is big business now and it's getting more expensive every day. A homeowner should acquaint himself with all new types available in order to give his lawn what it needs and at the same time to get the best purchase for his poor inflation dollar.

Fertilizer is available in organic and inorganic forms. The organic form is divided into what are termed *natural organic* fertilizers and *synthetic organic* fertilizers. The natural organics may be composed of sewage sludges from human waste, of dried blood from slaughtered animals, of soybean or cottonseed meal, or of fish scraps and even seaweed. Synthetic organics are chemical in origin and contain some form of urea, which is a weak nitrogenous compound synthesized from carbon dioxide and ammonia.

Inorganics—also called chemical, or hot, fertilizers—are available as liquids and solids. Soluble inorganics include urea, plus ammonium sulfate, ammonium nitrate, potassium nitrate, sodium nitrate, and so on.

The significant difference between the natural organics and the chemical inorganics is that nitrogen in the natural organics must be "released" by organisms in the soil before they become a food for the grass plant. Therefore, since they are not soluble in water, they are (a) less likely to be lost from the soil through leaching, (b) slow-releasing, and (c) nonburning. Natural organics contain a low percentage of nitrogen and phosphorus and a tiny bit of potassium, some iron, and other trace elements not found in synthetics or chemical fertilizers—all in natural form, derived directly from processed plant and animal sources. Since the natural organics are low in nitrogen, a homeowner applying only them always handles more bulk, but his lawn usually is safe from burning, if he follows directions. The natural organics have the lowest salt index, which practically eliminates all possibility of burning.

The blended, or "complete," inorganic fertilizers readily break down in the soil and thus quickly bring nutrients to the plants. This responsive action occurs because the complete inorganic fertilizers are *soluble* in water. They are often called "hot fertilizers" because they contain salts, various mineral compounds that can burn the grass if not handled properly. These soluble salts, although packaged dry and friable in the fertilizer bags, immediately begin to collect moisture when exposed to high humidity. On a home lawn, especially when the grass is wet, the fertilizer may stick to the leaf blades and act like a poultice. When the fertilizer salts start to draw moisture from the plant tissue, "burning" results, sometimes excessively.

To lessen the chance of burning your grass with this type of fertilizer, follow these three rules.

1. Calibrate your spreader properly before applying fertilizer, and test it in the way I suggested in the last question. An overdose can result in excessive burning, which means good-bye to your green lawn. I repeat, people tend to apply too much fertilizer despite the fact that the prescribed amount on the package is all that's needed to provide adequate plant nutrition. This usually is 1 pound of actual nitrogen per 1,000 square feet.

2. Never apply a complete fertilizer in hot weather (the same goes for some pesticides, like the arsenics).

3. Buy a complete fertilizer in pelleted or granular forms, even though it may be more expensive than the dusty ones. Granulated fertilizer distributes much better, it doesn't cake so easily, and it rolls off the grass blades onto the soil.

The chief advantage of inorganic fertilizer blends is that they contain a high ratio of the three main food elements that grasses require: nitrogen, phosphorus, and potash, which I will dwell on later in this chapter.

Another slow-releasing fertilizer that has gained popularity on golf courses and commercial areas is the straight nitrogen type of synthetic organic. These are ureaform compounds made by mixing urea and formaldehyde. They break down so slowly that the nitrogen becomes available over a period of time to the grass. (Straight urea by itself, even though it is an organic synthetic, is as hot as a firecracker on the Fourth of July.) These straight nitrogen sources are more expensive than the inorganic nitrogen sources or the natural organics, but fewer applications are required; therefore, the total cost (including labor) may not be much more than the others. However, this theory doesn't work with lawns that need a number of other important nutrients. The major drawback of these synthetics is that straight U-F (urea-formaldehyde) materials lack phosphorus and potash, so supplements containing these two (especially potash) might have to be fed to the lawn, which means extra work and money. Ureaform synthetics' resistance breaks down faster as daytime and nighttime temperatures get higher and more constant.

Another type of a synthetic organic—discovered and exported by the Japanese—is called IBDU (isobutylidene diurea). Its breakdown is caused by hydrolysis, which is the action of water on it, and it is regulated by the size of the particles. High temperatures supposedly do not affect the release of this fertilizer, only extremely slow solubility by water availability independent of temperatures. (However, I have always thought that as temperatures increase, water becomes more soluble.) These are the slowest-releasing nitrogen fertilizers on the market, it's claimed, and their reserves last longer than any other type of fertilizer.

I repeat, generally you pay a much higher price per pound for the synthetic-organic nitrogen fertilizer, whose significant benefit is gained from the slow release of nitrogen. Please understand when comparing prices between, say, a 50-pound bag of this slow-releasing synthetic form of straight nitrogen and a 50-pound bag of a blended fertilizer (or a natural organic), that the synthetic organic may have as much as six times more *actual nitrogen* available in the package. That's considerable if nitrogen is all that you want to apply, and you don't need any of the other important elements. But only soil tests can confirm that.

I want to impress indelibly one important point about using synthetic organics. It concerns application. Only a few pounds (usually about 3) of fertilizer material make up 1 pound of actual nitrogen. If the homeowner doesn't set his spreader to a perfectly accurate adjustment he may very well dump, in warm weather, more straight nitrogen on his grass than it requires. (This also applies to "hot" inorganic fertilizer blends that are high in nitrogen content.) Such a costly and careless mistake with a straight nitrogen synthetic organic fertilizer might not burn his grass, but it might produce a tremendous lush growth during the hot weather at the expense of root formation. This overly succulent soft leaf from overfertilization would make your grass more susceptible to insects and certain turf diseases, as well as making the turf too soft to take traffic. Remember, with synthetics and with most garden blends, you put on very little; with natural organics, you put on a lot, in order to get that 1 or 2 pounds of actual nitrogen necessary to keep your lawn healthy. You must be very professional in handling this expensive, slow-releasing nitrogen fertilizer, and have a very accurate fertilizer spreader.

Most homeowners like to clearly see *and* hear the fertilizer falling onto the grass blades. Therefore, they seem to get a better feeling of the pattern and overlapping they make when using natural organics, which have more bulk material. With synthetics and all high-nutrient lawn blends, you need a fine setting for very little output. This might mistakenly lead you to believe that nothing is coming out. And this can in turn lead you to dial a larger spreader opening, which will only result in much expensive fertilizer being wasted, with no real benefit to the grass.

The liquid fertilizers, which produce a sudden flash of very green growth and rapid depletion of nitrogen, generally are available as an inorganic fertilizer form, as a straight nitrogen-urea, and as a urea formaldehyde powder *to be dissolved in water before use;* this latter is available only commercially. Their forte is their quick discharge of nitrogen (as in ureas); or of nitrogen, phosphorus, and potash (as in blended salt form). It's like a "butterfly" allergy shot just under the skin. The reaction is immediate. This type of fertilizer can be absorbed by the leaf, but its action and effect are brief. I don't care for this type of fertilizer and do not encourage anyone to use it for his lawn, whether he does the job or has a contract lawn service company do it. I have seen too many lawns go out because nothing more has been added to their hungry turf than a fast-acting fertilizer in liquid form applied through hoses from house faucets or from lawn service trucks. Stick with the solid fertilizers. There is nothing better than fertilizer in granular form. Please understand, of course, that I am not discussing house plants. Liquid fertilizers (like emulsified fish oil) have to be in liquid form so they can be added delicately to plants in your house, but even they must be carefully measured. I should know: I always kill my house plants with too much fertilizer. But that's another story. Forget a liquid fertilizer for your lawn. You're paying for water and very little actual nitrogen.

Q.—Isn't there another new type blended fertilizer on the market that is 50-percent organic?

A.—The fourth form of lawn fertilizer now available to the

homeowner contains U-F (urea-formaldehyde) plus inorganic sources of N + P + K (nitrogen, phosphorus, and potassium). This blend of fertilizer is usually advertised as 50-percent nitrogen organic, which to a homeowner can be confusing. Do the companies mean 50-percent nonburning and 50-percent burning? Or 50-percent safer than blended inorganic fertilizer? Or what? Some homeowners have been led to believe they needn't water at all after applying this fertilizer. Then they find out (too late) that there is some burning—especially if they have been careless and overapplied. What 50-percent organic actually means is that 50 percent of the nitrogen in the bag is a nonburning, synthetic nitrogen fertilizer form, and the other 50 percent is a chemical, water-soluble nitrogen salt (this percentage burns). And then, of course, the chemical form's phosphorus and potash (the hottest of chemical salts) percentage also can be expected to burn if the fertilizer is not watered in. The advertising usually states boldly on the fertilizer package that 50 percent of the nitrogen is organic; however, this is deceiving, because it really is not natural organic, as most people assume, but a synthetic organic, and in my opinion it should be advertised as such.

One other thing adds to the homeowner's confusion. On many fertilizer bags are the capitalized letters *W.I.N.,* which simply refers to water insoluble nitrogen (and not some big endorsement). The higher the percentage of water insoluble nitrogen, the safer and longer-lasting is the nitrogen. W.I.N. does not mean that the nitrogen will never be usable, but simply that it becomes available at a much slower rate. The soluble sources of nitrogen provide the grass plant with an immediate source of nitrogen, while the supply of water insoluble nitrogen (W.I.N.) will provide nitrogen over a longer period. It's important for you to understand this clearly so you will get your money's worth and the grass will get it's proper nutrition.

One significant observation I've made about fertilizers in my twenty-five long years in turf management is that in hot and humid weather all fertilizers release damned fast—the organics, inorganics, synthetics, half-and-halfs, and what have you. This even applies to the oldest type of fertilizer known—manure. Manure and all other natural organic fertilizers release nitrogen by the action of decomposition. Generally the warmer and moister the conditions, the faster the breakdown is. So don't apply fertilizer during seasonal periods of stress to grass—unless you're a homeowner in the land of the nitrogen-devouring Bermuda grass, but even then apply it very carefully.

Since turf's need in most areas is greater for nitrogen and potash than for phosphorus (see the next two questions and answers), and since grass is most responsive to nitrogen, I like a ratio of 2-1-2, 3-1-2, or 4-1-2 of fertilizer grades for mature lawns. Established lawns in almost all of North America will *always* respond to more nitrogen and potash than phosphate.* This is because most plants use more nitrogen and potash than they use phosphorus. Also, nitrogen and potash are lost quicker in the soil due to leaching. So in most cases, unless a soil test indicates otherwise, use a blended fertilizer with more nitrogen and potash than phosphorus. I prefer combinations like 18-4-9, 24-6-12, 10-5-10, 20-5-10, or 12-4-8. Use one of these materials on your lawn *at least twice a year.*

Q.—How much fertilizer shall I apply per application on my bluegrass lawn? What kind do you recommend? Also please explain what is meant by actual pounds of nitrogen per 1,000 square feet.

A.—My recommendation for bluegrass lawns mixed with other cool-season perennial grasses and mowed sensibly at a 2½-inch cut is 1 pound of actual nitrogen ("N") per 1,000 square feet in the first two weeks of May and again at the same rate right after Labor Day. In order to better understand what is meant by actual pounds of nitrogen, or "N," take the percentage of total nitrogen analysis, which is always marked on the fertilizer bag, and multiply by the weight of the bag to get the total pounds of actual nitrogen. For example, with 50 pounds of fertilizer containing 20-percent nitrogen, multiply .20 by 50 pounds and the answer is 10 pounds of actual nitrogen. This enables you to fertilize 10,000 square feet with the contents of the 50-pound bag, or 1,000 square feet each time you apply 5 pounds of fertilizer material, which is one-tenth

* The homeowner never actually sees grass respond to potash and phosphorus.

of the 50. If you're confused, just follow the directions on the bag and you should be okay. Or hire a mathematician.

For pure or blended stands of those elite and regal varieties of Kentucky bluegrass such as Merion, Pennstar, Fylking, Warren's A-20, Nugget, and Adelphi (all mowed never lower than 2 inches), I suggest 1 pound of actual nitrogen applied in May. Then apply it again between Labor Day and October, but this time at *a double rate*—in other words, 2 pounds of actual nitrogen per 1,000 square feet. Don't change your setting for the higher rate; just go over the lawn twice in opposite directions. The elegant varieties of Kentucky bluegrass demand more fertilizer, especially nitrogen, owing to more growth and an exceptional rhizome (underground stem) development. They need adequate nutrition for best performance.

As to the type of fertilizer per application, I think I made my feelings clear in the last question. You'll remember that I like a blended commercial fertilizer—especially if potash is low by soil test—with a ratio of 2-1-2, 3-1-2, 4-1-2, and even 6-1-2 (10-5-10, 15-5-10, 20-5-10, and 24-4-8) a minimum of *two times* a year. These ratios will ideally give more nitrogen and potassium than phosphorus, and this usually is what better varieties of grass require—unless soil tests indicate otherwise. Always heavily water these fertilizers into the turf, especially the last application in the fall, which is to be double the rate (2 pounds of actual N per 1,000 square feet) for the elite Kentucky bluegrass varieties. The water-soluble fertilizer, you should keep in mind, will cause foliage burn in warm weather by drawing moisture out of the green leaves of grass. So you must water the fertilizer off the leaf and into the soil. There are many other complete fertilizer ratios and grades that should do almost as well—fertilizer blends such as 10-6-4, 16-8-8, 20-10-5, 15-5-5, 7-7-7, 15-8-8, and even 10-10-10, if you can find it. The important thing is for your lawn to get the three major elements—nitrogen, phosphorus, and potash—a minimum of twice a year. Where phosphorus and potash are adequate by soil tests, I recommend that you go with either a natural or a synthetic straight nitrogen slow-releasing organic fertilizer. Though the natural organics supply trace elements and phosphorus, whether you need them or not, they are by far the safest for the homeowner to use, especially a novice. In all honesty I have never seen a home lawn in poor condition adequately fertilized with only natural organics and nothing else. Oh, it might get just a wee bit smelly while it breaks down, but you never have to worry about burning your grass if you overapply. Their low-content nitrogen, along with a small percentage of phosphorus plus a few trace elements, all in natural form, are extremely safe to use.

My advice when using *all other types of fertilizer* is to add trace elements such as iron, calcium, magnesium, zinc, molybdenum, sulphur, and copper only if indicated by soil tests. Never before. Trace elements are rarely needed in most of the cool-region states or in Canada (except for iron, especially in the western states.) Soils in this zone usually need only nitrogen, phosphorus, and potassium, because they contain enough of the other plant micronutrients. If you are attempting to grow grass on "basement fill" or clay soil, then call in a county agent or advisor and have him check the lawn and advise you about what trace elements you might need. Sandy areas require more fertilizer than clay soils.

To conclude the answer to the original question, I should explain that many factors influence good fertilizer application and management—whether clippings are removed or not, whether the lawn is irrigated or not, and what the soil constituency is. Heavy rainfall and high temperatures definitely influence the fertilizer picture. The length of the season is another important consideration. If you want to be perfectly scientific in your method of fertilizer application, soil testing will give you most of the right answers, provided of course the results are interpreted by a knowledgeable grass man. But let's face it, this is not always practical or desirable for the homeowner. The average homeowner would never go the full route of applying fertilizer scientifically. It's tough enough to convince a homeowner to apply fertilizer twice a year. Even so, I'm giving you what I think is a good basic fertilizer program.

Q.—What do nitrogen, phosphorus, and potassium, the three main elements, provide for the grass?

A.—Most soils are deficient in nitrogen. Some are deficient in phosphorus. Many are lacking in potassium. Let's take them one at a time and learn what they do for your lawn.

Nitrogen is the single most important plant food for turf grass, but it should be used in a ratio that is balanced with other plant foods. It increases growth and dark green color. It is a growth regulator. Without nitrogen, grass thins and turns a weak green color. Grasses use lots of nitrogen. It is easily leached from the soil and quickly lost. Using a slow-release organic fertilizer can help prevent this condition. Oh yes, the observation many homeowners make after a rainy lightning storm, that their grass seems to be greener, is not a hallucination. Nitrogen comprises the major part of air by both volume and weight and some of this nitrogen is always released from the air during a lightning storm.

Phosphorus. A phosphate fertilizer gives better results when worked into the soil, because that way plant roots can make better contact with this source of nutrition than if the phosphorus is just applied to the soil surface and not mixed in. The reason is that phosphorus moves very slowly through the soil.

Phosphorus is a necessary element for young seedlings. It is essential for good root development and should be a "starter" fertilizer incorporated into the soil during seedbed preparation. One year after application, as the turf grass becomes established, excessive phosphorus usually begins accumulating in the soil; therefore, repeated fertilization with this element is not required more than twice a year (at the most), and then only in small quantities. Unless you live in a phosphorus-deficient area, don't waste too much of your money on this nonleaching, stored-in-the-soil element. Instead, spend your dollars on a higher percentage of nitrogen and potash content, as I recommended in my basic fertilizer program. Phosphates increase density of root development, and it is a recommended main diet for fledgling lawns to help them develop faster.

Phosphorus becomes the major factor in lake algae growth and premature "aging" of the lakes when it is discharged heavily into these bodies of water. Strict federal and state standards now require industries and municipal sewerage plants to remove certain levels of phosphorus. Recent significant evidence obtained by Canadian and United States weather scientists also shows that phosphorus contributes to the contamination of our atmosphere. Although homeowners don't have to worry too much about phosphorus doing anything but good for their lawn, it looks like the present heavy phosphate ground run-off and emission into the air will have to be much more tightly controlled by the U.S. Environmental Protection Agency.

Potassium provides substance to plant tissue and helps with the assimilation of other elements into the soil. It is absorbed by grass in an amount second only to that of nitrogen in clippings. Potassium (or potash) is needed for the metabolism of plant cells. Its effect on carbohydrates encourages the cell walls of grass to thicken and stand stiff and upright (thereby helping golf balls to sit up better on fairways). There is some scientific indication that potassium plays a strong role in winter turf survival, disease resistance, and overall hardiness. A recent survey of one Midwest area showed that over half of the lawns needed potash. Scientists say that leaf spot is considerably more prevalent on potash-deficient lawns than on lawns that have an adequate supply of this mineral. At first, potassium was derived from wood ashes. Today, most potash in the United States is mined in the South. The world's greatest supply comes from the Canadian province of Saskatchewan, near Saskatoon. I must impress upon you the fact that an overabundance of any element in the delicate soil/mineral/plant relationship may result in that element's becoming unavailable to the plant. Strange but true. Ideally all elements in the soil should be in suitable, adequate proportion to one another. Too much of any one element can sometimes upset the delicate balance of the soil/plant relationship of your yard.

Q.—Please explain what is meant by a "complete" fertilizer?

A.—A complete, or blended, fertilizer means it's a rapid-response inorganic fertilizer that contains nitrogen (N), phosphorus (P), and potassium (K). These are the *big three* elements that are necessary for good lawns.

The numbers in the formulas found on the fertilizer bags represent the different elements present and show an analysis of the fertilizer in percentage of the bag weight. Fertilizer "grade" refers to the guaranteed analysis; by law, the percentage of the elements (nutrient materials) in the fertilizer must be displayed on the package or bag. These "grade" numbers also show the ratio between the three major nutrients. For example, in a fertilizer bag marked 10-10-10, the first number refers to the percentage of nitrogen, the second to that of phosphorus, and the third to that of potassium (or potash). In general tnese are referred to simply as N-P-K. Thus there is 10-percent nitrogen, 10-percent phosphate, and 10-percent potash in the bag, and the ratio between the three is equal—1-1-1. In a 20-10-5 grade, or analysis, the ratio would be 4-2-1. A bag marked 12-4-8 has a ratio of 3-1-2, and so on.

Consider individual trace elements only when a proven need exists, such as when indicated by a top-quality soil test. Never before. Micronutrients (trace elements) should never be used unless you know positively that your lawn needs them in order to thrive better. Trace mineral supplements other than iron are seldom needed by turf grass. Most soils are good providers. If in doubt, check with your local county agent or farm advisor.

Q.—What do you think of fertilizers that are mixed with insecticides or herbicides?

A.—Not much. I have never been satisfied with combination feed-and-weed chemical applications, because for whatever reason you're applying it, whether for crabgrass, clover, dandelions, insects, or fertilizing, insecticides and weed killers are far more effective when applied separately at the appropriate time. I want to impress you with these points: some pesticides have to be washed in, and others must remain on the blades of grass to be effective. I have never found these "scattershot" combinations as effective as separate application. Apply what's needed when it's needed. What really gets my dander up are those fertilizer companies that advertise these strange combinations as a great convenience to you. But, I ask, what good are these ballyhooed conveniences if they don't do the job *right*?

Actually, though, I have no quarrel with the better fertilizer companies that sell a two-in-one package, which is usually a fertilizer and a dandelion control. That isn't too bad, but still not as good as separate applications. My quarrel is with the chemical packages that contain three or even four different combinations of fertilizer, insecticide, herbicide, and fungicide. That's too many at one time. To be most effective, the pesticides should be applied individually at the right time of the season. On *Mother Nature's time,* not *Mother Manufacturer's time.* Remember that all chemicals will shock grass to some extent when they are applied, no matter what the advertising states. Why add stress to your lawn? And why pollute your lawn with chemicals that (when applied at the wrong time) do nothing except kick the George out of your dollar and contaminate your yard? I hope that legislation in many of our states will soon prohibit the sale of these "glorified convenience" combinations. Keep in mind that the more chemicals you use, the greater the danger is, especially if you are not really sure whether you or your lawn needs them. The rule of thumb to help any plant should always be *to use chemicals as little as possible,* and only if there is a positive need.

If you do have to use the two-in-one weed and feed combination, be sure its nitrogen content is not high. The reason is that in a bag of weed and feed with high-content nitrogen, there are always fewer particles; as a result, you're less likely to hit all weed plants. In other words, the more bulk material that you apply per 1,000 square feet, the more pesticide particles cover the grass and the better chance there is of killing the dandelions or whatever.

Q.—Please tell me the really big difference between organic and inorganic fertilizer. Which is best to use?

A.—Actually there is no difference. To a hungry lawn there is no big difference between a natural organic and an inorganic fertilizer. Plants can't tell whether chemicals are prepared in factories or come from natural sources. Disregard the pseudoscience nonsense about organics being better than inorganics. Grass plants take up almost all nitrogen in the same form—as a nitrate. Organically grown lawns are not superior to those inorganically fertilized. I can grow good lawns with both, but I prefer the inorganic, or blended, fertilizers, which contain nitrogen, phosphorus, and potash. As I said before, I like this type applied in spring and fall. If you must fertilize in between in warmer weather, I suggest that you use the organics (or synthetic inorganics) because of their safety factor and their slower rate of release. However, I must give the observation of some turf experts: that the use of natural organic fertilizer has a beneficial effect in promoting bacterial activity, an activity required for the natural decomposition of thatch. On the other hand, the inorganic fertilizers are combinations of chemical salts, and salts inhibit bacterial activity. For example, in meat preservation. Remember that in the good old days of pre-refrigeration, the only means of preserving the hanging slabs of beef outside butcher shops was to use salt. The salt stopped bacterial decomposition of the meat. However, I can only say that I have never seen the blended fertilizers do any harm to anything, if applied properly. Applying anything heavily, whether it's salt on meat or salt on grass, is going to have an adverse result.

Q.—Is it my imagination or are the fertilizer bags getting smaller and the nitrogen content higher?

A.—It's not your imagination, my friend. And it's not bags anymore. More often it's a dainty package of fertilizer now, not the heavy bag of fertilizer your father once lugged from the store. The modern "package" weight fertilizer has become increasingly popular. For many years fertilizers were bagged by the hundredweight, then in 80-pound bags, then 50, and now they average 20 pounds or so per package. The nitrogen content, though, has greatly increased in percentage. The lighter package is easier and more convenient to carry, and the homeowner doesn't need help to carry it. Thus, the store doesn't need extra clerks to help the homeowner carry a back-breaking, 100-pound bag. The store saves lots of money. All this convenience makes me very happy, because the liberated ladies of the 1970s are now doing most of the fertilizer shopping (and spreading) and releasing the husband from this once important and manly duty. Now he can relax during the weekend and watch sports spectacles while consuming pretzels and foreign beer. Or (hopefully) spending more time on the golf course.

Almost all of the small fertilizer bags carry a higher nitrogen percentage, which means less bulk material but more actual pounds per 1,000-square-feet coverage than in the heavier and bulkier bags. This smaller size allows the store owners to use much less storage space for fertilizer products, and it costs the fertilizer manufacturer less for freight charges because he can ship more in less space. For example, it would take five times as much storage space to store two 50-pound bags of 5-10-5 than it does to store one 20-pound bag of 25-5-10. On the other hand, when it comes to application, it would take two 50-pound bags of 5-10-5 to cover the same area that can be fertilized with the more convenient 20-pound bag of 25-5-10.

There is a disadvantage to the homeowner. He has to be especially careful with the calibration of his spreader and with the measurement of his total lawn. The reason is obvious. Much less actual weight of bulk material is required to fertilize the regular prescribed area in order to get 1 pound of actual nitrogen per 1,000 square feet. The setting must be very fine and accurate when using a high-nitrogen-content fertilizer to apply the equivalent of 1 pound of actual nitrogen per 1,000 square feet. As a result, a miscalculation or carelessness can result in serious chemical injury to the lawn. For this reason, perhaps the safer, low-nitrogen-content natural organics should be considered for use as against the high-content nitrogen fertilizers. The heavier dose of material necessary to get 1 pound of actual nitrogen per 1,000 square feet using natural organics enables the homeowner to better see, hear, and feel (later on he can smell it, also) the fertilizer flying out, and this sensorial judgment is assurance that he is doing the job right. These have been my observations. With a high nitrogen content, a homeowner should not try to improve on standard rates of nitrogen application recommendation—1 pound of actual nitrogen per 1,000 square feet—except in the fall for the new Kentucky bluegrass varieties (as per my recommendation). Remember, too much nitrogen and not enough of the other fertilizer elements can cause deterioration of turf. The high-nitrogen complete fertilizers are generally low in phosphate and potash.

Q.—With fertilizer getting so expensive, how can I make sure that I get the most for my money before I go broke?

A.—Everything is going up, up, and away. Now it's seed and fertilizer. In fact, prices for all lawn and garden care products are growing faster than weeds. Seed brokers are blaming farmers, who are planting wheat and other high-paying crops instead of acres of grass that produce seeds for your lawn. What seed there is has nearly doubled in price, and some have even tripled. The fertilizer manufacturers would like us to believe that fertilizer is scarce and more expensive because of three things: exporting great quantities to foreign countries; lifting land banks, thereby opening up more land that needs to be fertilized; and lifting price ceilings on food. Maybe so, but actually, the main thing that has been lifted is the retail price, which has ballooned by more than 50 percent. As with everything else that has been doubling and tripling in cost, it's a matter of price raising by the big companies, accompanied by much double-talk. They feed us the bunk and we in turn always seem to fall for it and pay through the nose. This system of the sheep following the leader will never change.

The best method I know of to make sure that you're getting the most for your money when purchasing fertilizer is to count the total units of the analysis marked on one brand and compare the cost per unit with another brand. Be like the shopper who compares one company's can of beans with another's. But be sure to compare apples with apples and oranges with oranges. By that I mean both brands should cover approximately the same area (usually a standard 5,000 square feet). They should also be (as close as possible) of the same granular, or particle, size. Most important, they should contain nearly the same percentage of nutrient material and have a similar ratio, e.g., 2-1-1, 3-1-2, 4-2-2, etc. The best ones to compare are the blended commercial inorganics that contain the three major elements N, P, and K. There are more of them manufactured, and a better price is available for the smart shoppers. The urea-form fertilizer IBDU (doubtful if you can get them in pure form) and other slow-release fertilizers are a little more complicated to figure out, especially if there is a big difference in the W.I.N (water-insoluble nitrogen) factor. These fertilizers are priced considerably higher, but they have a greater safety factor, as well as a timed rate of release, or "breakdown." The natural organic fertilizers are easily compared, if you can find a couple of "natural" brands in your area to make price comparisons.

Now let's go back and figure out an actual case of unit-price purchasing. Recently a large department store in Chicago offered three different brands of fertilizer, but all had the same price and the same ratio. They were 20-10-10, 16-8-8, and 12-6-6. If we divide the units of the first one (20-10-10) into the price ($4.80), we get 12 cents per unit cost. The second one (16-8-8) comes out to 15 cents per unit cost, and the third costs 20 cents per unit. So naturally, you're getting the best buy with the brand containing the 20-10-10. Sometimes the cost difference can be as much as 10 to 15 cents per unit cost. The best buys for frugal homeowners are the brands that aren't big-name products. Remember, the fertilizer grade and nutrient analysis, no matter who puts them out, are guaranteed by law to be the percentage stated on *every bag*. So why be a sucker and pay more just because it's widely advertised, or because the bag is prettier, or because the clerk tells you it's the only thing to buy if you want a perfect lawn. Horse manure!! Your grass doesn't care who makes the fertilizer, or if the bag is nice and has a convenient handle on it, or if it was advertised on color TV last night. All this is bunk. Just follow the instructions on the money-saving fertilizer and your grass will do fine. Put the left-over money into groceries for the family. Now you're being a wise shopper and a good provider. Guide yourself to better buys by understanding the fertilizer analysis; count the units and don't be misled by Madison Avenue advertising or beautiful pictures of verdant lawns on the bag.

Q.—I seem to have wide spreader burns at the edge of my lawn. What am I doing wrong? Why does the fertilizer dump more here than anyplace else?

A.—You're dumping fertilizer because you're opening the spreader shutter before you begin walking. Always start walking first to get the fertilizer spreader in motion before opening up the holes. Otherwise you'll be dumping and burning. When you're finished, using the same walking rhythm do the short two- or three-step areas on the outside that you missed. Another good suggestion is, always know where you're going with your spreader by walking over the terrain first and examining it for bumps and sudden dips. You'd be surprised how many people burn their grass by hitting bumps, dips, tree roots, toys, and the like before they can shut the spreader off—meanwhile dumping excessive fertilizer on the grass.

6

Mowing

TODAY A GREAT VARIETY of mowing machinery is designed wholly for the care of home lawns. (The first lawn mower was based on a machine developed in England in 1830 by Edwin Budding for cutting the nap of a carpet.) Although in some parts of the world people still cut grass with the sickle, scythe, and machete, most of us do not. Modern mowing machinery, for both walking and riding, is now powered by gasoline or electric batteries. Some machines just being introduced even have remote-control systems. You just sit back in a lawn chair, press buttons, and the machine does the work. Still, a lot of people (myself included) like the small, uncomplicated reel mowers pushed by hand. Machines also come with special attachments —everything from leaf bags to snow blowers. There is some difference of opinion about which machine is the most satisfactory for the homeowner. I propose in this chapter to answer some of the key questions asked of me in the past few years concerning mowing and mowing machines. I will attempt to explain the good and bad points of the various types of mowing equipment now available.

Q.—What are the different types of mowers available, and which type do you recommend?

A.—There are four basic mowers available to the homeowner. The type you buy should depend on the size of your lawn and the size of your wallet. The four types are hand-push reel, power reel, power rotary, and power riding-mowers (rotary and reel types.)

The hand reel mower is my choice for small lawns of 3,000 square feet or less (even up to 5,000 square feet if you are energetic and like to work up a good sweat). For good healthy exercise, I recommend mowing a lawn with a hand-push reel over jogging any time. You make your lawn look good and yourself feel better at the same time. And there's some calorie loss. You'll not only be cutting down the grass but also your weight.

Hand-push reel mowers are your best, cheapest bet (if you can find them) and are easy to take care of. All that they need in the way of upkeep is annual sharpening, an occasional bed-knife adjustment, repacking with cup grease, and oil lubrication. They are quiet and they last forever. This is the only mower that I recommend for children to use. I have access to all types of mowers to use on our small lawn, but the only one that my wife and children use is the old, old push type that we borrow from a neighbor. Boy, does it whiz through the grass!

Rotary power mower. National sales figures indicate that the rotary mower is still the best seller year in and year out. It is about 50 to 1 in popularity compared with the reel power mower, mainly because it costs only half as much. A few manufacturers used to make a relatively cheap and dependable power reel mower, but no longer; at least I haven't seen any for a long time. It seems to me they all went on to make the more expensive power reel mowers, and as a result the rotary mowers have taken over. (Lovers of reel mowers, don't despair. Reel mowers always have one great advantage—they cut finer. See next question.)

Rotary blade mowers are improving considerably. I am speaking of the more expensive models. Keep away from the real cheapies. It's the new rotaries with the safety devices that are dominating the market. Always look for the safety features, and don't buy one that doesn't come equipped with them. One such feature in the better models is a safety door that drops down and closes the opening to the grass bag when the bag is taken off, so nothing can fly out of the hole while the mower is running. Another big safety feature is that you can't start the machine unless your foot is solidly on the deck. An extra "plus" on a good rotary mower is that when the horizontal rotary blade hits an object like a protruding curb, a friction disc causes the blade to give, which keeps it from breaking off and hitting someone. Be sure that the rotary mower you buy has a strong housing and a heavy-duty metal deck. The handle should be of heavy steel tubing that can't break. I am happy to say that many good rotaries have hard steel blades that hold a sharp edge longer. Rotaries are cheaper to sharpen than reel mowers, whose blades can number as many as ten or twelve.

Rotary blades can be sharpened at home with an inexpensive bench grinder or even with a good 10-inch file if the blades are of softer steel. But I prefer an electric grinder for sharpening rotary blades. (Be sure you have a safety guard over the grinder and a three-prong safety plug, and put on safety glasses when sharpening the blade). Cheap blade balancers are available so both blade ends can be balanced evenly. But there is a simpler method of keeping the blade ends at an even weight if you have a heavy hand with the grinder or file. Just drive a nail into a wall and put a wee bit of oil on it. Now hang the blade on the nail. The heavy side of the blade will always drop to the bottom.

When a rotary blade is dull, it pulls and frays and mutilates the grass tips, making the grass look whitish and unsightly. This tearing can lead to other problems. So keep the blade sharp, and good and tight when you put it back under the housing.

The whole secret of rotary mowers is a keen edge. Remember the sickle and scythe era? Of course not, you were too young. But the same principle prevailed. Experienced men and women could cut as low as 1 inch with them, but they sharpened the blade every hour, or less, and carried the honing stone in their pocket. People go year after year without sharpening their rotary blades while the lawn deteriorates. Then when they buy a new rotary, they exclaim, "Hey, my lawn looks better. How come?" "How come" is simply because the new rotary mower has a sharp blade. This is a good time to emphasize one key factor concerning homeowners living in the South and their mowers. Because the textures of Bermuda, Zoysia, and St. Augustine grasses are tougher than those of cool-region grasses, mowers, whether reel or rotary, must be sharpened much more frequently than in northern areas. The southern grasses can round off the edge of a sharp blade in a hurry. Friends of mine living in the South inform me that they have to sharpen their blades at least four times during the growing season. And we think we have it tough, honing a blade once a season or once in the mower's lifetime. I recommend that you sharpen your rotary blade after every eight hours of use. If you do this your turf will always be neatly clipped and attractive.

Rotaries are extremely hard workers and are the best mowers for cutting not only rough grass and weeds but your finer grasses as well. However, if you get into the heavy stuff, always check the blade for a sharp edge. A rotary can be easily turned or moved back and forth. I like this, especially at dead ends and around solid objects like trees, posts, walls, and fences. With a rotary, you'll never be caught in a tight corner. Rotaries don't jam or clog up like reel mowers do when they cut through long grass or when they hit sticks, twigs, and other debris. The blade rotates and chops like a machete. It swings unhindered by itself, while reel blades can only cut in a scissor-like (shear-like) contact with the bedknife. Anything that catches in between the reel and the bedknife will stop the reel blades from revolving and possibly knock the mower out of kilter. With a rotary blade, there is no worry with this; however, there is the possible danger of its throwing any object it hits like a deadly missile. So it's very important to pick up all foreign objects on the lawn before you mow with any mower, particularly the rotary. As far as height adjustment is concerned, rotaries are simpler to set up and down than reel mowers. The suction created underneath the housing of rotary mowers can disturb thatch lying in the mower's path by "vacuuming" stems and leaves and pulverizing them under the housing, especially when the lawn is good and dry. The slower you mow, the more this is likely to happen. It's always a good idea, if you don't use the grass bag, to throw clippings and other debris away from the sidewalks, streets, etc. You see, grass flies out from the discharge side of the housing. Point that side away from areas where grass isn't growing. Otherwise you'll have to do a lot of sweeping. Though I don't advocate picking up clippings most of the time, I would like to see more of it done when a rotary mower is used. The reason is to catch dangerous flying objects. Though stones, sticks, and other dangerous missiles can fly out from almost anywhere underneath the mower, most of the stuff takes the easiest way out, which is the opening for the grass discharge. I would much rather it hit the bag than a person. If you're careful, rotaries will usually chop up everything so small that disposal isn't necessary. However, if the grass is too long, a rotary mower will mash the clippings and drop them in unsightly windrow masses all over the lawn, causing grass to turn yellow underneath due to lack of oxygen. Rotary housings need periodic cleaning underneath, where the pulpy mass sticks like glue to the sides. Pry the green mass off with a stick or a screwdriver and then rinse with water.

In order to make mowing with a rotary more efficient, be sure when cutting long grass that the clippings are thrown onto the still unmowed grass. That way you will chop them up again still finer.

Recently, I saw ads for small rotary mowers in a newspaper. The ads stated something like this: "Top recoil starter with compression release starts engine quickly. Rugged wind tunnel steel housing has two baffles for grass discharge . . . clog resistant, too. Adjust wheels to cut in fine heights with finger-tip ease. Handle folds to store." There wasn't much difference in the ads, except for the fact that the models were either 20 or 22 inches wide and their engine sizes varied from 10 to 12 cubic inches. But boy, was there a gigantic difference in their prices! They ranged from $49.99 to $89.99 to $114.95 to two whose price was $149.95. None of them advertised any safety features, and only one of them came with a grass catcher. So it's always up to the homeowner to ask the dealer what the safety features are—and then buy the rotary mower that has the best all-around safety features, not the one with the lowest price tag on it.

Reel mowers. Their paramount feature is their cutting supremacy. Due to their scissor-like cutting, the grass blades are sheared cleanly and left with no ragged tips or fraying, provided the blades are properly adjusted and sharp. A reel mower is a precision instrument whose blades are propelled to revolve against a flat, stationary knife (bedknife); this action cuts off the leaf tips as a sharp scissors would. The number of blades on a reel mower can vary from four to a dozen (as on some machines used on golf course greens). Since the blades must slide by and make contact with the bedknife, there isn't much allowance between the reel and the bedknife. Therefore, a reel mower will clog up quickly if it hits high grass or picks up a twig or stick. The only thing to do when this occurs is to stop the mower, tilt it back (first disconnect the spark plug wire), and slowly rotate the reel and readjust it until all the blades cut strips of newspapers right across the length of the bedknife. It's important to adjust the mower in such a way that with little pressure the reel rotates very smoothly and cuts the paper cleanly. If a reel mower is dull or if the bearings are loose, it'll mow ridges in the grass. The washboard effect on turf is generally the result of travelling *too fast* (i.e., the "clip of the reel" is too long relative to the mowing height).

A reel mower *must* be sharpened by professionals each year after the last mowing is done. Don't wait till spring when everybody else remembers to have his mower sharpened and the engine overhauled. Take your mower to a qualified shop in your community and have the work done when they aren't rushed. Then be sure to get an itemized bill. Reel mowers are considerably higher priced than rotaries and are more expensive to overhaul and sharpen. But their major advantage is their superior mowing ability.

Another advantage of reel mowers is that they have a roller in the back that smooths down worm castings or any heaving or thawing that has occurred during the winter. The solid-front roller will also knock down the dew ahead of the reel blades. (Most reel mowers have front and back rollers.)

The best place to adjust a reel mower for its cutting height is on an even floor. Most books advise using a ruler and measuring from the floor to the tip of the cutting edge of the bedknife. This sounds like good advice but it isn't—and maybe that's why so many homeowners really don't know the actual cutting height of their mower. Let me ask you, have you tried sticking a ruler between the floor and the top of the bedknife? With the sharp reel overhanging? Well, it's almost impossible, not only because of the angle but because of the reel and the grass shield guard on top. Furthermore, you can damn near scrape your fingers off. The best way to adjust for height that I know of was devised by my mechanic, Tony. He took a large bolt whose length was exactly the height of the cut he wanted, then slid it under the reel (the reel always protrudes out forward first) and up against the bedknife shoe. By doing this, he could adjust to the height he wanted by making sure the top of the bolt was even with the tip of the bedknife shoe. That's all there is to it. Now put the measuring bolt away. Don't leave it on the grass. An even easier way is to use, on high cuts, a board shaved to the height that you want to cut your grass (2½ inches). Just slide it underneath and past the protruding reel and up against the bedknife shoe. When the tip of the bedknife is exactly even with the height of board, tighten the nuts. You now have the desired height of cut. Simple?

Just one more hint about reel mowers, or for that matter, any type of mower. If the grass is extremely long, don't make a full swath each time. This usually plugs or stops the overworked mower. Instead, take half the width (or three-quarters, depending how deep your grass is) rather than the full cut or bite.

Riding mowers, whether reel or rotary, are for serious mowing and should be considered only for larger-than-average lawns and estates. They are a nice lazy way to mow large areas, but they are quite expensive and more difficult to handle than they look. Children should neither be allowed nor encouraged to ride them until they are able to, which is usually when they are 14 to 15 years old. Nothing is more stupid than parents being talked by their kids into letting them use the riding mower when they don't know the first thing about them. I never forgot the one that overturned with two young boys riding it. The kids were sitting on the seat motorcycle-fashion, with their legs swinging all over the place. It was a miracle that something wasn't chopped off. They did run into the neighbor's new car, which caused bad feelings and expense, but they got off lucky. What possesses parents to permit their little children to take such chances is beyond me. These mowers are for use by *adults only*. They are easily overturned if you aren't careful, especially the rotary ones. The riding reel mowers are the best-riding mowers. They have three reels, one in front or underneath the machine and one on each side. But they are beyond the reach of most pocketbooks and are used commercially and extensively only on golf courses. Three-speed transmission riding rotary mowers are the most popular units, and they cost considerably less than the triple-reel riding mowers. However, I dislike the cheaper rotary riding models because they cause too many frustrating problems with the cutting assembly and the maze of belts underneath the mower. Most rotary blades on riding mowers are rotated by a V-belt drive. On the cheaper belt models, the belts are forever slipping off or getting too loose, or the pulleys bend, or something else goes wrong. It's best to buy the more expensive, high-quality riding rotary mowers that have good V-belt devices. I recommend that you always look around for units whose V-belts are stocked at automotive parts and supply houses in your community, rather than buy ones that are available only in oddball sizes (this goes for odd-shaped batteries also) from the dealer. (This is usually the case now.) The cost of V-belts at an automotive supply house is but a fraction of the cost you pay for them from the mower dealer. Of course direct shaft attachment drive eliminates the maze of belts.

It is very important that riding mowers have the best of safety features. Here are some of the things to look for:

1. If you get off or fall off without setting the brake, the engine should stop.

2. For protection of kids, the mower should have a key to start the engine. This way, you can always hide the key.

3. Safety chain guards that form a 360-degree shield around the unit. These chainlike guards touch the ground on all sides even when the unit is mowing high. This safety feature prevents ejection of grass, bottles, cans, and other debris onto adjacent grass areas or people.

4. A wide floor deck between you and the mower housing.

In conclusion, I would like to state that the demand for reel mowers, both hand and power, has dwindled to such a sad degree that most companies selling lawn products to homeowners don't even carry them in their catalogues. It's too bad in a way, because as I said earlier, the cutting action of reel mowers is superior to rotary blade mowing. Most of all, I miss the good clean exercise and the smell of fresh cut grass (not the smell of gas fumes), plus the release from tension. Nothing will ever beat the old, uncumbersome, hand-push reel mower. Good-bye, little old friend.

Q.—Please tell me which is better: gas, electric, or battery powered mowers? Our yard is average-sized.

A.—First, think about noise pollution. There are only a few places in the world today where it is quiet. Noise has become inescapable in modern life. So if you want to do your share to keep the noise level down, buy an electric mower with a long cord attachment. Wait—good news!! *Cordless* electric-powered mowers are also available. Their batteries are charged by the ordinary home electric current, which gives you enough juice to finish cutting your lawn and then some. Don't worry, the battery (power pack) lasts a long time. Their principle of power is similar to that of the electric riding carts on the golf course that have successfully been in operation ever since golfers got lazy and decided walking wasn't part of the game. The cordless electric mowers are the latest innovation in lawn mowing and will increase in popularity as time goes on. Your neighbors who love quiet will applaud you.

Be careful if you use the electric models with the trailing cord. Don't get tangled up in it or cut the wiring in two. Perhaps you can have somebody lift up the cord and walk behind you to keep it out of the way of your mowing. We do this at my course when we are spraying greens with fungicides, using a 200-gallon power sprayer and a 100-foot hose. One man sprays and a helper walks a short distance behind him, keeping the hose from getting underfoot. You can use the same method with an electric mower and cord. Get one of your family or the next door neighbor to help you. (Just be sure her husband isn't home!) I don't recommend an electric mower with a cord for lawns with many trees. These shaded lawns usually have too many roots, knobs, dips, and bumps, so I suggest a mower without a cord. A gasoline rotary mower set at 2½ to 3 inches is the best solution.

I like the electric mowers for several reasons. They are never hard to start up, and when you're using them, you're not troubled by noise, smell, vibration, or involvement with messy gas and oil. As far as being free of pollution, they're the closest thing to the old hand push mower. Though these mowers are considerably more expensive, it is almost effortless to use them and they are extremely dependable.

For large areas, I recommend a battery-electric riding mower. The battery starts your mowing unit just like your car battery starts your car. All you do is turn a switch, press a button, and away you go. The battery-electric starter mower and the regular gasoline push-type power mower should be used in the evenings or after ten in the morning on weekends. Be considerate of those in your neighborhood who like to sleep late. Besides, a lawn mower, no matter what type, will always do a much better job of cutting if the grass is dry. Mowing the evening is best of all. Hot afternoons are not. With the gas type and the battery electric starter mower, more service and adjustments are required, which results in more expense to you. I think once the popularity of electric power for home lawn mowing units is fully established, sales will increase and this new type mower power will give the gasoline models a run for their money. Once you try the electric mowers, you'll appreciate their quiet operation, their 100-percent starting dependability, and their other conveniences such as no fuel storage and cheaper maintenance. Electric power is the coming concept in lawn mowing machines, whether in reel or rotary types. (*Note:* Don't cut wet grass with a direct current cord electric mower.)

There will soon be a federal law to reduce noise below a certain decibel level. Abrasive noise is being outlawed in residential areas. You might as well start doing your part now.

Q.—My lawn is predominantly Kentucky bluegrass. How high should it be mowed? Also, I would like to know your recommendation for an ideal mowing height of cool-region grasses.

A.—At universities, experimental turf plots that have been mowed at different heights show that the higher the mowing cut, the stronger and deeper is the root system. The shorter the grass is mowed, the shallower and more reduced is the total root system, which eventually weakens turf. This goes for all grasses that are mowed too low. In my opinion, this should be a special warning to the cool-region homeowners, who frequently mow upright rhizome grass lawns far too low for the good of the grass. When mowing is low, the total leaf surface available for photosynthesis is reduced. Consequently, the root and rhizome growth, as well as the plant's recuperative powers, are impaired because of reduced carbohydrate reserves. You see, grass develops a balance between the leaves and the root system, and a sudden upset of this delicate balance can cause severe shock to the plant. A home-owner should keep in mind one simple but very important fact—food is produced in the leaves, so removal of too much leaf surface is damaging. Therefore, low mowing is the quickest way to make your lawn weak and sparse and to produce a shallow root system that has difficulty reaching moisture in the soil. When this situation occurs, weeds come in and unsightly brown thatch at the soil base is exposed; so are sticky earthworm mounds, knobby tree roots, and numerous dips and mounds that your extremely low-set mower might hit, scalp, or tear. This damage to the lawn's appearance and health will not occur if the grass is mowed at a sensible high cut. Turf experts have decreed that low mowing also makes lawns more susceptible to diseases such as melting-out (*Helmintho-sporium*), and less resistant to insects and drought (the shallower the roots, the harder it is for the grass to reach moisture and with-stand the stress of temperature extremes). Furthermore, a short-mowed lawn will always need more water, fertilizer, and other cultural practices (which nowadays can be quite expensive). The worst thing homeowners can do to their lawns is mow the grass too low and then not follow through with the required cultural practices. There is a range in height of cut that is considered satis-factory for each lawn grass species, certainly. But many times the homeowner unwisely disregards the advice of turf experts and chops his lawn grass way down. There is always more damage to the plant when the grass is under stress for moisture, but there the unknowing homeowner is out there foolishly mowing in the hot sun, as happy as can be. It's not good judgment to cut a lawn even at a sensible high cut in the hot sun. But with short grass, mowing low and exposing the sensitive, newly cut grass to the direct sun can lead to disaster.

If I had one big wish to help homeowners in the cool-region zone, it would be that mower manufacturers could not sell ma-chines that could be set to mow below 2½ inches for home lawns. (And not as low as that in the South and in transition zones where the upright cool-region grasses sometimes grow.) But that's wish-ful thinking, like wishing car manufacturers would make cars that could not exceed 65 miles per hour. It's too bad; there is nothing lovelier than grass uniformly mowed at a high cut, and believe me, nothing more durable. Higher-cut grass plants are larger and generally more tolerant to environmental stresses.

Have you ever stopped on a windy day and watched a field of long grass on a golf course rough or in a park? If you haven't, just stop the next time and listen to how the wind softly sighs and ripples swiftly through the grass, bending it down with its force, teasing it, allowing it to stand up, and then rippling through it again and again. Have you ever walked out in long wet grass and felt its gentle tickle under your bare feet instead of feeling the brittle prickling of grass mowed at stubble height? Long grass feels cool even when temperatures are high, because it helps keep the soil temperature down, thus reducing moisture evaporation. When the lawn is mowed too low, you feel the hot ground, not the grass. With long grass, you won't see the exposed ground with its yellow thatch and brown stems. Instead you will see, if you bend down and look closely, an ant hurrying to some secret project, or a beetle wandering through on an endless journey, or a grasshopper stealthily hiding but ready to leap. Believe me, in the majestic, flowing beauty of long grass, there is a wonderful and exciting ecology going on—more than you can study in a lifetime.

Above all—and I think this should be a paramount objective for any family—lawns that are mowed high will take heavy traffic considerably better than lawns mowed ridiculously low. And scars sustained on that long slipping slide home will heal faster and hardly show if the grass is the proper length when your ten-year-old son or daughter is playing baseball. Try it this summer.

Q.—Please explain to us the best way to mow a lawn. Like what should we do before we even start mowing? What are some of the important practices we must know about mowing and what preparations must we make to get a uniformly clean-cut, attractive lawn? This is our first home and the lawn is about two years old.

A.—The best way to mow a lawn is with a good lawn mower. I know that isn't exactly what you meant by your question, but let's start with that important premise. A good lawn mower with a sharp edge is not only the best way, but the only way. Otherwise, you're wasting your time and hurting your grass. All the good that a homeowner can possibly do with other management practices is undone by using a dull or bad mower that's in poor condition. All right, now that we have that cleared up, let's proceed to good lawn mowing practices.

Always make sure all debris is cleared off the lawn area—sticks, stones, toys, cans, paper. It's much smarter to pick up a whole piece of paper before you mow than twenty little pieces after you have shredded it. Don't mow wet grass. A mower will always do a cleaner and neater job when the grass is dry and drops to the ground, rather than lying in a pulpy mess and smothering the grass. But if you do have to mow when it's wet, take an end of the hose, give the other end to a member of your family, and then drag it in a U-shaped loop slowly over the lawn. This will knock the dew off as you pull. Then drag the hose back again. If you have a small lawn, you can knock off the dew with a bamboo pole or a long slim stick. At the golf course we drag a long hose pulled by a tractor or scooter over the fairways, and on the greens we use bamboo poles to knock the dew off before we mow. This helps prevent clumping of grass clippings and accelerates drying time. Why not try it at home if you must mow in the morning? Don't mow in the heat of the day and expose the newly cut, sensitive part of the grass to the direct sun. I recommend waiting until after five o'clock. Besides, it's not good for you to stay out in the hot sun too long. Not only can it result in sunburn, but also in allergic reaction and even heatstroke (we all know about those mad Englishmen).

A lawn likes to have a good soaking once a week (see next chapter). Why not soak it right after mowing? It looks so fresh and attractive, especially next morning. Of course you know by now how I feel about the height of cut (see last question). I recommend that you never mow lower than 2½ inches, unless you have bent, Bermuda, or Zoysia turf. Don't fill your mower gas tank to the brim. Give it a little air space. This will prevent gas trickling from your mower onto the grass. *Never* fill the tank on the grass itself, and never fill it while the engine is running. Fill the gas tank when the motor is cold, and do it on the sidewalk away from the grass and other vegetation, just in case you have an accident. If you run out of gas in the middle of mowing a lawn, take the machine to a bare area, turn off the motor, let the engine cool, then carefully fill the gas tank to about 1 inch from the top.

Remember, gas that leaks onto the grass will kill whatever it hits.

Clean off both gas caps before replacing them, and be sure you put the right one on the proper tank, not the other way around. Paint the caps a different color, or put a distinguishing stripe on one. This is not meant to be funny. I am serious. The gas caps sometimes appear very similar. Many times, both fit snugly on either gas tank. But there is one major difference in them. There is a tiny breather *air hole* in the mower gas tank cap and *no hole* in the gas can cap. Here's what happens if you put the gas cap with no air hole on your mower's gas tank. Your mower runs for a few minutes, then conks out. Without that little breather hole, the gas does not get to the carburetor and the engine stops. Later on, it starts again, runs a few minutes, then stops again. The homeowner by now is so upset that he calls the dealer or the store that sold him the mower, and either blasts them for selling him a mower that doesn't run or pleads with them to come out and service the thing. I know people who are in the business of lawn mower service, and they get (so they tell me, believe it or not) up to fifty calls or more a year from people who get gas caps mixed up. Most homeowners, they tell me, who mistakenly switch the caps call them to come right over or they bring their mower to the repair department and proceed to chew the heck out of the clerk for selling rotten mowers. Of course, when the right gas cap is put back on the mower, they sheepishly stand back with disbelieving eyes watching the mower run smoothly. It's frustrating, and yet according to my friends in this frustrating business, some of the homeowners just don't believe this could happen, and actually—actually!—do it over again. How dumb can you get? I've done it once, too, a long time ago when I was apprenticing as a greenkeeper.

Always keep gasoline stored in a safety can, not in a jar, pail, starch bottle, or bleach bottle. Be sure always to carefully clean the underside of the housing with hose and water. Some mowers now have hose attachments to the under deck just for easier cleaning. Any standard garden hose can connect to the washout post for a quick cleaning. Don't let the bottom of your mower get all clogged with a clinging, pulpy grass mass. Clean it off. If it doesn't come off, use a long screwdriver or stick to wedge out the grass sticking to the housing. Periodic cleaning assures that grass buildup will not occur. Don't ever, when washing the mower after cutting, splash cold water on the hot block of the engine. You might crack it. Another hint: if your mower suddenly conks out, don't try to start it on grass that is long. The rotary blade engages and starts whirling around just as soon as the engine starts. In thick long grass, you aren't going to have much success starting the mower, because the blade won't rotate. Instead, be smart and take the rotary over to the sidewalk or a bare area to start the engine. If, for one reason or another, you have to turn the mower over, don't do it on the grass. Watch out for gas leakage, and see that the oil doesn't leak out of the air breather.

If you use an electric mower with a cord, be sure the wiring isn't frayed or nicked anywhere. Also be careful that you use a three-prong grounded connection.

It's very important that children and other important people are kept at some distance from your mowing, just in case you chip a stone or hit gravel. These things can fly a considerable distance out from under certain mowers. I've not only seen it; I've been hit and wounded. Disengage the cutting blade when moving the mower across asphalt or cement walks. Shoo everyone away. Even your mother-in-law.

If you must stop for any reason, even for a moment, also stop the mower. This is for two reasons. One, a running mower can prove a danger to curious onlookers, particularly those under four feet tall, who are too young to understand that there is a blade whirling at a tremendous speed a few inches away underneath the mower. The other reason is that it is a danger to your green grass. If you let the mower run even for a minute while it is standing still, the grass under the mowing deck will turn brown by next morning due to the friction and bruising of the whirling blade. Another precaution concerns mowers (I know of one very popular, publicized mower) that have exhausts directly under the housing. Each time they get hot (after just a few minutes) and the homeowner stops or briefly slows down, the exhaust burns off and kills the grass. The dead spots aren't large, just the size of the small mower exhaust, a few inches, but on a green lawn they look awful.

When mowing, walk at a steady pace; do not run or hurry with your mowing. If you haven't time to do a proper job and observe the safety precautions, then wait until you do. I don't want you rushing out in all directions like some hay-burning Don Quixote. Take your time. Make proper moves and turns at the perimeter of your property, especially with a riding mower. Be sure you have enough room to turn. Don't mow if you drink. Periodically check your mower to make sure that all bolts and mountings are secure. When putting on a special attachment for some other job (such as a cultivator, disc harrow, spreader, seeder, fertilizer, sprayer, lawn roller, leaf rake, plow, rotary broom, spiker, aerifier, thatcher, vacuum sweeper, snowplow, or verticutter), do it yourself. And never allow children to monkey around with the attachments. Be sure that the kids don't try to adjust the mowing height, at least not until they are old enough and you have instructed them in procedures and safety. And never, ever monkey with the mower when it is running. I know many people with fewer than ten fingers, and a couple of nice kids who've had toes cut off.

When mowing your lawn, take a different path each time. Frequently, on alternate weeks, cut at right angles so the grass won't bend just one way and develop a grain. At my golf course, we always keep changing our direction of cut, even on the rough. Grain on golf courses affects a rolling ball, especially on the green. Going always in the same direction on a home lawn can also cause compaction and patchlike trails. Your mower will do a better job of cutting grass that is upright than grass that is flat and drooping. (Don't worry, healthy, well-kept grass will stand up and reach for the sun and is beautiful at 2½ inches high, unless it's a stoloniferous type like bent or Bermuda, which must always be cut below 1 inch.)

If for some reason your grass is deep and long, don't cut a full swath. Take half or three-quarters of the width of your mower, not a full width. There is no reason to overwork your mower and have it conk out or choke up with clumps every few minutes.

If you are using a rotary mower, discharge the clippings on the return cut into the path of the mower. This way you are chopping the long grass blades into tinier bits, and they can easily shift down into the zone of decomposition. There now are rotary machines that can chop up grass clippings much more finely than the old rotaries, even in deep grass. They use a multipitched blade that cuts the grass and then allegedly cuts and recuts the airborne clippings into fine mulch particles that are blown down onto your lawn.

Of course, mowing in the opposite (perpendicular) direction will accomplish the same purpose if you aren't using a grass catcher. Always study the instruction manual for the manufacturer's recommendations for care and use of the mower. And don't ever start a new mower without checking the oil level in the crank case. Last of all, wear sturdy shoes, for protection not only from mower accidents, but also from the messy excrement left on the lawn by man's best friend. And since in this modern, enlightened age we are still spending more money on the feeding and care of pets than on mental hospitals, orphanages, and school lunches, there is plenty of *that* lying around.

Q.—I would like to know once for all whether picking up clippings does any good when I mow the grass. It's a nuisance and a waste of time to stop frequently and empty the grass into a disposal bag, leaving the full bags at the curb to have them hauled away. Sometimes kids on bikes come by and puncture the bags, which spills the leaves all over. Can I leave the catcher off every time and not have to pick up the clippings?

A.—This question is frequently asked and I've read some interesting answers. To pick up clippings or not to pick up clippings has been bothering homeowners for a long time. My feeling on the matter is this.

Lawn turf that has a stoloniferous growth (crawling horizontally, similar to a strawberry plant) must be cut low in order to look attractive. It should have its clippings picked up every time it is mowed. I am talking specifically about lawns that are composed of creeping bent, Bermuda, and Zoysia grasses, which are mowed under 1 inch high. You see, these low-growing grasses, when properly cared for, form an extremely tight "carpet" of turf, with many more actual plants per square foot than any other species. Therefore, if leaf clippings aren't picked up each time the low-growing grass is mowed, but are allowed to drop on the tight texture of the turf, they don't shift down to the soil base (the zone of decomposition). When this happens, the grass clippings lying on top will start to brown off the foliage and make it look unsightly with leaf burn (yellowing underneath due to lack of air —suffocation). On the other hand, when and if the clippings finally do drop down through the top of the tight leaf surface, all they do is add to the accumulation of undecomposed blades. This frequently compounds the thatch problem and promotes a thicker, even stronger, barrier to good air and water circulation in the soil. Any heavy clippings or clumps that remain on top of the tight texture will smother the turf and turn it yellow or brown. With a living green lawn, an excessive accumulation of thatch will not only deteriorate the looks of your bent, Bermuda, or Zoysia lawn, but eventually help to wipe it out. So pick up your clippings whenever mowing a lawn of stoloniferous, low-growing grasses like the ones I mentioned. (Also, as I mentioned in chapter 3, dethatch these lawns at least once a year.) This advice also goes for any future grass that eventually will be perfected to grow nice and green *through the whole summer* at a very low height, but which now still has to be cut high during the stress times of the summer.

With upright grasses that grow by rhizome and tiller, such as Kentucky bluegrass, the rye grasses, and fescues, I recommend that you pick up the clippings in spring (or rake them off cleanly if you don't have a grass catcher) when turf growth is sometimes extremely heavy. Also do this each time you mow soon after fertilizing, when growth usually is profuse for a short time. The reason for picking up clippings during this time is this: when lush growth occurs and clippings aren't picked up, the heavy clippings that are discharged from the mower will collect on the grass surface, where they turn brown, make the lawn look unsightly, create windrows, and suffocate the green grass (leaf burn) wherever they are heaviest and cannot get air.

Also, please remember that in the periods of your lawn's most vigorous growth (in spring and after fertilizer stimulation), not only are more leaves cut off, but the leaves are longer, so an adverse situation arises. (Please don't promise that you will cut the lawn twice a week or more during this period of heavy growth. That's one promise I have never seen kept by a homeowner.) Something else happens, too. As the heavy, long clippings accumulate on the lawn's surface during its zesty growth, they cannot be expected to decompose as rapidly as the fine leaf particles are decomposed by the soil organisms (bacteria, fungi, and earthworms). There's just too much clipping material at once. It's an overload. It's not an ideally balanced situation, and nature just can't cope with it.

Heavy clippings contribute to thatch, which provides a base for fungi and insects to breed in, instead of providing nutrients to stimulate the grass. The grass eventually becomes sparse, intolerant of drought, and hard-hit by temperature extremes. Certain wise and industrious Japanese homeowners and gardeners insist on mowing their grass every day, and immediately afterward they water lightly. This washes the tiny clippings down to the soil base and provides the moisture to initiate decay. It also causes shallow rooting and reduced vigor—but a finer-textured, denser turf.

In this ideal situation, the clippings are so minute that decomposition is no problem. Most of us, though, are not as industrious as the Japanese, and the best we ever do is to mow once a week, which brings us to the third time that clippings must be picked up—a time that, in my opinion, develops the worst situation of all.

This third time is when you mow less than once a week. When this happens, you're not cutting grass—you're almost cutting hay. So if infrequent mowing is your bag, with long intervals when the grass grows out of control, then I suggest you pick up the lawn clippings every time you mow with a catcher, or rake them, or use a leaf sweeper. But get rid of them. Besides suffocating your green lawn, the infrequent removal of a large portion of grass blades also can sometimes cause damaging shock to the grass plant. The whole secret of whether or not to pick up clippings each time depends on the length of the clippings, which comes down, simply and plainly, to frequent mowing and other good lawn management, such as an adequately balanced fertilizer program and sensible irrigation of your lawn (next chapter). Actually, if lawns were cut just twice a week in periods of abnormally long growth, you would never have to pick up the short clippings. But as I said before, I've yet to see a homeowner push himself to this horrid extreme even though in some periods the grass grows faster and heavier than at other times.

It has recently been determined by some very qualified turf researchers that clippings are of insignificant importance to the accumulation of thatch. It is only when other good management practices are not carried out properly that clippings, along with other thatch present at the soil base (like singular grass plants that in the natural life cycle of all grass plants are continually dying and being replaced with new growth thatch), do not decompose at the rate they ought to. All lawn practices are important. If your lawn is already shoddy and in a state of neglect, heavy grass clippings will add further to its decline. On the other hand, if your lawn is well managed and mowing is frequent, lawn clippings add a *little* nutrition (about 2 pounds of nitrogen per 1,000 square feet per year and a lot of potash, also).

It's interesting to note that during the preenvironmental era, some lawn maintenance companys sold many homeowners on the importance of bagging the clippings every time the grass was mowed. They said disposal was extremely important, and homeowners went along with this theory. Of course, all this did was to increase the working time for the lawn maintenance companies, whose employees were stopping frequently to remove bag attachments, empty the contents, replace the bags on the mowers, and then restart the mowers, and maybe have a cigarette in between. But as soon as the Environmental Control Agency restricted the burning and dumping of lawn debris, except in a few state-approved dumping sites (as far as 20 miles away), the lawn maintenance companies quickly changed their tune and advised their customers about the ecological and organically sound recycling practice of returning clippings back to the soil. The fact that the lawn maintenance companies also had to pay a high dumping fee each time they hauled debris to the far-away dumping sites naturally made it impractical for them to continue their former "advocacy."

Q.—I have always been told there was a revival of grass growth in the fall and that clippings should be picked up at this time the same as in spring when there is usually heavy growth. Yet you recommend that a homeowner who mows a minimum of once a week doesn't have to pick up clippings in the fall.

A.—That's right. He doesn't have to pick up clippings in the fall, except for the few weeks right after he has fertilized his lawn for the last time, a time when the grass is stimulated and its growth is heavier than normal. Let me clear up something. Grass growth in the fall is never as heavy as most people are led to believe it is. If you don't believe me, make a test. Check the weight of your clippings in the summer and then again in the fall. You'll be surprised at the difference. I agree, there is a slight growth at this time that is more, perhaps, than in the hot summer. But this is never heavy, compared with the spring. What usually happens as the nights get longer, the days shorter, the sun lower, and the soil temperatures cooler, is that cool-region lawn grass begins to get much greener and more beautiful after the stress of summer. This condition leads people to believe it is growing vigorously again. It isn't. It's actually slowing down quickly—but in a lovely green condition—as late fall and early winter approach. The grass gets only moderately heavy for a short time, if you have given it that important fall feeding. (I talked about this in the last chapter.) The root system during the fall develops more than the foliage. Also, grass has a more prostrate growth orientation in the fall. This is a perfect situation.

Q.—What is the safest method to mow a slope?

A.—The safest and best way to mow a slope will depend on the degree of incline. A gentle slope can be mowed either parallel to the face of the slope or up and down. However, slopes of 45 degrees or more cannot be mowed safely with any type of riding mower in an up-the-hill-and-over-the-dale fashion. The same thing goes for a walk-behind mower, especially the popular rotary mower. Going up, the mower can fall back on you; going down, it can get away from you and hit someone. Remember, grass is always slippery, and the slope's danger is compounded when grass is wet with rain or dew, which makes it even more slippery than normal. (Red fescue turf on slopes is especially slippery.) In the hands of a strong adult who is wearing spiked golf shoes, a walking mower could be used up and down. But I don't recommend that slopes be mowed in this way by anyone, strong or weak, especially children. If possible, avoid having steep slopes constructed on home lawn areas. They are not only unsafe to mow, but in the hot summertime they're susceptible to drought, localized dry spots, and scalping. However, if you have a slope, mow across the face of it.

Q.—What is the best way to prepare the mower for winter?

A.—A power mower should not be put away for the winter until it has been cleaned of grass clippings, dirt, and grease. Then take the mower to a qualified lawn mower shop for repair and sharpening. Don't wait for this important checkup and overhaul job until spring—when everyone else is rushing to the same lawn mower service shop with nonstarting mowers. (Remember how hard yours was to start last spring?) A lawn mower in good condition is the important final touch in any lawn management program. Because it really is so close to your grass, it deserves proper care.

If you intend to use the all-purpose power mower for snow removal in the winter, then specify the date you want it back, but give them plenty of time for the overhaul. If you're not going to use it for snow removal, fill it with fresh gasoline and oil when it comes back. Then you can put it away until spring. I know this contradicts everything you have ever read or been advised to do. The usual and accepted practice is for the homeowner to drain the fuel from his gasoline-powered equipment before storing it away for the winter, that is, run the engine dry to prevent gums and varnish from forming in the fuel tank, carburetor, and fuel lines. The problem is that *most of the time* the homeowner does not really run all the fuel from the engine. He thinks he has used all of it, but what commonly happens is that some gas remains in the carburetor and fuel bowl and in the pickup inlet at the bottom of the fuel tank. When this remaining fuel dries, it leaves gummy deposits in these critical places. In addition, the seals and the rubber gaskets dry out and tend to cause gasoline leaks in the spring. For this reason, my golf course mechanic, who is considered not only by me but by his peers and Chicagoland equipment dealers to be one of the best in the region, recommends that you fill the power mower with fresh gasoline and 3 ounces or so of "heet" or a similar gas additive. Then drain the crank case and refill it with new oil (don't overfill). Take out the spark plug and pour about an ounce of SAE-30 oil into the cylinder (combustion chamber). Crank the engine slowly to distribute the oil. This will coat the piston and cylinder walls and prevent rust. Then replace the plug. Also clean or replace the air filter. If you have a riding mower, put it on blocks so it is not resting on its wheels during the winter. I further suggest that you cover the mower unit, but not so it is airtight. Never store it near heated places, like furnaces and heat vents, because this will cause above-normal evaporation. Of course, mowers stored in damp wet places will suffer a lot of internal rusting. One last important hint. Close the fuel tank shut-off (if you have one) so tightly that in the event the gas ever by-passes (escapes the carburetor), only the fuel in the carburetor will leak. This will greatly reduce the chance of fire.

Frankly, though, most of the homeowners I know don't do anything to their mowers after the last mowing. Nothing at all. They just put the old mower away, usually with some gas in the tank. If you fall into this category, then I advise you strongly to drain all your old gas in the spring and refill the tank with new fuel. Put 1 percent of Gumout in your tank and "crank it."

Q.—Why do they always advertise mowing machines (and other garden equipment) with pretty women (in tight clothes) sitting daintily on the mower?

A.—Because men in tight clothing can't sit daintily on a mower. No, seriously, I guess it is to show the potential buyer that the mower was safe and easy to handle, even by the wee lady of the house, which is alright by me. I'll tell you why. It seems to me that before women's liberation, the tired husband always did the mowing. I am glad that wives now sometimes take their turn and mow the lawn. It's about time. Give the mighty lord of the house a chance to push the dish-washing machine button once in a while.

7

Watering

THERE ARE heavily populated areas in the world today that are extremely short of water. Conservationists and soil experts tell us the situation here will increasingly worsen and eventually become very critical. This is directly due to the tremendous volume needed for daily public consumption and for heavy industrial use, which is expanding by leaps and bounds. Of course, the modern homeowner, with his two to four bathrooms, showers, swimming pools, automatic dishwasher, automatic washing machine, and automatic lawn irrigation, contributes to the water shortage. We soon might be putting out the rain barrels again to catch a little extra water, as some countries are doing now. We might even have to ration water, as some of the arid western states are doing now.

Q.—Water is very expensive in our community. Please explain to us how we can economize and still have a good healthy lawn.

A.—The best money-saving advice I can give you is never to mow your grass below 2½ inches (preferably 3 inches) going into the hot summer. Keep your cut high. Here's why. Grass that's been mowed high meets less stress in a drought because it has more leaf area. Thus the photosynthetic ability of the plant is greater to provide carbohydrates for production of a deeper root system. As a result, a lawn with deep roots is better able to reach the water in the subsoil. Also, I might add, with a higher mowed lawn, the rate of evaporation of water from the soil is drastically reduced, and the grass can shade itself by providing ideal insulation from the rays of the hot sun. All this adds up to one big plus for the homeowner and his wallet. There's another plus: an established lawn in reasonably good condition mowed 2½ or 3 inches *doesn't* need watering more than once every week or ten days. (This of course depends on cloudy weather, drying wind, heat, showers, and other weather patterns.) Infrequent watering, if you mow your grass sensibly high, will save you money and many headaches.

The other smart, sensible way to conserve water (and money) is not to water until the last of June or, preferably, just before the Fourth of July. Put aside your urge to water until this time—and then only if needed. Of course, as I have repeated so many times before, I am recommending this procedure only for established cool-region lawns that are *mowed at 2½ inches or higher*— not less.

Don't be alarmed if your grass goes a little off color before its first watering in July (or, later on, between waterings). This is a natural and normal stage for all cool-region grasses, because grass starts to slow down and conserve water and energy when the heat and the humidity get high. But don't worry, the turf will survive. If you are a golfer in the Midwest, you know what happens with the golf course rough; it turns brown in the hot summer but becomes green again with the first heavy rain in the fall. However, this is a purposely extreme example. For, you see, we *never* water the rough. You at least *will be watering* your lawn once a week, once July comes along.

So don't worry—save money on the water bill during the safe lawn period of April, May, and June. I promise you, a good lawn mowed high won't go out during these months. (Naturally, if you live in the South, Southwest, or the dry West, you'll have to water sooner.) But it's a different matter with a short-mowed lawn and its shallow root system. You'll have to baby it every time the weather gets dry. A lawn short-mowed and camouflaged with weeds and undesirable grasses usually is nice only early in the spring; but later, weeds and deterioration will show vividly during the hot weather. I predict that with a short-mowed lawn, you'll be outdoors all the time watching for every brown spot that occurs and watering frequently, which will naturally result in a costly water bill. And if you finally get fed up with the poor lawn, as some people do after spring fever, and let the lawn go, then my question is: Why have a lawn in the first place? Put in cement or asphalt.

The last hint to reduce heavy bills is to water only the front lawn—the public view. This really is the choice part of your lawn as far as eye appeal is concerned. If water costs get too high and restrictions frequent, keep the front green and the back dormant.

Q.—What is the best way to water a lawn? How frequently? And how can I tell if the lawn is watered adequately?

A.—In the cool-region area of the Midwest, July is the time to do serious watering, and once a week then is enough if you irrigate heavily. Irrigate heavily so you soak the subsoil deep down. Don't just surface water. The best way to know when your lawn has had enough water (forget about setting out coffee cans to test the amount) is to feel water squishing under your feet when you walk over it. In other words, if when you "press" on it as you're walking, the water comes up easily and squishes under the soles of your shoes. You don't get this condition after 20 minutes or so of watering. You get this only after soaking the yard for from two to four hours *in one spot,* depending on your soil constituency. Believe me, after you're through, you'll know that you've watered there and not sprinkled. Heavily is the only way to water your lawn—once a week or every 10 days. You'll be delightfully surprised at how many times a good heavy rain comes along and soaks your lawn (run out and catch some in a rain barrel or pail to water your indoor plants). I've seen this wonderful free gift from Mother Nature occur so many times during the 7-to-10-day interval of no watering that a few times I have never had to water my lawn *all summer long.* That's the truth. And this, let me tell you, is saving money in water costs. (Of course, I live in Lake Bluff, Illinois, and not in Salt Lake City, where it gets pretty dry.)

Remember, daily watering not only accumulates high water bills and wastes effort in setting out and moving sprinklers, but it also begets a shallow and weak root system and therefore reduced turf grass vigor and quality. Lawns in this sad condition (usually short-mowed during soaring temperatures, too, with no rain in sight) lose their moisture faster from the leaf surface than the shallow roots can replenish it. It's also very difficult for them to go into semidormancy as a healthy lawn does. Instead, what usually happens is that the grass plants begin to "footprint," wilt, and brown out. As a result, you'll end up with a lawn full of bare spots, which will rapidly fill with weeds, disease, and perhaps even bugs. Its tolerance to heat, cold, and drought will also be greatly reduced. Then you'll really have troubles.

I have never known a lawn with a weak root system and top foliage mowed too low to maintain a *good condition* throughout a hot July and August with just frequent light sprinklings. (On the other hand, frequent excessive watering can result in a waterlogged condition, which leads to compaction, loss of oxygen, leaching, and, of course, diseases.)

Frequent watering also encourages the growth of treacherous *Poa annua,* which I have noticed comes in more and more abundantly with daily light sprinkling and low mowing. This extremely shallow-rooted "grass" (see chapter on weeds) comes in beautifully in spring and fades in the summer, then recovers to take over the lawn or some of the lawn in the fall. But it declines so rapidly in the summer that all you have is irregular patches of brown grass. Water-loving creeping bentgrass also thrives and flourishes in lawns that are watered every day. And believe me, all you need is a couple of seeds in the soil to get bentgrass spreading its stolons all over the lawn. Then you really have a dilemma: two different kinds of grass growing together, except one is upright and grows by rhizomes and needs to be mowed sensibly high and watered infrequently, and the other grows by spreading stoloniferous growth and needs to be mowed extremely low and irrigated almost every day to look attractive. North America is full of lawns smack in the middle of this dilemma. Remember, in pure lawns of only one type of grass, everything else growing can be considered a weed, even if it's another grass. Therefore, in a pure Kentucky bluegrass lawn, bentgrass can be considered a weed just like a dandelion. A weed is any plant growing where it is not desired. So take my advice: keep the grass long and water the lawn every week or 10 days, so that between the waterings the roots can grope downward to where the moisture is usually available. That's a secret of a healthy lawn: a deep root system.

Q.—When is the best time to water the lawn—night or day?

A.—The grass doesn't care if you water in the day or night, nor does it have a preference or a say-so about when rain will fall. Just as long as you supply the plant with water when it is thirsty, it will survive. But if your low-mowed or new lawn is severely going off color (dark bluish green in appearance) and footprinting during the high temperatures of July and August, don't wait until evening. Throw on the water right away. "Footprinting" is a visible and dire indication of dryness when the turf is walked on; the footprints stay wilted. Low-mowed lawns, new lawns, and poor lawns should be watered right away, because waiting until evening to water might just be too late. Mature lawns mowed at 2½ inches or higher going into the seventh day or so of no moisture will look peaked but will survive till evening, at which time I recommend that you water deeply and heavily.

I would prefer that you water during the still evening hours or at night for several reasons. Less spray evaporation occurs at this time, and due to lower wind velocities, a better and more uniform water pattern is distributed. All this adds up to a wise economy, plus more effective water use. It has been my observation that any wind intensity picks up by nine o'clock in the morning. Therefore, watering when there is a wind (unless absolutely necessary) wastes moisture owing to quicker evaporation, and when daytime temperatures are up, it results in a waste of water and an uneven watering pattern. The sprinklers always throw more water downwind and much less water into the wind. As a result, unless you're very vigilant and overlap accurately, you'll end up with dry spots in a few hours or days all over the yard. Another disadvantage of daytime watering is that a lawn is normally used then for recreation by your family and friends (but not during the night, unless you're nocturnal wanderers from Transylvania). So water in the evening (usually the best time is after seven o'clock, when the wind activity subsides). You'll be getting a full 100-percent "green color" value from your watering at this time in two ways—dollarwise and grasswise.

Another big reason now for evening watering in summer stems not from a homeowner's preference, but from an ultimatum handed to communities by the village or city waterworks to water only at certain times of the evening (usually after everyone has taken a bath, which can get to be pretty late) and on certain days. This is getting to be more the rule than the exception. City Hall wants you to water at night when there is more pressure. Eventually it might come to compulsory night watering for city homeowners during certain months of the year. Water is becoming scarcer every year, not because of any horrible prolonged drought, but because more of it is being used by people and industries.

For this reason, my prediction is that many homes in the future will be built with automatic irrigation systems, even though they are expensive. Pop-up sprinklers with watering heads spaced in the lawn to distribute water evenly. The automatic irrigation system will be turned off and on by electric timers inside your home. Many homeowners already enjoy this convenience. It's better than setting the alarm clock and waking your wife at 3:00 A.M. (or when you come home) to water the lawn.

I want to end this discussion with a reassurance to those homeowners who have this doubt about night watering: Does watering at night favor disease infection? The answer is, *Absolutely not.* If you water heavily just once a week, chances of disease are almost zero. However, if you water frequently, keeping droplets on the turf grass for prolonged periods, especially during high humidity, your chances are greater of getting some fungus germination (see chapter 10).

Q.—Which type of sprinkler do you recommend for watering a home lawn?

A.—Although an automatic system is best and can be wonderful if you can afford one, its disadvantage is the homeowners. They can't keep their hands off the controls. They want to run them every night at short intervals, babying the grass with light sprinklings instead of soaking heavy and deep once a week. Homeowners with automatic systems sometimes are like big kids playing with toys. Besides being proud of the expensive systems and wanting to show them off, they get a kick out of seeing the heads pop up all over the lawn. This, of course, uses more water than is necessary, as well as more electricity to start and stop them. But worst of all, the grass gets spoiled and frequently develops only a short and weak root system. Then, if for some reason the system breaks down and the repair service is slow, the lawn begins to suffer. During a harsh winter short-rooted grass will suffer damages. It is well to keep in mind that some grass species like the fescues do not tolerate high soil-moisture levels. They don't tolerate too much water. (Common and some other varieties of Kentucky bluegrass also do best with infrequent soakings.)

I like the oscillator sprinklers, which are still inexpensive. They slowly irrigate back and forth in almost a square spray, rather than in the circle of a rotary sprayer. I like the square pattern, because, well, aren't most home lawns square in shape? With an oscillating sprinkler you can get the borders of your property watered better because it doesn't leave any unwatered triangles along the perimeter of your lawn. Best of all, they throw out water through minute, multiple holes, and the pressure moves the sprinkler back and forth in a swaying motion. This slow-motion spray enables the water to penetrate the soil with no runoff or flooding. An oscillating sprinkler (or, for that matter, any sprinkler that gives good coverage and throws water slowly) is far superior to the sprinklers that whirl in circles like mad. Sprinklers that throw out water too rapidly usually flood everything in no time, which deceives the homeowner into thinking he has watered enough when actually he has hardly penetrated the soil surface. So the homeowner quickly moves the sprinkler to another spot and next day wonders why the lawn that was "flooding" yesterday is so dry again today. This type of irrigation is a waste of precious water.

Pulsating sprinklers that throw the spray in circles are fine *only* if they revolve slowly. Otherwise forget buying one. Traveling sprinklers, in my opinion, are fine for estates and other large areas. I don't care for them on small-sized lawns. There are several kinds of crawlers, guided by a cable or hose or both. These sprinklers string out in any direction you want them to go. When they have eaten up the length of cable or hose, they may automatically shut off. I know of one incident where the traveler sprinkler went through one tiny yard and into another yard, giving that happy homeowner free water *all night,* without shutting off!

The last type of sprinkler is the hoseless manual sprinkler with snap valves into which sprinklers can be inserted. This is the second most expensive installation. It has to be installed underground and spaced much like the pop-up automatic heads—strategically, to give good, even coverage. The difference is that you have to insert the sprinklers yourself, manually, and then you have to take them off again. If you're considering this type of installation, go a step further and install an automatic system.

I want to leave you with a story about a recent experiment that I conducted. I proved through tests that, compared with another liquid, water for your grass is really only second-best. Let me tell you what happened.

I like to putter around with plants, even on my vacation. During my holiday in Fort Lauderdale recently, I conducted some hydroponic tests with stolons (runners) of St. Augustine grass that I had pulled off the hotel lawn. Hydroponics is the process of growing plants in a water solution. However, I changed the method slightly. Instead of using water alone, I added a couple of shots of alcohol to each glass. One glass contained a solution of scotch, another of bourbon, another of rum, another of gin, and so on—ten in all, the last one being plain water. All solutions were carefully marked and placed on the big windowsill of the room, in full view of hotel guests walking by. They were delighted with this unusual test, after I explained what I was doing, and eagerly watched the progress of the stolons each day.

Well, after 14 days it was "scientifically" found that the stolons survived quite well in this "potted" solution, and they successfully expanded a root system as good as the one growing in water alone. But to the amazement of all, the root system of the stolons in the solution of gin and water broke forth profusely and astonishingly. I haven't analyzed to date what the consequences of this test proved exactly, except the interesting fact that growing grass can, in certain circumstances, drive people to drink. For the rest of my vacation stay, the bar downstairs did a record business selling gin drinks to the hotel guests who were so kindly disposed to, and interested in, good grasses. I guess there is nothing better than a healthy drink; even grass laps it up.

8
Weeds

WEEDS are some of my best friends; to me they are much more interesting than lawn grasses. They come in different shapes and sizes, and many of them (like my favorite, Queen Anne's lace) are beautiful. The only problem with weeds is the old brother-in-law syndrome: if you don't watch out, they'll move in with you. Even so, as long as they don't blemish my lawn or invade my garden, weeds are welcome to grow anywhere else. They do no real harm, except for ragweed—the Great Achoo—one of Mother Nature's rare mistakes, poison ivy, and a few others. Most weeds do a lot of good; in fact, their good points may outweigh their drawbacks.

A few years ago, I got a phone call from a newspaper reporter on one of the large dailies in Chicago. He had a "weedy" assignment and needed for his article my expertise to identify the "awful" weeds and "wild" grasses growing tall along the verges and banks of the highways. The article was focussing on a highway scandal in suburban Cook County. Allegedly, the grass and weeds were not being mowed off highway shoulders, medians, and intersections as prescribed by contract, nor was mowing being done along roadsides and in fields belonging to the county's highway department. Of major concern to the newspaper, on behalf of the taxpayers, was the vast sum of money annually allocated for this work to certain landscape companies who weren't doing the job. Why weren't the highways mowed? Where was the money going? Well, eventually the situation was resolved, thanks to the newspaper, and the roadsides and fields were once again mowed.

But as I drove with the reporter that day, surveying many miles of suburban highways and stopping here and there to identify clumps of high grass or weeds, I mentioned to him my thoughts on the matter of mowing highways. I said it was ridiculous and a waste of money and time, even when it was done honestly. Why chop down this wild, beautiful growth, I questioned, and leave mucky ditches, shredded litter, beer cans, and garbage? Why mow these areas and brutally expose the shoulders and banks? Why cover them with ugly windrows of brown and decaying foliage? Why contribute to their erosion by heavy storms? Why destroy the natural habitat and the hiding places of wild animals, birds, and insects? So much of their kingdom has been progressively destroyed by bulldozers that for many of these wild things, the highway right-of-way was a haven, in spite of the noise and pollution from traffic, at least until they tried to cross to the other side.

I am happy to say that since that time the Illinois Division of Transportation has revised its weed-cutting practices, which used to be strict adherence to pavement-to-fence mowing of weeds, wild grass, and domestic grasses. Although a lot of cutting continues, especially in urban areas, much mowing has been eliminated in the rural areas. All of the shoulders and intersections are still trimmed, but the trimming stops at the ditch line, and steep slopes and hazardous slopes are left alone, as are the vast expanses between shoulders and fence lines. The Department of Conservation has also wisely joined in support of reducing the mowing of weeds along roadsides and adjacent areas in many Illinois parks.

Certainly the decision not to mow was influenced by the energy crisis and the high cost of labor and equipment. However, I would like to think that the decision makers also considered the environmental gains, the protection of roadsides from erosion with a better root system and the preservation of wild animals. I remember one newspaper's cartoon, showing the highway officials in a car and—hiding deep in the long grass just off the road—little animals holding up placards thanking the officials for not cutting down their shelter.

I hope other states and park departments will soon follow suit. It would be good to know that along roads and in fields belonging to the highways meadowlarks, pheasants, bobolinks, quail, honeybees, mice, possum, rabbits, and other animals once again had a place to survive and perhaps flourish. The motorist, in turn, would have an aesthetically pleasing view of the natural look, especially at today's reduced highway speeds.

To me, weeds and forages are friends. They can never be ugly. As long as I live, I want to see the wild daisies and clover and the blue haze of chicory in late afternoon, along with rose milkweed, black-eyed Susans, and goldenrod. I want to see the old Eurasian herb, Queen Anne's Lace, and stands of foxtail swaying in autumn breezes, and the tough burdock standing guard at fences. Also soft velvet weed, Indian paintbrush, and the children's flower with the golden bloom, the dandelion in the spring. How much lovelier these plants are, growing massed in uncultivated fields, than ground up and reduced to stubble.

Of course my sentiments run to such out-of-the-way places as highways, roads, and fields. Our society frowns on any wild, unkempt growth that propagates in yards and streets. It wants a weedless landscape of manicured lawns surrounded by trees and flowers, and considers weeds nuisances that take away from the beauty of a verdant, uniform turf grass cover. The control of undesirable weeds and grasses in North American lawns annually costs homeowners millions of dollars. Even though no one chemical has been able to control all undesirable weeds and grasses, scientists are always developing newer and safer herbicides for homeowners to use.

What is important when using an herbicide is to properly identify the weed and to know the ability of the herbicide you are using.

Q.—What is a weed?

A.—Most definitions state that a weed is any plant growing where it is not desired. To me a weed becomes a *floram non grata* if it's in a place where I am trying to raise another plant or grow nothing at all. In a meticulously kept golf course, weeds are any plants—even if they are cattleya orchids or tropicana roses—growing in the manicured turf grasses used for golf play. In a large sand trap, Kentucky bluegrass or creeping bent seedlings trying to establish a root system in the soft sand (and boy, do they) are weeds to me. If I were going to grow a pure field of beautiful dandelions (whose seeds are now sold at certain stores) to eat as greens, I would consider the best grass in the world a weed if it interfered with the growth of my dandelions.

Q.—What is meant by broadleaf weeds and grassy-type weeds? What is the significant difference between the two? Is there a chemical to kill both?

A.—The weeds that invade lawns are classified in two categories, monocots and dicots.

Monocots. This is a classification into which all grasses fall, even bamboo, corn, and wheat. The notorious lawn weed grass examples are crabgrass and quack grass; others are barnyard grass, Dallis grass, nimbleweed, sandburs, tall fescue, *Poa annua,* and creeping bentgrass. The most distinguishing characteristic of all monocots is that they have veins like railroad tracks—they run parallel to each other. *Mono* means one and *cot* (short for *cotyledon*) denotes a seedling leaf that emerges from a seed. The monocots include weed grasses and—except for crabgrass, foxtail, and Dallis grass—are very difficult to kill with present-day herbicides once they get established in your lawn. Any chemical that kills them usually wipes out all other plant life with which it makes contact.

Dicots. Weeds in this category are often referred to as broadleaf weeds, and they are completely different in appearance from the grassy types (monocots). The word *dicot* indicates that two seedling leaves emerge from each seed. All dicots have a network of delicate vein patterns, their distinctive characteristic. Because of this, even extremely small-leaved weeds, such as knotweed, clover, and chickweed, are designated broad-leaved weeds. In no way do broad-leaved weeds resemble narrow-leaved grass weeds (except as undesirables).

The best examples of broadleaf lawn weeds are the dandelion, common buckhorn plantain, ground ivy, chickweed, clover, knotweed, and bindweed. Most broad-leaved weeds are extremely easy to eradicate with present-day herbicides.

Q.—How do weeds occur? Why do I have weeds in my *new lawn*?

A.—There are thousands upon thousands of weed seeds buried in the soil you walk on. Some have been buried for many years, just waiting for an opportunity to pop up and greet you. The majority of these weed seeds never germinate, because ideal conditions are lacking most of the time for them to sprout; these conditions are adequate light, moisture, moderate temperature, and proper movement of air. However, as soon as the soil is disturbed by cultivation, the weed seeds are brought to the surface, where germination suddenly becomes more favorable and they proceed to grow like anything. That's why, when a new lawn is cultivated and seeded with a turf grass recommended for your area, weed seedlings often seem to appear overnight like magic. The weeds usually appear much faster than your hoped-for grass. Fortunately for homeowners, most of these oddly shaped and often interesting weeds don't survive constant low mowing, so they vanish. Those that adapt themselves to low mowing and persist and those that usually appear where grass is thin and sickly will be the subject of further discussion in this chapter.

Q.—Why do I have weeds in my *old* lawn? It's about ten years old.

A.—Weeds probably discourage homeowners more than any other lawn problem. The usual reason for the deterioration of a lawn and the subsequent weed invasion, I am sorry to say, is poor lawn practices—improper feeding, mowing, and watering, and not cutting the lawn high enough. A starved lawn is the result of miserly fertilizer application or none at all, or of watering every night, or of dull mowers pulling up or tearing the grass, or worst of all, of low mowing. A skimpy lawn develops bare spots. As soon as this occurs, dormant weed seeds that have been waiting patiently in the soil for years suddenly begin to grow and spread. Lawns with exposed bare spots are also invaded by "outlaw" weeds. These quickly germinate and root in the open spots of a weak lawn. Some weed seed pods (like oxalis) actually explode when ripe and throw their seeds helter-skelter. So you can't win, except by good cultural practices—mowing, watering, fertilizing. A healthy, dense turf grass that is managed properly keeps out most weed competition. You might as well know now that weeds don't really come in from your neighbor's lawn or in purchased grass seed mixtures (unless they're cheap bargain types). I want to state once and for all that there is no such thing as being lucky with a lawn. Your chances with Lady Luck to keep weeds out or to a "hand pulling" minimum are not good. Your chances are improved and realized only through diligent lawn upkeep and management, combined with a successful weed program.

Q.—How do I get rid of weeds?

A.—By two good methods—hand weeding and control by chemicals.

Hand weeding is still the best and safest method. Don't use chemicals when you have just a few weeds here or there. It's a waste of time and money. A lawn with just a few weeds, either grassy or broad-leaved, can easily be weeded by hand. Let your wife get the exercise. Tell her to be sure to remove all of the roots, not just the crowns or most of the tops; otherwise the weeds will spring right back up. There are also easy-to-use weed bars of soft wax, which rub off some wax and herbicide on weeds (no drift hazard), and a weed "cane and wand," whose hollow tube device is filled with herbicide solution or pellets. Both of them effectively spot-treat weeds. There are even aerosol cans (use gloves) and flame throwers (have a fire engine stand by; I know a guy who burned down his garage with this open flame) for spot-treating weeds.

Chemical control. The best method for eradicating weeds that are growing *heavily* and vigorously is to use herbicides (or weedicides). It is much less laborious in a large lawn than the hand method. Except for the use of nonselective weedicide bars and cones to eradicate grassy perennial weeds, I still prefer hand pulling in a lawn with just a few weeds. Herbicides are more complicated and necessarily require proper identification for weeds to be controlled. After positive identification of the weed come proper selection of a chemical and then careful application to ensure successful eradication. All three steps are extremely important and I can't emphasize them enough. Many excellent herbicides are effective and safe if used according to directions on the label, but their misuse by the homeowner results in overkill, which is drastic to a lawn and often to trees, shrubs, and flowers in the area.

The defoliation and massive damage by herbicides to South Vietnam's high farmland woodlands, which are so vital to the country's economy, is about the worst (and saddest) example I know of chemical misuse.

Q.—What is a selective weed killer and what is meant by a nonselective herbicide?

A.—A selective weedicide, if used properly, kills only certain types of weeds. There are now selective weedicides to safely kill most broad-leaved weeds (dicots). There also are excellent chemicals for safely eradicating a few of the annual weed grasses such as crabgrass and Dallis grass. Selective herbicides can effectively eliminate weeds without killing or noticeably injuring turf grass—if properly applied. These herbicides usually affect the growth of certain other weeds (broadleaves).

Nonselective weed killers. Look out! These kill everything in sight; that is, everything they contact. This type of herbicide usually is used for spot-treating weedy perennial grasses. Since weedy grasses and desirable grasses are in the same group (monocots) and therefore are almost identical in shape and makeup, the scientists in universities and in industry are having an extremely difficult time developing an herbicide that will selectively eliminate the grassy perennials but not affect the desired lawn grasses. The fact that we now have safe selective chemicals to kill crabgrass and foxtail, two very bad grassy weeds, is a remarkable and noble achievement.

Q.—Please comment on some of the selective herbicides now available to the homeowner, along with the weeds they kill.

A.—The best selective herbicide available to homeowners is 2, 4-D. This old standby is still the most spectacular weed killer since World War II (the beginning of the Herbicide Age) and it is completely safe when properly used. (This warning goes for all chemicals, even the aspirins you use to stop your headache.) 2, 4-D is an effective hormone-type killer that eradicates broad-leaved plants by overstimulation. The weed poison (hormone, here) is absorbed through the leaves and soon after the broadleaf plant twists and curls. The amine form of 2,4-D is preferred for home lawns over the ester formulation, which is more volatile and thus has a higher drift hazard. In some states, 2,4-D is restricted (e.g., Orange County, California) and you must have a permit to purchase it. You can buy no more than one pint per 24-hour period—like some cough medicines at drugstores. When I think about some of the careless homeowners in our country, it's a good idea. For further protection, I would also very much like to see companies put safety caps on all lawn chemicals they sell, like those on prescription drugs. Though the most effective herbicide for most broadleaves (dicots) is 2,4-D, many commercial formulations of broadleaf weed killers also contain another very good chemical, called 2,4,5-TP (Silvex), which increases the range of controllable weeds. 2,4,5-TP is absorbed through the foliage and acts by upsetting the growth mechanism within the broadleaved weed plant. These two old chemical standbys, along with other new and outstanding herbicides recently introduced, are excellent for controlling broadleaf weeds when used in two or three combinations with newer materials and give better control of numerous other weeds. Two of the best new herbicides are mecoprop (MCPP) and dicamba.

MCPP is a safe weedicide and works efficiently, with 2,4-D in equal parts, to better control clover and chickweed. It is as good as 2,4,5-TP—and less harmful (due to its somewhat lower potential for foliage burning during warm weather).

Dicamba (trade names Banvel and Banvel-D) is by far the most effective chemical I have ever used for such "small-leaved" broadleafs as knotweed, chickweed, yarrow, clover, and henbit. If you apply this weedicide by itself, do it in early spring when there is plenty of moisture in the ground. Low temperatures have little if any effect on this herbicide. It is sold extensively in combination with 2,4-D (about 5 parts to 1). However, be very careful; use dicamba only for *open clear areas*. If shrubs and trees absorb this weedicide through the root system, it can seriously injure them or kill them completely. Dicamba is mobile in the soil, so it's best to avoid using this chemical near the root systems of shrubs and trees. The combination of 2,4-D and dicamba is the best possible combination a homeowner can purchase to kill broad-leaved weeds. But once again let me warn you, *don't* use it near the root zones of desirable trees or shrubs.

For a good rule of thumb, do not water or mow the grass for 24 hours after application of any of these chemical combinations. And for best effectiveness they should be sprayed when day and night temperatures are above 60 degrees. Dicamba is not leached out by moisture right after application, 2,4-D and 2,4,5-TP are affected by possible leaf washoff, and all of these herbicides are considerably less effective if the grass is mowed too soon after application. More of this later.

Here are the broadleaf weeds that 2,4-D kills effectively when it is applied properly and by itself only: dandelion, common and buckhorn plantain, wild geranium, ground ivy (creeping Charlie), pennywort, thistle, shepherd's purse, curled dock, oxalis, and spurge.

Dicamba, 2,4,5-TP, or MCPP by themselves kill clover, chickweed, knotweed, oxalis, yarrow, and spurge. But if you are wise, you will buy a combination of 2,4-D and either one or two of the other above herbicides; I promise that this formulation will give you the most effective one-two punch possible, and it will eradicate almost any common broadleaf weeds with a couple of applications.

One precaution: 2,4-D or 2,4,5-TP should never be used on creeping bentgrass or on St. Augustine grass home lawns. They are highly injurious to these species.

Q.—How do you control weed grasses in a Kentucky bluegrass yard? I have quack grass (or something) all over the lawn. Please comment also on the nonselective herbicides (which I was told by a clerk in a store to use) in order to stop this horrible weed taking over my lawn.

A.—I am glad you enclosed (wrapped in plastic) a sample of your "weed" problem. It isn't quack grass but tall fescue, which is just as bad if you're attempting to grow a pure stand of Kentucky bluegrass. Tall fescue in southern parts of the country is sometimes a desirable and respectable grass and does very well where other grasses fail, but it's not as popular in the cool regions where attractive Kentucky bluegrasses thrive. The best way I know to get rid of any tough or weedy grasses is by pulling or digging them out with a sharp knife or shovel hand hoe. This is also the safest method.

There are no selective chemicals to kill coarse weedy grasses (except crabgrass, Dallis grass, etc.) The only method besides hand digging is to use nonselective chemicals like dalapon (Dowpon). Be sure you don't get any on your desirable grass. If you use a dalapon wax bar for spot-treating and effectively kill the patches of tall fescue, I recommend that afterward you spot-sod the larger bare areas with Kentucky bluegrass (green side up). Of course, if your whole yard is covered with a weed grass, then either kill the whole lawn, remove all the sod, and start over, or consider having the best (and only) predominantly tall fescue (or whatever) lawn in the neighborhood. Fertilize it and mow the tall fescue frequently (twice a week at minimum) to keep it down and camouflaged and nobody will ever know. I hope.

Weed grasses, such as tall fescue and quack grass, are very tough grasses and very hard to kill. Once they take hold, it's almost impossible to remove them without resorting to drastic measures. Nonselective herbicides are good, but extremely dangerous, especially when applied over the whole lawn. They can kill off everything, including your desirable grasses. Nonselective herbicides like dalapon, Paraquat, Amitrole, and Cacodylic acid should be used carefully and only for spot treatment. These materials may come in liquids, powders, aerosol foams, and wax bars. With some of them you have to wait a stipulated period before seeding or sodding again. This wait will be an inconvenience, and an eyesore if you wiped out large areas of the weed grass. However, a few spots treated here and there (better still, pulled or dug by hand) will hardly be noticeable. I would like to make one more comment. There are two grasses, one respected (in its place) and one a black sheep (always out of place), that like to invade Kentucky bluegrass lawns that are mowed low and soaked frequently. I see this encroachment problem with these two grasses more and more often. They are creeping bentgrass (great on a golf course) and *Poa annua* (annual bluegrass). Though both can be knocked off with frequent applications of 2,4,5-TP and 2,4-D, it's just as easy to extract them in summer by digging them out. Reseed or sod right after. Generally the homeowner doesn't realize he has them until the hot summer, when either one or both of these "weeds" start showing up in a Kentucky bluegrass lawn. The thatchy, creeping bentgrass appears in puffy dense patches of brown, and the treacherous, short-rooted *Poa annua* in yellow or light green blotches (with frequent white seed heads common any time that cool weather persists). As soon as hot, droughty summer comes along, the *Poa annua* dries out and turns into dead brown blotches in the lawn. At this time, both are easily pulled out or skimmed off with a sod knife and gotten rid of.

Poa annua is a terribly deceiving weed grass, because it is beautiful and attractive in spring and fall but dies in the first spell of hot, dry weather. It is the golf course superintendent's worst problem when it is not kept in check. Many superintendents have lost their jobs over it.

Q.—Please explain what a preemergence herbicide is. Also, what is meant by a postemergence herbicide?

A.—A preemergence herbicide is applied over the lawn to keep certain grass and broadleaf weed seeds from becoming established in the spring. (Death occurs *during* germination following absorption by the seedling). Crabgrass (which we will discuss in the next question) is a prime example of a weed that is killed by a preemergence herbicide before it gets a chance to become established. A preemergence herbicide is usually applied in granular form and inhibits seeds from coming up. It can also be applied as a wettable powder or an emulsifiable concentrate.

Postemergence herbicides are to be applied only after annual weeds sprout in the lawn. They work well in spring and in very early summer, when the soil is moist, temperatures are warm, and the often tender plants are growing vigorously. At this time, the chance of total weed kill is highest. Fall is also an excellent time to use postemergence herbicides for most annual broadleaves and grass weeds.

Q.—What do we do with a lawn infested with crabgrass? We have a rampant growth of crabgrass every spring. Especially in the front yard. This year my husband is finally going to do something about it. Please tell us how to successfully wipe this weed out. Permanently, if possible.

A.—Crabgrass is an annual weedy grass that dies and turns brown with the first frost. It is an unsightly broad-leaved grass plant with purplish seed heads. Crabgrass cannot tolerate shade and is a paramount example of a weed that will germinate quickly and grow vigorously in a lawn that is mowed too low. This is why I have been harping over and over again about high mowing in the past chapters. A thick, dense Kentucky bluegrass lawn that is mowed no less than 2½ inches throughout the growing season will retard not only the emergence of shade-hating crabgrass, but of many other unwanted weeds as well. In fact, crabgrass hates shade to such a degree that many times I have actually seen a perfect tree shape outlined on the ground. Wherever the tree's branches spread out and shaded the ground, there was absolutely no crabgrass infestation at all. But right outside the shade pattern, the lawn was completely covered with purplish crabgrass growth. Crabgrass can be controlled easily with a *pre*emergence herbicide. However, most homeowners wait two or three years before taking any action against heavy crabgrass infestation. Then suddenly, one spring, they become worried and start using chemicals, usually a *post*emergent. However, I think that using *pre*emergence herbicide control in spring before crabgrass germinates is by far the best and easiest control. Never wait until crabgrass appears to apply a *pre*-emergence herbicide. (They only work before the emergence of the crabgrass.)

If you continue diligently with a preemergence herbicide for a few years and control the seed production of crabgrass with the recommended chemicals, then the viable seeds in the soil will be reduced to a point where crabgrass is no longer a serious threat. Always make a chemical crabgrass control shake hands with a proper turf management program.

Some of the best preemergence herbicides for crabgrass control —in April—are bensulide (Pre-san, Betasan), benefin (Balan), terbutol (Azak), and siduron (Tupersan). I like DCPA (Dacthal) best of all. I have never seen injury to established grasses with this chemical. DCPA is a super crabgrass control. All of these herbicides (except siduron) will have a warning label on the package stating how long you must wait before it's safe to reseed (usually till fall). You see, the crabgrass preemergence herbicides will also inhibit any lawn grass seed from germinating. The best method I have found to get around this problem, if you have open spots already in a lawn, which will be compounded by more exposure after the crabgrass control takes effect, is to spot-reseed the lawn the preceding fall (see chapter 2). Then the following spring, when you must apply one of the crabgrass preemergence herbicides and can't reseed for 6 months, don't worry. Last fall's grass growth will be filling in most of the lawn's spots while the preemergence herbicide keeps the crabgrass from germinating. Siduron is an excellent herbicide because it can be used when seeding. It will not "burn" lawn grass seeds in a new lawn, but it will control the germination of crabgrass seed. In fact, both the herbicide and the seed should be applied at the same time if you're seeding a new lawn in the spring. Siduron can be applied safely to all newly seeded upright grasses as well as to established lawns.

I always like to sprinkle the lawn with water right after applying any granular pesticide. This washes the chemical off the leaves and into the soil (even those whose labels say not to sprinkle after use).

I don't like midsummer crabgrass control with postemergence herbicides. It's hard on your turf during this time, and the chances of injury are more frequent than when using a preemergence herbicide. But if you must apply them, remember to use a little wetting agent. One teaspoonful of household detergent per gallon of spray mixture will help if you don't have a commercial wetting agent. The postemergence crabgrass herbicide controls (DSMA, AMA, MSMA) are available in liquid or water-soluble powder forms. One name fertilizer company I know also has them in granular form. The best success with them is achieved with a carefully calibrated and uniform application two or three times at seven- to ten-day intervals. These postemergence chemicals should be applied only at recommended rates. Repeated applications will also control goose grass, Dallis grass, and foxtail. Never use the arsonates DSMA or AMA on St. Augustine grass if you're living in the South and nurturing this fine old grass.

Q.—Is it better to treat broad-leaved weeds with a liquid or with a dry herbicide?

A.—For control of broadleaves, the herbicide formulation that is diluted with water and a little wetting agent (if they aren't already included in the formula) is the most effective means of weed eradication in my opinion. The dry formulations are not only more expensive, but the overall total weed kill is always slower and less effective. You need more chemical in the dry form for effective kill. They often come with weed and feed combination. Also, granular dry herbicides that are spread on slopes and hills sometimes may move downhill and pile up at the bottom after a heavy rainstorm. However, I do like a dry herbicide application when it is used as a preemergence control for grassy weeds, such as crabgrass. But since most preemergence crabgrass herbicides are combined with fertilizer as a carrier (the best sellers), this conflicts with my recommendation of applying a straight fertilizer only and never before the first two weeks of May (chapter 5). Try to find one that isn't mixed with fertilizer.

Crabgrass herbicides have to be applied early (in April, before the forsythia blooms) in most parts of the cool-region area in order to effectively inhibit the germination of crabgrass seeds. If you wait until May to apply preemergent crabgrass herbicides, the crabgrass seedlings may already be emerging. I advise the homeowner to shop around for preemergence crabgrass killers that use calcined clay, fine shredded corncobs, or vermiculite as a carrier. As I have stated so many times before, I like to apply fertilizers and pesticides separately, at exactly the time they can do their job best. To me, timing is everything, whether you're applying fertilizers or pesticides or planting a tree. Herbicides are not as effective when they are combined (supposedly for your convenience) with fertilizer or other pesticides.

I have observed that some homeowners with small lawns like to use only dry herbicides that are applied with a small fertilizer drop spreader. They find it uneconomical and impractical to invest in a special liquid-type sprayer just to use for weed control in a tiny yard. (I suggest that homeowners with very small lawns pick the weeds by hand.) Remember when using dry herbicides that dust drifts, so if you use a dry form of herbicide that has a dusty formulation, don't apply it on a windy day. There is also a real danger of drift with a liquid spray. A good rule is to be careful with both. I am happy to say that there now are some excellent lawn spray service companies available at reasonable costs to homeowners. If you are having weed problems and don't wish to mess around and knock them off yourself, or haven't had much success in eradicating them with your present methods (or mine), perhaps trying a good spray service would be a wise thing to do.

Q.—Is there some secret or best way to completely wipe out the broad-leaved weeds in my lawn? I spray every year but never seem to get good results. What am I doing wrong? When is the best time to spray for weeds?

A.—Provided that you calibrate your spray application properly at the recommended rate for the size of your lawn, the secret of complete weed eradication is to do it again with the same application *two weeks later.* If you're using the right herbicides, you'll find to your delight that weeds die out totally when hit by two applications. This "two punch" spray application is usually not practiced by the homeowner. He sprays only once, which is one reason postemergence crabgrass control usually fails.

Homeowners should be wary of overdosing with hormone-type herbicides like 2,4-D and Silvex, because then they don't translocate the chemical throughout the whole plant. Instead, these hormone types may get only "pinpoint" kill. By this I mean the overdosed herbicide solution becomes so strong and lethal that it kills the tissue by an immediate direct contact, rather than moving throughout the whole plant when applied with exactly the prescribed dosage and thus effectively killing the whole plant. One other thing to keep in mind: if you overdose with fertilizer, the grass may be only temporarily injured, but an overdose of herbicide might cause fatality to grass.

Broad-leaved weeds should be knocked off with my recommended two-punch application in spring or fall—never in the summer, when they have hardened off. Get them in the spring, when they are young, tender, and growing vigorously, and when the grass is in its most recuperative stage and thus better able to recover from a possible overdose. Get them before they develop deep roots and seed heads that will reinfest your lawn. It's best to stop weed growth when the weeds are small and not so competitive. Get them before they get "summer tough" and twice as hard to kill, because at this time they don't translocate the herbicides as well. I like best spraying for weeds in the spring, when temperatures are at least 70 degrees. Autumn is the second-best time for killing broad-leaved weeds if you don't get them all in the spring.

Last of all, keep in mind that no matter how many times you spray for weeds, if you don't properly carry out this and other good cultural management of your turf grass (see next question) your lawn will always have some infestation of weeds (plus other problems). If you don't correct the problem that caused the weed in the first place, there is no use spraying.

Q.—What other good tips do you have to limit weeds in a lawn?

A.—1. Mow your upright cool-region grasses (like Kentucky bluegrass and fescue) 2½ inches or higher, but never lower. Predominantly bluegrass lawns that are mowed too low have poor color and vigor; in this condition, they cannot take the stress of a long hot summer. (Of course, cutting height varies with the other turf grass species, like creeping bentgrass, Bermuda grass, and St. Augustine grass. These species must be mowed at lower heights to be healthy, dense, and attractive.) As short-mowed, predominantly bluegrass lawns decline in the heat of summer, they often become more susceptible to disease and weeds. The usual compensating practice of most homeowners is to water low-mowed lawns with frequent light sprinklings, which only causes weak root systems, soil compaction, and often overly wet soils, all of which help to bring on disease and further weed infestation.

2. Fertilize a minimum of twice a year (more in the longer growing seasons of the South. See chapter 3.).

3. Spot-reseed sod or plug in the fall (see chapter 2).

4. Starting in late June or early July, water deeply once a week or so (unless you're in a western Kentucky bluegrass state like Colorado, where you must start earlier because the climate is very dry and rain infrequent). Never water before this time unless you are nurturing a new lawn or a renovated lawn, or unless an exceptionally long drought hits your area. (I consider no heavy rain for two weeks a drought in this period.)

5. Always use a sharp mower. A dull mower tears leaf foliage and opens the weakened turf to disease and weeds.

Q.—What is the best safety measure you can give us when we are using weed killers? We are conscientious about environmental problems but think that chemicals properly used by people are not a hazard.

A.—A good question and a sensible philosophy. The best advice I can give you for using garden chemicals is to take the three minutes' time necessary to read the label on the pesticide container. I mean *really read it* and comprehend the entire instruction. Don't just glance at the print. Understand completely how the dilution is to be made in order to get a safe uniform coverage and a best possible kill of weeds. Nothing else. (Most of these recommendations are based on 1 ounce per gallon per 1,000 square feet.) Many millions of dollars and many years of time have been spent in research to bring homeowners the instructions and warnings on these labels. Read them.

While we are on the subject of pesticide safety, let me list some more precautions and advice about using garden chemicals. All garden chemicals should be stored under lock and key. Keep pesticides in their original containers with labels *distinctly* showing what their names are. If you are no longer going to use the pesticides, get rid of them in such a way that they are no longer hazardous. Better yet, buy what you need and use what you buy. If you are moving away, don't leave garden chemicals behind (especially unmarked ones) for the new homeowner or his child to possibly misuse.

Don't ever use spray pesticides while munching a sandwich or smoking a cigarette. Don't use pesticides if you are feeling ill or tipsy or hung over. It's always safer to wear rubber gloves and old clothes with long sleeves and long pants that can be washed immediately if a chemical spray wets you or a pesticide solution spills on you. Take a good soapy shower right away if you accidentally spill some on your skin. Never wear bermuda shorts or a bathing suit while spraying with pesticides.

Following a pesticide application, always wash your hands even if you have had no contact with the material.

In order to keep a spray mist from descending on valuable plants, lay plastic coverings (like dry cleaners' suit bags) over the valuable plants, especially if spraying the edge of the lawn close to flower or garden beds. Never spray into shrubs, flowers, or trees with materials meant for *lawn* use.

Pesticides should never be applied on a windy day, because the pesticide can cause damage and even fatality to surrounding landscape. Spray only when the wind velocity is low, or calm. If you do injure any plants, don't wait, but immediately cut back the damaged tissue before further translocation of the chemical takes place in the plant. Translocation is usually quite rapid, but you might save the desirable plants if you cut back immediately. Weedicide chemicals are very hard to wash out, especially 2,4-D-type materials. I recommend you use a separate sprayer exclusively for weed control. Mark it *For Weeds Only.* If you don't heed this good advice, then wash out the weed spray with a strong solution of household (chlorine) bleach, and rinse the sprayer and its hose several times.

I have just told you how tough it is to wash out weedicide sprayers. Keeping this in mind, don't ever ever use children's water pistols or trigger-type squirting oil cans or watering cans or anything similar to these as a container for weed control. Use only pressure spray tanks, which are especially designed for weed applications. Believe me, a good sprayer is a justified expense. Remember, weed control chemicals are tools for management. Use them carefully, in conjunction with other cultural practices that have been designed (and described) to provide a dense, healthy turf grass for your lawn. In order to have the chemicals do their jobs safely, read the labels first. Lawn weed killers must be used within the limits specified on their labels. It's best not to mow your lawn for two days after weed spraying; this will allow time for the transfer of the herbicide to all parts of the plant. If it rains heavily less than four hours after application, respray your lawn. But don't rush right in and spray. Wait a day or so; sometimes the killing action has set in even before four hours. One way to tell if the chemical is working is to look and see if the weed starts to look droopy, twisted, and misshapen. If you're not sure what the weed is, don't start monkeying around with herbicide until you make a positive identification. Have it identified by the county extension agent or a local golf course superintendent. Always use the right chemical for the right weed. Measure your lawn accurately. Then make a good test measure (as you did in fertilizing) to make sure the recommended dosage (the amount of spray material) for 500 or 1,000 square feet comes out exactly right. First measure the amount of square feet, then "treat" the plot using only *water* in your sprayer the first time for calibration. Not only will you find out the correct square footage and distance, but you will also find out if your sprayer is in good condition. If it is plugged up or dirty, and the water barely trickles out, take off the nozzle and run clean water through it. Don't apply any chemical until you have a perfect spray pattern. If you are using wettable powders, shake the tank frequently to keep the herbicide properly mixed. Don't use more than the recommended dosage for the area to be treated. I don't care if you vary the amount of water for making the solution (often the more the better) but extreme caution must be taken that the dosage recommended for the area is *never varied*. Be very careful in all adjustments and calibrations. Heed all precautions for storing, mixing, applying, and disposing of herbicides. Finally, in case of a serious mishap, such as when the pesticide has been swallowed, immediately call for medical help— a doctor or a hospital or a poison center. You should always have the hospital emergency phone number on the wall. When calling, tell the emergency ward the name of the pesticide involved. Have the package or bottle in front of you so you can read from the label, giving the hospital all the pertinent information. Don't try to pronounce the long, hard words; spell them out.

Before I close this chapter, I would like once again to express my admiration for weeds. Anything that withstands frost, high temperature, heavy traffic, and drought has to be respected. You really have to admire their remarkable ability to adapt to all kinds of soil conditions. However, weeds will dominate any area they invade and slowly rob the desirable plants there of water and nutrients. Even so, weeds heal the scars of the earth; that's their whole purpose, I think, and it is because of their rapid growth and tough constitution that damage from erosion is much less after man's cultivation in the name of progress.

Many times I have walked along in late summer or fall with a good book on weeds and tried to identify the many different types growing in Lake Bluff. Weed study is very interesting; it takes a vast amount of time and keen observation of weed shapes and growth peculiarities to really get to know them. I know only two men who can really tell most weeds at a glance or even just by looking at their clusters or seedpods.

9
Insects

THERE PROBABLY ARE more different kinds of insects in the area where you live than ever before. The reason is that very often insects come from other states on fruit and vegetables and nursery stock. They also "hitchhike" cross-country on cars, trucks, trains, and even jet planes. Some insects, like the fierce fire ant from the South and the devastating gypsy moth from the East, keep spreading closer and closer to the Midwest not only by their own lateral movements but by transportation on campers and boats. A few, like the dreaded European elm bark beetle, were transported by boat in the early thirties across the Atlantic to the eastern United States; since then this beetle has been moving across our country, devastating most of our beautiful elm tree landscape in its path.

Actually only a few hungry insects with a terrific appetite for grass are responsible for home lawn turf injury. When these insects attack, they can cause extensive damage. Unfortunately, the homeowner has difficulty diagnosing early signs of insect infestation. As a result, he doesn't often recognize an attack until the problem is out of control. The insects' irreparable damage may leave the homeowner no choice except to resod or reseed the damaged areas.

189

Another hindrance to immediate recognition of damage by the average homeowner is that many times the injury caused by insects produces symptoms similar to those caused by disease or even poor soil conditions. For this reason, it's very important to confirm the presence of injurious insects before using a specific insecticide.

Q.—How can I tell if I have insect damage? My lawn this August is covered with blotches of whitish, dead patches. The turf also seems to be detached and comes up very easily when I pull on it.

A.—It sounds like you have a serious grub infestation. But please don't take my word for it. Make this check first. Grip the sod again, lift, and pull back. If you have grubs, the sod will roll back easily like a carpet, because the roots will have been devoured. Now poke and scratch with a trowel a few inches down into the soil. If you have grubs, you'll see their fat, white, C-shaped bodies (up to ¾ inch in length) in the top few inches of soil. Another sign of grubs in a lawn is animal life. You might begin seeing lots of birds pecking in your yard. Also, moles, raccoons, and skunks (yes, skunks) will invade lawns to feed on the juicy, fat grubs and on other insects. Be very suspicious of grub infestation if one morning you see your old lawn torn up by animals. I have seen lawns literally ripped up and pulled apart by hungry night animals in search of grubs. However, once a good insecticide is used, their food supply is removed and they won't bother your lawn. *Maybe.* (The bigger animals may move to your garbage cans if you don't keep the lids on tightly.)

Another method you can try to determine the presence of insects is to apply one tablespoon of commercial pyrethrum in one gallon of water on a small plot of ground about one yard square. If you have sod webworms, cutworms, or other caterpillars, they should come to the surface within 15 minutes. However, this test will not show the presence of grubs and certain other lawn insects. Sometimes a household detergent mixed with water in a watering can and poured over a suspicious area will force out insects. Mix about 2 tablespoons of detergent per gallon of water and pour it over about one square foot of lawn. Give the insects time to come out. Sometimes in very thatched grass, you might have to wait longer than the usual 10 to 15 minutes. Some detergents work better than others.

A good test for the almost microscopic chinch bugs is to take a piece of pure white paper and drag it over the grass. Chinch bugs will soon reveal themselves on the white paper.

The best and surest way of finding out if you have an insect problem in your lawn, and the specific type, is to call an insect expert, an entomologist. In your area, this might be the local county extension agent or, if you're lucky, an area agent-entomologist. The local golf course superintendent can also help you. You see, during the golf season golf course superintendents must carry out an insect prevention program. For both diseases and insects, we spray with proper chemicals and right equipment (every week, ten days, or two weeks, depending on weather and temperature) all through the golf-playing season. Overall, the homeowner's turf grass problems aren't as complex as ours. Usually, for the homeowner, an insect attack is infrequent. But when one does occur, it usually is an advanced problem; before he discovers he has insects, therefore, he must apply control measures. One application of chemical is usually not enough (unless you use insecticides like chlordane) to do the job. Total control of an advanced stage of infestation will require several follow-up insecticide applications about a week or two apart. That's the *whole* secret of insect control when insects infest your turf grass—the follow-up.

Q.—Please explain the difference between below-ground insects and above-ground insects.

A.—One group of lawn insects is categorized as below-ground, or subsurface, insects (e.g., grubs). These insects destroy grass by devouring its vital roots below the ground. Because of this ruthless destruction, they are usually the most devastating.

The other group of insects is the above-ground, or surface, insects (e.g., sod webworms). These pests are foliage-feeding insects. They destroy turf grass by partially eating grass blades and stems on the surface of the ground or by sucking the plant juices (e.g., chinch bugs). Damage by these pests results in discolored grass with a ragged appearance.

Immediate identification before either group reaches a stage that would cause turf grass deterioration is necessary, and then the purchase and proper application of an insecticide are the next two important steps. A rapid determination of the correct treatment may mean the difference between saving and losing large areas of your lawn.

Q.—Please describe the various below-ground lawn insects and what chemicals to use for their control.

A.—Grubs are the larvae of Japanese, May, and June beetles, as well as several other insects. Grubs hibernate deep in the ground during the winter and come up to feed in the spring. They stay in the 1 to 3 inches of soil around and below grass roots. They stay in the soil from 90 days to as long as 3 years. They are light grey and white, C-shaped, with dark heads. Grubs are usually ½ to 1 inch long. In lawns heavily infested with grubs, the turf appears at first yellowed and then, in the final stage, as whitish, dead patches. These patches can be effortlessly rolled back like a carpet or rug, because the grubs have fed on the roots and there is nothing to hold the grass down. In my opinion, the best control is with chlordane. A single recommended dosage, followed by another in 10 days, should provide control for 3 to 5 years. However, the extremely effective chlordane is a hard pesticide that also wipes out the beneficial earthworm. I like chlordane on a golf course, but for the homeowner I recommend diazinon, a recently discovered insecticide that will control below-ground insects but won't completely wipe out earthworm populations. For best control, diazinon and other insecticides (with the possible exception of chlordane) should be applied every week or so. However, a homeowner should keep in mind that control is always slow when an insect problem is in an advanced stage of destruction, especially in thick matted lawns and heavy soils. With below-ground insects it's very important to thoroughly water your lawn immediately after applying the insecticide; otherwise, if it stays on the surface, the chemical won't do any good. Water two days later and then again for the last time two days after that (unless, of course, a good rain washes everything in). This procedure of repeated application will ensure that the insecticide will move into the subsurface, where the pests are. Keep all children off the lawn until you have watered in the insecticide at least once. Let the grass dry out before allowing the children to play on the lawn. After the grub infestation is more or less under control (you can never kill every single one of them), you'll have to decide whether to sod or reseed the dead patches. Don't wait for the whitish dead patches to regrow. They won't. With the root system devoured, there is absolutely no chance. The best way to proceed is to lift up the dead sod and haul it away, then apply fresh insecticide to the soil, and spot-sod or reseed. Then soak everything. Keep the ground moist until the grass seed germinates or the new sod takes a good hold.

There are three other interesting and much less damaging types of insects. They like to dig holes and throw up unsightly mounds of earth. These insects are cicada-killer wasps, ants, and our friendly earthworms. Diazinon will control the ant colonies. The yellow and black, bad-tempered Cicada-killer wasps, with a body 1¼ inches long, may sting people. These sinister creatures, where they make nests, burrow into the ground and leave mounds topside at the nest entrances. The best control is to apply chlordane into the nest at night and then tightly seal the entrance with dirt. Don't worry about the earthworms. Every lawn and garden should have these good creatures, who help aerify and mix the soil under the lawn.

Q.—Please describe the various above-ground lawn insects, their habits, and the best way to get rid of them.

A.—The above-ground insects destroy grass areas either by chewing off the leaves and stems or by sucking out the plant juices and killing the turf grass.

Sod webworm. The adult sod webworm moth is a dull tan color, but the moth itself is not damaging (nor pretty to look at). When moths are present, they are stirred from their hiding places in the grass as you walk on the lawn. They fly a short distance in a jerky, zigzag manner and then quickly hide in the grass again. At night the moths come out of hiding; they are attracted by light. The moths lay eggs around and on the grass plants, and within a short time the eggs hatch into larvae.

The sod webworm is destructive only when it is in the caterpillar, or larval (worm), stage. (So are the other "worm" moths, like the cutworm and the armyworm.) In the caterpillar stage, however, they feast on homeowners' lawns at night. These worms leave grass ragged by chewing or clipping the grass blades at soil level and leaving large brown spots (about the size of a baseball). The patches, if damage is severe, may run together and form a single large area. (Keep in mind, however, that large dead patches are also commonly the sign of white grub damage, disease problems, etc.) Sometimes the webworms pull the grass blades into their tunnels to feed. Sod webworms get to be about ¾ inch in length. One worm can munch around and chew up to 4 square feet of turf during its life cycle of about 35 days. Sob webworms are not only a problem of golf and home lawn turf grasses, but they are a very serious problem in range and pasture lands, where they may destroy thousands of acres per year with their ravenous appetite for grass leaves and stems. (The close clipping by the insects sometimes does not directly kill the grass. The hot sun beating down on the exposed crowns is what actually kills it.) Sod webworms are best controlled by using carbaryl (Sevin), diazinon, or chlordane. Adequate watering and fertilizing, which keep lawns growing vigorously, will also lessen the amount of damage resulting from webworm feeding. One thing is important to remember when spraying for above-ground insects: to get good control you must thoroughly and uniformly cover all the grass blades and stems with the insecticide. The poison must be left on the leaves as well as at the soil-surface stem level. Although most recommendations say never to water in an insecticide, they will say that for surface insects you should water the lawn well *before* application. I discovered that I have better success if I moisten the grass with just a very light sprinkling (not soaking) right after treatment. This helps to move the insecticide application further down on the stems and onto the lower part of the grass blades. Then let the grass blades and grass crowns dry out, and don't mow for at least three days.

Another thing I advise for successful control of above-ground insects is to repeat the application of insecticides a week or so apart. Remember, the below-ground insect application will stay in the soil, whereas the above-ground insecticides will stick on the leaves and stems and then be mowed or washed off before doing a complete job. Children and pets should not be allowed to play on lawns sprayed for above-ground insects for 48 hours after treatment—or better yet, until the lawn has been watered a few times.

Cutworms may reach a length of 1 inch or more. Their usual color is greenish gray. The cutworm is another insect that likes to feast on grass during the night and hide in the thatch in daylight hours. This voracious insect can devour a square yard of turf in its life span of about three weeks. The female adult moth can produce 300 or more hungry offspring.

The insecticides recommended for the control of cutworms are carbaryl (Sevin) and diazinon. I find at my golf course that cutworms are slowly developing resistance to chlordane, which I have been using. Cutworm control is most effective in 70- to 80-degree temperature. Use the same watering and mowing management after the treatment as recommended for sod webworms.

Armyworms. Unlike the cutworms, who are solitary feeders, armyworms attack in Genghis Khan hordes and destroy everything in their path. They render extensive damage to home lawns and other grassy areas. Thank heavens armyworms don't attack every year. But when they do attack, they are devastating and leave patchy dead areas all over your yard.

Armyworms in the caterpillar stage are green when small and dark brown when fully grown. They also have a dark stripe marking each side and a stripe in the center along the back. Armyworms have one other distinguishing marking—an inverted *y* on the head. Use the same insecticides as recommended for sod webworms and cutworms. Also carry out the same postmanagement care; don't water and don't mow for a few days after application. Repeat the same application a week later.

Chinch bugs. Adult chinch bugs are black with white patches and have wings neatly folded over the back. These tiny sucking insects are only about one-fifth of an inch in size, and they have piercing, beak like, sucking mouth parts. They feed at the base of the grass plants, attacking the stems. Their favorite dish is common St. Augustine grass, but other St. Augustine grass varieties (with perhaps the possible exception of the newly discovered resistant variety, Floratam) are severely damaged by them in hot dry weather. The attacked turf grass occurs as patches with brown, dead centers and yellowish margins. The chinch bug population can be hundreds per square foot. The best method for eradication of these bugs is to first aerify the St. Augustine lawn in order to penetrate the dense, thick turf. Then mix a wetting agent with the insecticide and water to make a closer contact to the base of the soil after aerification. If the lawn is not going to be aerified, use a powerful sprayer to penetrate the tough turf, the sprayer should be used at a minimum pressure of 200 pounds per square inch. It's a wise policy to switch chemicals with chinch bugs so that they won't develop resistance. Turf grass should be moist before application of an insecticide for chinch bug control, and best results are obtained when the entire lawn is treated uniformly. The safest, yet potent, materials to use are carbaryl (Sevin), Trithion, VC-13, diazinon, Elthion, Dursban, and Aspon. Akton is a more dangerous insecticide and should be applied only by licensed pest control operators. Though we don't recommend watering after applying insecticides to control surface insects (except for a very light sprinkling to move the insecticide to the stems), it is practical to give a good soaking after applying the chinch bug insecticide. The reason is obvious. Since the chinch bugs feed at the base of grass plants, it's best to get the insecticide spray down through the dense turf to where the action is.

Well, I have mentioned to you some of the worst above-ground insects. Others less troublesome, like lawn moths and flea beetles in dichondra lawns of California, can be wiped out effectively with repeated applications of malathion, diazinon, or Dursban. Sow bugs can be killed by applications of diazinon or Zectron. Leaf hoppers can be controlled with methoxychlor. Chiggers, which are very annoying to people (and whose scars I carry on my legs), can be knocked off with either chlordane or malathion. These tiny insects attack when you walk through long grass, and cause severe irritation and extreme itching. If you intend walking through chigger country, spray your legs with a nongreasy, nonstaining chigger repellent (absolutely effective). The repellents also keep off ticks, mosquitoes, and sand flies. Get a good repellent, the kind that comes in a pressurized container and that can be safely sprayed over pant cuffs, socks, and shoes.

Snails and slimy slugs aren't really in the insect category, but sometimes they are a nuisance in lawns and ornamentals. The best way to control these larger pests is with a combination slug and snail chemical formulation, like mataldehyde plus calcium arsenate, or metaldehyde plus Sevin. The recent sensational articles stating the alleged control of slugs by putting out saucers of beer are questionable, and the control a rather nebulous and ineffective one. Instead, I suggest the homeowner indulge in the good American pastime of drinking the beer, and let the slugs and whatever else crawls about in the yard at night drink something else.

Q.—I am in trouble. My lawn looks awful. I think I have both the above-ground insects and the below-ground insects. What do I do now? Move away?

A.—Don't move yet. The first thing you must do is to make sure you *definitely* have both kinds of insects in your yard. Positive identification should be made before any application of insecticide. That's step one. Once you have properly identified the problem and learn definitely that you unluckily have been attacked by both insect categories, then here is what you should do. Use a good insecticide that is recommended for both above-ground and below-ground insects. Measure out the recommended dosage of this broad-spectrum insect poison, mix it with lots of water, and apply it uniformly over your lawn. After you treat your lawn, in order to knock off the above-ground insects, *don't water* and *don't mow* for 3 days. After the 3-day waiting period, soak the insecticide material off the blades and stems and into the soil, where the subsurface insects are having their root feast. Repeat the "double-kill" treatment one week later and then once more after that in order to get effective control of both insect categories. Remember to cut your grass just before each new application.

Q.—Please explain what is meant by an insecticide and what is the difference between dry insecticides and liquid insecticides.

A.—The Illinois Department of Agriculture describes an insecticide in this way. "Insecticide means any substance, or mixture of substances intended for preventing, destroying, repelling or mitigating any insect." Our concern in this chapter is only with insects that destroy turf grass.

Dusts and granules are prepared for direct application in *dry form*. The granules can be spread with either a cyclone or a small drop-type fertilizer spreader. The dusts usually are applied with a hand duster.

Emulsified concentrates and wettable powders are applied in

liquid form after they are thoroughly mixed with an adequate amount of water. Apply them either with a small walking-type sprayer that you push or with a sprayer that sprays by means of a garden hose and jar (hose-end sprayers). I don't like the over-the-shoulder, or knapsack, compressed air sprayers that sometimes get the applicator wetter than the lawn. (However, larger centrifugal sprayers—pressure piston pumps—with either boom or hand guns are good for large turf grass areas.) If you use these and get some spray on you, be sure to take a bath and change clothes right after. Another thing. Some old-type insecticide concentrates are extremely harsh on bentgrass and fine fescues if not carefully applied, especially if they are carried with an oil base. Many years ago, an oil and gas company that went haphazardly into the business of home lawn insecticide application during the summer to boost its business, found that out. (This was back in the days when gas and oil were cheap and plentiful and consumer demand wasn't too great.) The company used a liquid emulsifiable concentrate insecticide with an oil base mixed with water in the 8,000-gallon truck tank. (Also, I suspect the insecticide was mixed with some leftover home fuel at the bottom of the tank.) They did a good business until they sprayed a certain lawn in Skokie, Illinois (one of their winter fuel customers). Well, sad to say, they burned most of his grass. The oil company called me in to look at it. I examined the Skokie lawn carefully on my hands and knees. After diagnosing the problem, I informed the company official that the lawn, which was of Kentucky bluegrass, fine fescue, and creeping bentgrass, had been burned by an overdose of an oil-based emulsified concentrate that was applied by a careless operator. I pointed out to the concerned homeowner and to the fuel and gas representative that the Kentucky bluegrass was unharmed but that the fine fescue and creeping bentgrass turf, in sporadic patches, was dead, wiped out, from the overdose. The gas company man drove me home in silence—and I didn't blame him. The large lawn had to be replaced. Much later the oil company frankly informed me that they hadn't believed my diagnosis at first, and had called in a consultant from Purdue University as well as a man from the Illinois Co-operative Extension Office. Both confirmed my suspicions with tests and a technical report. In the end, it cost the company not only the complete sodding but also the travelling expenses and consultation fee of the Purdue lawn expert. (The Illinois man was free. The Co-operative Extension Service provides service for those in the county or state without charge.) *So be careful when using pesticide.* Be sure it isn't harmful to a particular grass or grasses. Also, be sure that when you hire a lawn service company, it knows what it is doing. Keep away from the "quickie" lawn maintenance companies. I want to leave this last advice impressed indelibly on your mind: before applying any insecticide, *always* measure the length and width of your lawn. Then pace off 500 or 1,000 square feet, or better still, use a measuring tape to get the exact test-area measure. Now go over the test area first with sprayer and water only. Then carefully check the instructions on the insecticide bottle and formulate with the amount of water used in your spray tank or jar the exact amount of insecticide required for the actual insecticide application to the 500 or 1,000 square feet you have measured out. (Measure out a smaller ground area for hose-end jar sprayer.) Now mix well and apply.

Precaution: Always fill spraying equipment half full with water before pouring in the insecticide. Then fill to the top with water and mix really well. If you don't do this, the insecticide will stay in the bottom of the sprayer. Remember, the same precaution of measurement and precise application must also be carried out with the granular insecticide formulations. Never guess.

Q.—Isn't there another method besides insecticides to kill lawn insects? What about biological controls?

A.—There has been some success with using milky spore disease to control Japanese beetles. The Japanese beetles in their adult stage are harmful to gardens, and in the grub (larval) stage to turf grass roots. The experiments involve methods of making the unwanted insects sterile, thus preventing the females from producing young. Also, some scientists are experimenting with tiny wasps imported from Europe to eradicate the elm bark beetle. These wasps prey on the European elm bark beetle. They lay their eggs right on top of the bark beetle's larvae. Thus, when the wasp larvae hatch, they immediately begin to feed voraciously on the beetle larvae. However, it will be a long time (if ever) before biological controls will be discovered for all the terrible insect problems in the world today. Insects are man's constant and eternal enemies, and some will always be around to plague us.

Many of us get unnecessarily overemotional about our environment and the problems of ecology. When this happens, we sometimes take it out unfairly on the pesticides. This is deplorable. Pesticides are effective lawn and garden management tools if used as recommended. Insects, weeds, and plant diseases are fierce competitors for our food supply, and our decisions must take this into account. Doomsday prophets in newspapers and other media, without authentic documentation, give you a one-sided, sensational story about the horrible dangers of pesticides. The next time you read something by these doomsday people, keep in mind one thing: have you ever seen a pesticide actually kill a bird or animal? Have you ever known of anyone made sick or killed by pesticide poison (positively proved) except, perhaps, in rare cases of suicide or premeditated murder? Okay, now let me ask you to do something the next time you ride to work or go for a pleasant Sunday ride in your car. If you are observant, it won't be pleasant. Count the dead birds and animals killed by cars that are lying at the side of the road or highway. Killed or worst yet, wounded and left to die. Nobody is running around yelling and screaming and writing about banning cars and careless drivers because each day they are destroying countless animal life. I'll tell you something, my worried friends, even sadder. Go out to where a rich developer (or any developer) is uprooting virgin land and building homes, shopping centers, or industrial parks in the name of progress. How many birds' nests and animal burrows do you think are destroyed along with trees, shrubs, and wild grass, by man and his bulldozers? Where do you think the uprooted, frightened, and displaced animals and birds go to after the destruction of their home and sanctuary? But I have yet to see work stopping on a building development because somebody is concerned about the wild creatures, great and small, no matter how many animals' homes are dug out and destroyed. And what about the majestic trees growing here since the time of the American frontier that have been destroyed or hauled away to a burning site? If you want some sad and positive proof of animal and plant destruction, think about this.

My friends, if you want to go crusading about something, crusade about something sad that you can see, not something that is being checked and rechecked to keep problems to a minimum. Sure, go ahead and try a little organic gardening on a plot of land. I think it's great fun and most enlightening. Some people have excellent success and I wish them luck. But if you had to depend on organic gardening, you'd never see vegetables and fruit as plentiful, clean, healthy, and insect- and disease-free as what you now buy in your favorite store. Furthermore, the cost of everything would increase by unbelievable leaps and bounds, and regardless of cost there would not be sufficient food to meet our needs. Food quality and yield would decline along with farm profits. Without chemical assistance (fertilizer included), the hardworking farmer wouldn't have a chance. The abundant, clean, cheap, and pest-free food available in the United States is a result of man's ability to control his environment. Think about this the next time you are munching a juicy red apple or having a bite of buttery wheat toast.

10

Diseases

THE AVERAGE HOMEOWNER has more difficulty correctly diagnosing lawn disease symptoms than he has with any other problem. Frequently what he thinks is a lawn disease turns out to be another lawn problem not caused by disease organisms at all, such as localized dry spot, chemical and fertilizer injury, chronic wet spots that turn brown and rot, brown spots from not watering when grass is desiccated, whitish and ragged leaf tips caused by dull mowers, scalping, lack of fertilizer, too much fertilizer, the natural tendency of grass to go dormant, dog urine injury, insect damage, and light-exclusion injury (suffocation) from rugs, mats, boards, tents, piles of leaves, and other objects, especially during hot weather. These are some of the *minor* lawn problems. They often make the homeowner think he has a serious pathogenic disease (fungi, bacteria, viruses, or nematodes) in his yard, when actually it's some other problem, perhaps physiological. At least, that has been my frequent observation and experience with home lawns that I have examined. Many times the owners have called, very worried, insisting that their beautiful lawn is being attacked by a sinister disease-causing organism. Once in a while, they are right. In fact, if the problem has become acute, usually there is more than one disease conniving to knock off the lawn. A disease complex is common and often functions to cause an advanced stage of deterioration. When this happens, it's hard for even some turf experts to diagnose what specific organisms are attacking the grass and then prescribe the proper treatment without a good pathological test in a laboratory. But let's hope this never happens to you. Handling one disease at a time is enough of a headache for anybody—even *expert turf managers* like golf course superintendents.

There are more than 100 fungi that can attack and infest turf grasses. Thank heaven only a few of these microscopic organisms are capable of causing severe injury to home lawns. And these diseases can often be controlled with proper turf grass management by an alert homeowner who seeks help before they get out of control. You see, controlling turf grass diseases is normally a preventive rather than a curative measure, with turf professionals like golf course superintendents, but the cost and time needed for an effective, desirable fungicide program has made such control impractical for most homeowners. Usually, when homeowners finally realize they have disease problems, it's too late to treat. By the time of diagnosis, severe damage and dead and dying spots appear all around. Sometimes a complete renovation program is necessary to obtain a healthy lawn again. Therefore, correct and expert identification of diseases and other turf disorders *before* they become too extensive is essential to the control with proper chemicals. A correct identification always provides a basis for the choice of the best fungicides. Remember, though, *if you can afford it,* that a well-planned, season-long *protective spray program* is still the best assurance of maintaining healthy turf free of disease, especially in the South.

Turf grass diseases vary from area to area, but some, like fairy ring and snow mold, are easy to recognize. Many, like stripe smut and certain kinds of leaf spots, are extremely difficult for a home-owner to recognize. The further north you live, the less lawn diseases there are to worry about and the shorter the season. The further south you live, the more disease problems there are and the longer-lasting they can be unless promptly and properly treated.

Attacks of disease depend on air and soil temperatures, humidity, shade, moisture, species and varieties of grass plants, fertilization, and other cultural factors. Fungus spores can be spread by lawn equipment, wind, water, shoes, and infected plant material such as grass clippings. Most turf diseases are caused by parasitic forms of fungi that live not only in the soil but in thatch (the tightly intermingled layers of living and dead leaves, stems, and roots of grass between the soil surface and the grass vegetation). Since fungi don't manufacture their own food, they attack the living tissue of turf grass when conditions are favorable. Luckily for homeowners, only a few fungi are capable of extensive damage to home lawns. Most of the devastating fungi are indigenous to the special, closely mowed turf grass (bentgrass and Bermuda) on golf courses, bowling greens, and other intensively cultured turfs. In order to keep golf courses green all season long without a blemish (some of these smooth, verdant "carpets" are mowed (as low as $\frac{3}{16}$ of an inch), golf course superintendents in most four-season areas spray with preventative fungicides starting around midspring or earlier, depending on weather conditions. Otherwise, these areas would be seriously blighted with diseases. I would guess that at least once during the growing season your home lawn is affected by one of the diseases that is common to your locality, without your even realizing there is a disease problem; the grass usually heals up without any assistance when the weather changes from hot and humid to cool and dry. Dry air is a particularly big discouragement to parasitic fungi activity. Mycelium threads, the vegetative portion of a fungus, grow actively when moisture is liberal—high humidity, saturated soils, heavy dew in the morning—but are so delicate that at the slightest hint of dryness, they stop developing. The ideal incubation of some destructive fungi usually occurs in a prolonged spell of extremely hot and humid (or wet) weather. At such times, even home lawns are vulnerable to certain types of fungi attack.

A homeowner should become suspicious when the weather stays hot and damp for a long time during summer. In fact, even in spring, examine your lawn carefully if the weather stays wet and overcast for a long time, because that's when you should start worrying about leaf spot attacks. But please get expert advice before you start applying fungicides to your lawn. Get it from the county extension agent, golf course superintendent, or local sod nursery. Look at the full-color disease illustrations (easily available from extension agents, commercial golf course supply houses, or lawn and garden centers), but only after the disease in your lawn has been properly identified and a specific fungicide recommended. Don't look at pictures and guess; too many people, trying to be experts, get fooled. Depend on someone who knows. What I am trying to say is that, outside of fairy ring or snow mold, the average homeowner isn't able to diagnose with any certainty the disease harming his lawn, so he shouldn't try.

I will tell you in the question-and-answer section what things to look for if you're suspicious of disease in your lawn.

Although research has brought some fine new varieties of grasses that are resistant to some of the major lawn diseases, none of them is immune or completely resistant to all diseases. The search for varieties within each species continues in order to develop better grasses that are resistant to diseases under many weather conditions. The sad and frustrating fact is that if this ultimate solution does occur and a "super grass" is developed, it will someday be attacked by a new disease as yet unheard of. In the past few years some of our top turf grasses have been seriously attacked by diseases that a decade ago weren't around to infest the grass and frustrate the homeowner and the professional turf manager. However, I feel that the homeowner's best bet in the future will not be one outstanding variety of grass, but a blend of several super grass varieties growing together in a lawn (see chapter 2). Many of my friends in the field of professional turf management feel the same way.

I hope this chapter will aid homeowners in maintaining beautiful, disease-free lawns, or at least in keeping diseases from ever becoming a serious nuisance.

One last thing. Disease likes company. Once a particular disease intrudes, it is followed by other fungi. The infection then becomes so unidentifiable that even the turf specialists have difficulty in separating out the real culprits. Without proper diagnosis, the collective disease sometimes wipes out a lawn before even the best turf experts know what has happened. Visual identification becomes next to impossible and only laboratory analysis, which takes time, may be able to reveal the specific diseases.

Q.—What are fungicides?

A.—Fungicides are chemicals that control disease-causing fungi. They act as protectants in that they prevent infection of the turf grass tissue from occurring. Fungicides are just one more material, one more excellent weapon, in a good gardener's armory. A good gardener knows that a preventative spray schedule offers the best protection against severe lawn damage—but a protective spray program is expensive. Something else also, fungicides even properly applied only stop the disease; they do not heal injury already done to lawn grass.* However, a good fungicide will prevent further damage to the grass plant itself and stop the spread of certain fungi into healthy turf areas. A homeowner should also understand that in certain intensive disease areas of North America, it is critical whether preventions or curative control measures are necessary. So accurate identification of the disease is very important.

The two types of fungicides available to the homeowner are *contact* (foliar protectant) fungicides and *systemic* fungicides. Contact fungicides are more easily purchased and should always be used with a little sticker for good foliar coverage. The contact fungicides have to be applied more frequently since the surface chemical is removed with irrigation, mowing, or precipitation. The recently discovered systemic fungicides, which are absorbed mostly by the plant roots, should be watered in for distribution of the material within the plant. The fungicide that is taken within the plant then destroys or controls the particular disease-causing organism for weeks at a time. The one drawback is that diseases sometimes become resistant to a systemic fungicide that is used repeatedly. Therefore, for the control of many lawn diseases, systemics shouldn't be used exclusively. For best results, they should be alternated with other types of fungicides such as some of the excellent contact fungicides. A baseball pitcher wisely mixes his pitches to strike out a good player; in much the same way a homeowner should mix his fungicides (contacts and systemics) in order to strike out a particularly tough disease.

When using fungicides, be sure to follow the directions and observe the precautions on the container. Fungicides are poison-

---

* There is some recent proof that systemic fungicides do enter the plant and "heal" certain diseases.

ous. Use lots of water—don't skimp. Skimping with water can lead to poor or partial control, because much water is needed to ensure an adequate coverage and penetration of the fungicide spray solution. *Note:* None of the fungicides recommended in this book contain mercury or cadmium.

Q.—Is there any one good way that I can tell the difference between insect damage and disease damage just by examining the grass plant?

A.—Keeping in mind that the natural color of a healthy grass blade is deep green, look for this: an insect-chewed grass plant is green (especially if freshly chewed) but the leaves look ragged because it has been partially eaten. Now, if the leaf plant is diseased, then the natural healthy green hue of the leaf blades turn another color, with spots and blotches. Sometimes they turn purplish red or brown. Sometimes the leaves develop unnatural black spots and dark margins. When this happens, it's time to be alert and get professional advice from a turf expert. *Do not* apply chemicals haphazardly before you have the disease identified and are sure you know what you're doing.

Q.—We have fairy rings in our front and back yards. Some are just dark green circles (or half circles), and some have mushroom rings. What causes fairy rings? The yard and house are about five years old. Is there a cure for these odd-looking circles?

A.—Fairy rings range from a few feet in diameter up to one mile. That's right—one mile. I once saw one that size in southern Alberta, Canada. Usually a dark green band of turf occurs in a circle or semicircle. The fruiting, or spore-producing, structures (mushrooms or toadstools) may or may not be present. The band of grass forming the ring is usually greener than the grass in the center. Frequently just behind the dark green band is an area of sparse, brown, dying grass caused by lack of water penetration and air movement in the soil due to a mass of mycelium formed by the fungus. Weed invasion usually follows the thinning of the grass. Fairy rings infect all lawn grasses; they don't discriminate. There are three common symptoms of fairy ring. *Number one* (most frequent) is a ring of dead grass each year (some growths have been found to be over 100 years old!) which is usually visible for long periods but is most noticeable in summer and fall.

Grass is often greener just inside and outside the ring. This stimulation of the grass is due to the availability of nutrients resulting from the decomposition by the fungus of organic materials in the soil.

Number two is a very hard green ring, especially in the spring. It is stimulated by the nitrogen from the decaying organic matter in the soil. Grass inside the vigorous areas, if unsightly, is in a state of decline.

Number three is the visible mushrooms (the fruiting bodies), which do not affect the grass. Knock off the mushrooms and dispose of them. Don't let kids handle them.

A characteristic of some fairy rings is the presence of toadstools and mushrooms in the infected area. Control is difficult after fairy rings are established. *Control* can begin in the initial construction and development of a lawn. Fairy ring is caused by a fungus that grows in decaying matter below the surface of soil that contains a lot of undecomposed organic matter such as roots, stumps, and boards. Such debris should not be buried but hauled away, because it provides a site for these fungi. Thatch can also favor unsightly fairy ring development. Years ago, in grandpa's time, when good topsoil was inexpensive and easily available, there was very little fairy ring problem. Now both homeowners and contractors timidly apply a few inches of soil ("on the cheap") over a clay subbase and buried debris. In a few years, of course, fairy rings appear in the yard.

I suggest you try a good management program of fertilization and annual deep aerification after Labor Day. Aerify twice, in different directions, then water heavily for 3 nights. *Really pour* the water into the holes. But wait—there is something I should mention before the watering. Since Labor Day is a good time to begin fertilization, give the lawn a good feeding *after* you have aerified the yard twice. *Then* throw some good seed into the aerified holes of the dead ring. (It works for me on the golf course.) After this, wash the fertilizer nutrients and seed into the numerous holes. These hints will help lessen the unwanted outline of fairy ring. Another treatment you can give for a very ugly fairy ring is to take a narrow tool 1 inch in diameter and just inside the circle and outside the ring punch holes 1 to 2 feet deep at

1-foot intervals. Presoak the ground before punching the holes; it makes for easier penetration. Then flood the holes every day for a week. If the ring is larger than 6 feet in diameter, a good strong root feeder is easier to use than a penetrating tool. Attach the root feeder to the end of a hose and work it deep into the ground. Circle the fairy ring in the same way as I have described above. Water 1 to 2 feet deep, and be sure to soak the ground well. Also, it's a good idea to use a commercial wetting agent while soaking the ring. Some people I know have had good results with tree service companies, which have powerful "jackhammer" root feeders to penetrate and soak the "monster" with water and soluble fertilizer. Some people dig out the soil with garden augers or posthole diggers and then refill with fresh soil.

The last resort, if you have a really ugly ring, is to dig out all the infected soil and get to the bottom of the problem, which is usually a decaying stump. Pull it out and replace it with good topsoil. Better yet, as I said earlier, don't let the lawn get into this situation in the first place.

I don't recommend fooling around with chemicals for fairy ring control, and I am surprised that some university bulletins recommend methyl bromide, a soil sterilant, which is extremely poisonous and dangerous to use. If you are going to experiment with something, try formaldehyde; it's less dangerous. Methyl bromide should be used *only* by professional turf people.

Q.—We just moved to Bismarck, North Dakota, from the Deep South this spring. Our new house is nice but the lawn is just awful. It's all covered with something called snow mold disease. What is it? Please tell us how to get rid of it. I am pregnant also.

A.—I think you have typhula blight, commonly called grey snow mold. (Fusarium patch, a pink snow mold, doesn't strike bluegrasses too often in your area.) Grey snow mold develops best under snow cover and is commonly found in the cool region of the United States. It is usually observed when the snow melts in early spring, although it can occur in late fall or during the winter. This easy-to-recognize disease is caused by a fungus that thrives in moist and freezing conditions. The disease first appears as a cobwebby white or grey matted film of tight growth as soon as the snow melts. These bleached rings are so tightly sealed to the ground that the grass underneath is destroyed. As the leaves of the grass die, the patches of turf turn brown. The size runs from a few inches to a foot in diameter. Snow mold, like fairy ring, attacks all grasses, but the further north, the worse and more profuse the disease becomes.

Snow mold is common in low areas, and damage is worst when snow covers the turf for a long time. The best thing to do in the spring, if you get an attack of snow mold, is to loosen the matted film that seals the grass with a bamboo "whipping" pole or a leaf rake in order to provide air circulation. Then, when the ground warms, *double-fertilize* to make the surrounding unaffected grass spread and help cover the damaged areas. Water in well. Even so, you may have to reseed or plug-sod the worst spots.

To prevent attacks of snow mold, it's best not to make heavy nitrogen fertilizer applications in late fall but rather to spray with a thiriam fungicide or with a systemic like benlate. I usually recommend that the Chicago-area homeowner spray for snow mold just after the first snow melts in Chicago, which it always does. As you go further north of the Chicago area, treat the turf before the snow falls. Treat again as soon as you can in late winter or early spring.

Q.—Please tell me what is the difference between dollar spot and brown patch disease? Is it possible to have both diseases in my Indiana Kentucky bluegrass lawn at the *same time*?

A.—Although I have observed severe dollar spot damage in almost all species of grasses, I have only rarely seen brown patch attack a bluegrass lawn in the cool region, and then only in a shaded and wet portion of a yard with absolutely no air movement —a microclimate sometimes conducive to brown patch in warm weather. The few times I did view minor brown patch development, it wasn't of serious concern to the homeowner in a higher-mowed Kentucky bluegrass lawn. In the cool region, light attacks of brown patch in Kentucky bluegrass lawns do not seriously affect the bluegrass root system, and the plants recover usually soon after the attack. Brown patch is much more commonly found in such extremely low-mowed northern turf grasses as bentgrass (on golf courses) and in such southern home lawn grasses as Bermuda, Zoysia, and St. Augustine. *Frankly,* dollar spot and brown patch are two good examples of diseases that thrive under totally different conditions. In fact, they are opposites, not only in appearance but in development. As a warm season disease, brown patch attacks in the cooler regions of North America only in the hot, humid weather of summer, when the grass is saturated with water and is growing lush and soft leaf blades. In the South, where it's much more prevalent, it can be a problem even during the warm winter months, especially on overseeded turf. Dollar spot, on the other hand, is mostly observed in late spring and late summer on all types of home lawns during periods of cool nights and humid warm days. *Low nitrogen* can favor dollar spot development, and dollar spot is also more severe on home lawns where soil moisture is usually low; in comparison with brown patch disease, which thrives on grasses that are overfed with nitrogen, retain a high moisture level, and are exposed to daytime temperatures that persist in the 90s. The ideal condition for dollar spot development on grasses, especially in the South, would have low nitrogen levels with a low soil moisture, temperatures of 50 to 80 degrees, and early morning fogs or dews. Dollar spot looks like its namesake in bentgrass golf course greens and other closely mowed grasses, such as the Bermudas and Zoysia, and its round, cobwebby spots are usually sharply outlined against the surrounding healthy turf grass, especially early in the day. Following infection, these spots first are usually grey, then turn straw-colored. In home lawns, parks, and industrial lawns of higher cutting (Kentucky bluegrass, fescue, ryegrass), dollar spot's roundness is replaced by a much more irregular shape about the size of a large maple or linden leaf, which gets even larger, especially if they merge together. On the Briarwood Golf Course, where I am superintendent, I have observed dollar spot attacks in my unwatered Kentucky bluegrass rough areas. I don't much worry about these infections and never spray them. The Kentucky bluegrass in the roughs always recovers. But I certainly do worry when dollar spot (sometimes in spite of an expensive preventive program) strikes my closely clipped turf grass—usually fairways. I then spray with a good fungicide, such as anilazine (Dyrene), chlorothalonil (Daconil 2787), benomyl (Benlate, Tersan 1991), or thiabendozole (Tobaz). I also use cycloheximide (Acti-dione-thiram, Acti-dione-RZ). Right after I treat, I always fertilize with a high-content, slow-release (urea-formaldehyde) nitrogen source (38-0-0). The nitrogen works to fill in the diseased spots by causing the grass to spread more rapidly in the thinned areas, while the fungicide keeps the disease in check. Using a dollar spot fungicide and then following with a fertilizer application is a smart "one-two punch." Remember, lack of soil nutrition might be a significant cause of the dollar spot attack in the first place.

There is one precaution you should take with dollar spot fungicide applications. In some cases, if you use a fungicide such as benomyl repeatedly, the dollar spot organism may become highly resistant. So switch (or alternate) once in a while to some other fungicide available in the lawn and garden centers.

Now let's look more closely at brown patch, the disease that I call the opposite of dollar spot. As I noted, this disease is rarely a serious problem in the cool-region Kentucky bluegrass country. It is a bigger problem down South, where it attacks all major lawn grasses and may account for almost 75 percent of the homeowner's lawn disease problems. Heavy nitrogen application, excessive thatch, lush growth, and moisture and humidity make the foliage of the shorter-mowed grasses in the South much more susceptible to brown patch attack.

The first symptom of brown patch is a slightly bluish, hazy smoke ring that turns brown after a few days. Some rings are irregular and some are almost perfect circles. Some spots stay small, but most will enlarge quickly to several feet in diameter during warm humid weather. Damage in hot humid areas occurs mostly on tender, lush (overfertilized) grass. The higher the nitrogen levels in the soil and the longer the humidity persists, the more the brown patch fungus is apt to strike an overfertilized moist lawn, especially one that is not sprayed with fungicides for preventive disease control. Though there are many good fungicides to stop brown patch, the best (and cheapest!) control is a change to sudden cool weather. I have seen this disease strike on a few occasions. Once it was on one of my poorly drained, shaded greens (in spite of preventive spraying) when the day temperature soared over 90 degrees and the night temperature was over 70; but then in the afternoon, when the wind from the lake switched, the temperature dropped into the cool 70s (and 50s at night), and the brown patch disappeared as if by magic. My only reminder that I was "hit" was some interesting smoky rings that soon disappeared. A limited attack of brown patch may sometimes only damage the leaves, causing a thinning and browning of the turf. The lawn will recover. Sometimes, when there is no attempt to control brown patch, the smoky rings turn brown and the grass inside the ring pattern dies. New leaves may emerge in the center of the circular patch in ten days or so, giving the disease area a "doughnut" shape. Sometimes the entire spot may become green during a long growing season. Of the southern grasses, St. Augustine is damaged more by brown patch than is Bermuda grass or Zoysia.

In the North, bentgrass is the most susceptible to this disease. The best controls for brown patch are benomyl (Benlate, Tersan 1991), chlorothalonil (Daconil 2787), pentachloronitrobenzene (PCNB), tetramethyl thiuram disulfide (thiram), thiabendozole (Tobaz), methyl thiophanate (Cleary 3336), and anilozine (Dyrene). However, the best control that I have ever used is mercury (Caloclor). Turf management plays the most important role in brown patch control. Don't fertilize excessively with *nitrogen,* and water only when the grass is dry and moisture is low.

If you think you have one or both of the diseases described above, consult with the turf expert in your area for positive identification. If he finds both diseases in your Kentucky bluegrass lawn, call me; I would like to see that phenomenon! It's extremely rare, but can happen in very closely clipped Kentucky bluegrass.

Q.—Please tell us what causes those small leaf spots on our Kentucky bluegrass lawn in the spring. We live on the Indiana-Kentucky border and would like to know the specific turf grass management program we can follow to prevent this disease from recurring every year. It causes our Kentucky bluegrass lawn to thin out, and some years it is worse than others. What do you suggest?

A.—Most leaf spot and leaf blights are caused by species of the *Helminthosporium* fungus. This varied fungus usually causes what the average homeowner will frequently call *leaf spot* disease. Other common names for this disease are melting out, dying out, fading out, brown blight, leaf blotch, root rot, and crown rot.

Leaf spot can attack most grasses. This disease produces

distinct, elongated, purplish or reddish, irregular semicircular spots or lesions on the leaves. These spots have significant borders. As the lesions enlarge, straw-colored centers develop. If ideal (overcast and cool) weather for this fungus persists, sheaths, crowns, and roots become covered with a dark brown rot. The entire plant is killed when the root rot phase of this disease develops.

In a home lawn, leaf spot infection (spores) may start in the fall, survive over the winter in thatch, and develop rapidly in the cool moist weather of spring and late fall. Leaf spot occurs during long periods of cloudy, misty, overcast weather. When this "ideal" situation occurs, the turf grass is infected very rapidly with *Helminthosporium* fungus. When the weather turns warm, sunny, and dry, *and most of all, windy,* the lawn's vigor suddenly decreases, and it fails to respond to fertilizer and water. Then the plant usually dies of crown infection. When this unhappy situation occurs, the turf thins, dries out, and dries up, leaving by the end of June those brown, "melted out" patches of various sizes. On the whole, a very unpleasant and unsightly appearance in any yard.

In the summer, there is considerably less chance of new leaf spot attack. The fungus (*Helminthosporium*) produces fewer spores during the summer and warmer weather of late to early autumn. But, sad to say, the infections of spring continue to destroy a homeowner's grass (normally by mid-June, leaf spot has run its course), leaving unsightly bare patches of ground, which usually are subject to easy invasion of crabgrass and other summertime weeds.

Positive diagnosis of leaf spot is tedious and difficult for the average homeowner and sometimes even for turf specialists. Samples should be submitted to a county agent for positive identification as soon as you get suspicious (which should be whenever overcast, wet spring weather persists from a week to ten days). Remember, leaf spot normally starts early in the spring and is tiny in size, but if not controlled, it progresses from this phase to severe crown and root rot by the middle of June or before. In home lawns that are left unchecked, the appearance is one of sudden and general thinning and decline. It was for me, once at Briarwood, the worst disease that I ever experienced. I'll never forget it. By the time it was identified positively, I had almost lost three greens. The problem started when I changed fungicides. I failed to check out all the great, heralded qualities of the new, "wonder" fungicide. It was a newly discovered systemic, which controlled several diseases (the ones I had always sprayed for) for a much longer period than the old proven mixture of contact fungicides. What I didn't know was that this new systemic had absolutely no control over the *Helminthosporium* species. Of course the chemical company didn't say that on the label, but I wasn't worried since I had never experienced the troublesome *Helminthosporium* before. Oh, I had had a little leaf spot in the spring before that (like everyone else), which the contact fungicides held in check with no trouble. Well, the systemic fungicide kept the other diseases under satisfactory control alright. But since it had no control over *Helminthosporium,* a disease that had never given me trouble before, leaf spot now became a monster.

Against leaf spot, I prefer Daconil 2787 over all other fungicides. That's the only one that finally stopped my *Helminthosporium.* Other excellent fungicides that a homeowner can safely and effectively use are Acti-dione, Thiram, Fore, Dyrene, Tersan LSR, and Maneb. Use systemics, such as benomyl, only for specific diseases that they "strike out" (read the label for advice), but even then, don't use them repeatedly. Change off the systemics with contact fungicides so immunity or resistance doesn't develop.

Much of the leaf spot disease incidence is greatly influenced by homeowner management. Disease incidence is considerably greater under *close mowing.* Close mowing tends to deplete food resources, thus weakening the grass. Lawns receiving high rates of nitrogen fertilizer too early in the spring also risk the greater possibility of damage. Avoid overstimulation by excessive fertilization in the spring.

If you mow sensibly at 2½ inches or higher (I repeat and repeat and repeat), your chance of severe damage from leaf spot will be reduced. Your higher lawn also will have less crabgrass, maybe even none at all. This goes for other nuisance weeds as well. Use blends of several grasses that are resistant to leaf spot if you live in a climate that is particularly conducive to this disease (like Kentucky and even Chicago's North Shore). Some of the new

Kentucky bluegrasses and hybrid Bermudas possess resistance to *Helminthosporium*. The *Helminthosporium* disease is not a big problem on St. Augustine or centipede grass. Bermuda grass low in vigor or receiving excessive traffic in summer stress can be severely damaged by leaf spot and other diseases.

In the Deep South, *Helminthosporium* diseases mostly hit common Bermuda grass lawns; they cause dark-colored flecks or streaks on the leaves, sheaths, and crowns. Believe it or not, *Helminthosporium* fungus mold can be a problem to people with allergies. I know. I have taken shots for it.

Q.—In my area of Maryland we have what my neighbors call "frog eye." It's some sort of horrible lawn disease. Since we are newlyweds, please tell us what to do.

A.—(First, pull down the shades.) "Frog eye" is fusarium blight, and is caused by the fungus *Fusarium roseum*. It first appears as light green patches a couple of inches in diameter, of different shapes and forms. Then in a few days, these spots may become generally 6 to 8 inches in diameter and turn dull tan, then finally straw-colored.

These first symptoms of fusarium blight may occur after several days of hot humid weather followed by a prolonged dry period. The grass areas that die rapidly form circular patches (in a week or so), which may have healthy-looking green tufts in the centers. These bizarre spots of green grass that center the dead patches give a "frog eye" appearance. *Important:* This appearance is the key feature in your lawn to diagnose fusarium blight. If not treated immediately, patches continue to grow outward. The disease always first reappears in the areas where it has been active. "Frog eye" is definitely more severe on areas with excessive thatch, and there is sound speculation that excessive fertilizing also contributes to this disastrous disease. Keeping a heavily thatched lawn damp (until dethatching can be effected in the fall) may help. Experts tell us fusarium blight is usually more severe in droughty lawn areas. The best solution to control a severe attack is to spray with systemic fungicides like benomyl as soon as symptoms appear. (Remember to get an expert's advice before treating.) Water the turf well the day before the application and water the fungicide in *well* to wash it down to the roots, where it can be absorbed by the plant.

Q.—(A phone call.) I live in Deerfield, Illinois, where you work. My lawn, composed mainly of Windsor and Merion Kentucky bluegrasses, has grass blades that are beginning to curl. The leaves have black stripes (streaks) running up and down the length of the leaf blades parallel to the veins. When these black stripes are touched, a black "soot" rubs off on my fingers. Please tell me what this "stuff" is. You have a lovely golf course.

A.—From your description, you must have stripe smut. I must compliment you on your vivid description of this "new" disease. Although it's hard to answer a question concerning disease over the phone, I'm quite sure it is stripe smut. This particular disease has been quite prevalent this year for the first time in Deerfield and the Chicago North Shore area. Previous to your telephone call, I made several area "house calls." After your phone call, just to make sure, I went over to your house, and finding no one at home, I took a few samples of the infected grass plants and sent them out for verification by a well-known turf pathologist. (There is no charge for this service at most "friendly" sod nurseries.) The report came back positive for stripe smut.

Stripe smut is very tough on Merion and Windsor. This disease is one of the most destructive of all diseases attacking Kentucky bluegrass. Homeowners rarely can tell in the initial stage of this disease just what (if anything) is troubling the grass. By the time they decide something is wrong, the turf may be in a serious condition. Stripe smut takes a long time to become evident to the novice. Usually the lawn ceases normal growth and slow deterioration sets in. When it becomes very bad, the sick lawn looks yellowish black. A close-up look and feel will show pale green, infected, stunted plants with long black stripes down the leaves. These stripes contain spores of the disease. This sootlike powder, which rubs off on your fingers, is the spore of the stripe smut fungus. The tips of the leaves wither, turn from black to brown, and are curled at the very top with whippy tips, or "ribbons." The worst thing about this most destructive fungus is that it becomes a *perennial* once it attacks your lawn. In other words, once your turf grass has an internal infection of this disease, it may remain in your lawn for the rest of its life (which may be very short). If you suspect that stripe smut is a problem in your area, ask your local golf course superintendent or county extension agent what the latest "disaster" befalling turf grasses is this year. If he informs you it's stripe smut, then here are some things you can try doing before it intrudes into your yard (as I said before, very slowly and deliberately).

Reread all the portions of this book dealing with good turf management. The better shape your lawn is in, the better chance your grass has of surviving a disease attack. Keep thatch at a minimum. Don't let your lawn *ever* dry out. Keep it well watered —soaked heavy once a week (more often in the arid West). In spring and fall, treat with a systemic fungicide labeled for stripe smut control. Soak completely with water right after treatment. A good systemic fungicide for smut control is benomyl. Actually, several repeated applications 6 weeks apart is your best bet. Even this doesn't always work, because as yet there is no sure cure for this serious disease. *Let me repeat,* turf areas must not be allowed to get dry. The saddest part of this awful disease is that if your lawn gets hit before you notice anything, other diseases may band together in the devastated area that has been weakened by stripe smut and give your poor old lawn the coup de grace.

I recommend that new homeowners plant a blend of three or more bluegrass varieties (see chapter 1), which together may resist stripe smut attacks or at least help slow the development of this destructive disease. There are varieties of Kentucky bluegrass that are resistant to strip smut. But I must warn you that even these presently superior and resistant grasses, as they get older (3 years or so) in your yard, may eventually lose this resistance and be attacked by some future strain of stripe smut fungus. Scientists have found that the treatment of seeds before planting with a fungicide, such as benomyl, maneb, or captain, will sometimes help.

Q.—Our common Bermuda grass lawn (in South Carolina) was beautiful until just a few days ago, when extremely hot humid weather, accompanied by rain, persisted for three days. Right after this, our lawn became completely blighted by ugly-looking, "streaky" spots, as if someone had poured hot grease off the stove all over the whole yard. We can't believe it happened so suddenly. The man at the lawn and garden center says it's something awful called "grease spot," then sold us a fungicide to spray on the yard every three days. Isn't there any way to prevent this horrible stuff from attacking the lawn? And must we spray every three days?

A.—Pythium blight (or grease spot or cottonly blight) is the most swiftly destructive grass disease I know, and it attacks Bermuda grass and bentgrass with extreme severity. It is much more troublesome in the home lawns of warmer climates than in the bluegrass cool region of the northern states. Some varieties of this fungus do strike the upright grasses, such as Kentucky bluegrass, perennial ryegrass, and fine fescues, especially in the seedling stage. The homeowner in the South, however, not only has to worry about pythium in the hot summer, but also when he overseeds his lawn for winter color with ryegrass in the fall. (The later the better.)

Pythium is normally a disease of high temperature, high humidity, and wetness, especially when all of these conditions exist at once. Severity is greatest during periods with *no wind movement.* This is one disease that is extremely difficult to prevent or control, and the above weather conditions are quite conducive to its development. I know this very well from firsthand experience, having suffered through enough junglelike pythium weather. On a few occasions, pythium has completely wiped out some of my predominantly bentgrass and *Poa annua* fairways. One chronic low area in particular on #6 fairway, where the water and air drainage isn't too good, is a frequent problem area. The clay soil is impermeable and the air circulation even on a windy day is blocked by heavy and dense shrubbery. I lost this area almost every year when the "dreaded" combination of water, high humidity, and extremely hot weather developed (usually the third week in July). I tried everything, but to no avail in this particular area. Finally, in a desperate, drastic move, I resodded that hopeless disaster area with Warren's A-20 Kentucky bluegrass, which can be mowed low. Before laying the sod I improved the soil drainage. Well, I am happy to say that did it. No more problems to date. Oh sure, we still get some pythium every couple of years when hot humid weather comes to this sheltered and airless fairway, *not on the Kentucky bluegrass,* even in the low, low area. What is so amazing and interesting, since we "appended" a half acre of Kentucky bluegrass to our bentgrass-*Poa annua* fairway, is that a greasy streak will run right to the border edge of Kentucky bluegrass, then halt, turn at right angles, and proceed to run parallel to the Kentucky bluegrass border until stopped by the Kentucky bluegrass rough— never touching a spot of Kentucky bluegrass, but making a line of pythium destruction on the bentgrass and *Poa annua* line. However, homeowners who have any variety of Kentucky bluegrass usually don't have to worry about "old grease spot" in the yard. But young seedlings of all grasses (planted anywhere) can, under the right conditions, be very vulnerable to pythium, even in the cool, midwest region.

The first signs of pythium disease are most visible in the early morning. At this time the blades turn dark and appear to be water-soaked and greasy (or slimy), and the usually small patches are covered with a cottony mycelium fungus. (Golf course superintendents in the Chicago area sometimes call it "wool.") I have on occasion seen this growth rapidly develop throughout the day like a cobweb. Once the mycelium disappears, spots ranging from the size of a dime to 4 inches in diameter appear as if a drop of oil or hot lard had fallen on the grass. As the leaf blades collapse, they become matted, turn blue grey, and in a day or so the grass bleaches to straw tan color, depending on sun intensity. The spots usually are irregular in shape, and the areas they dominate always tend to spread (run) downhill in the direction of water flow (or streak following the mowing pattern). Pythium thrives in low spots that remain wet and stagnant. Reducing shade and improving soil drainage help to reduce the problems caused by this disease. Treat with fungicides, such as chloroneb (Tersan SP), ethazol (Koban), or ethizol (Terrazole). Timing is of utmost importance for control (unless you spray every week). For best results, a lawn should be treated prior to a pythium attack. But that sometimes is like picking a horse after the race. In the cool season, the homeowner with a bent lawn should be very suspicious of pythium attacks, especially when the temperature persists in the high 90's and the nights are hot and muggy. A combination of a few days of rainy weather followed by hot, humid, windless days and nights is a common cause of this disease. In the South, the disease can strike at any time, even in wintertime on overseeded lawns (ryegrass seedlings are very prone to pythium). The surest control when a devastating pythium attack hits your area is a fast prayer—for a quick change from hot to cool, cool temperatures.

Q.—Is rust a serious disease?

A.—No, it isn't. Just don't get it on your white shoes when walking across the lawn. Rust is an easy disease to diagnose. When examined closely, orange bumps (pustules) are evident on the leaf blades, and when rubbed with your fingers, the orange spores come off easily. In the cool region, rust can do minor damage on the leaves and stems of bluegrass and ryegrass lawns. It is a certainty in inadequately fertilized Merion lawns. In the South, rust will probably attack ryegrass and Zoysia. Although you can use chemicals such as Acti-dione-thiram and Maneb to control rust, if grass is severely attacked (usually in August and September), I suggest forgetting chemical contact. Fertilizing the grass to stimulate rapid growth is the best solution, followed by irrigation and frequent mowing. Use a catcher for the clippings until the disease grows out and disappears.

Q.—In the shady part of my lawn, the grass looks like it has been dusted with flour or talcum powder. Is this serious? We never before had trouble with our lawn.

A.—I believe you have powdery mildew. But double check this with your local county extension agent. Powdery mildew is seldom serious except in shade, where it can sometimes overcome and kill the whole lawn. This disease usually attacks in cool spring and fall nights. It is predominantly a problem of cool-season grasses, and is most frequently found in the too-shady areas of a Kentucky bluegrass lawn. The powdery mildew fungus always appears as a white powder on lawn grass. Growth is mostly on the very tip of the leaves. As the intensity of the fungal growth continues, general chlorosis (yellowing) develops. Usually, when shade is cut back to admit sunlight and air circulation, chemical control is not a necessity. (Shade environment normally has more disease, because humidity there is usually high, dew stays on the lawn longer, there is also less air circulation, and usually the grass is lusher.) Chemicals like cycloheximide (Acti-dione-thiram), benomyl (Tersan 1991, Benlate) and wettable sulphur will control powdery mildew.

I think this is a good place to stop and say that the lawn diseases we have discussed up to this point are generally the most serious ones to be found in North America. I am sure I have missed a few "baddies" here and there that are peculiar to certain sections of America, but my signal intention was to discuss the most unpopular lawn diseases.

I would just like to mention one other disease in particular— iron chlorosis. Iron chlorosis results from iron deficiency in the soil. In extreme conditions of powdery mildew disease, the leaves are solid yellow. Often green and yellow streaks of chloratic grass intermingle. This disease, as I mentioned earlier, is very damaging to centipede lawns in the South. Iron chlorosis is also very common in the West. In the North, it isn't often damaging except occasionally on golf courses and bentgrass lawns. Sometimes, when there is excessive liming (apply only when soil tests indicate) and high phosphorus application, iron, which is a trace element in the soil, becomes chemically bound in insoluble iron compounds that are unavailable for plant use. Chelated iron and ferrous sulphate are two good materials to stop this disease immediately. Using a little commercial "sticker" will increase the effectiveness of application.

Q.—What sound and sensible practices should a homeowner carry out to prevent disease or lessen the chances of an attack?

A.—Several well-timed preventive applications are required to control most diseases, but spraying for fungus won't do the job alone. Basic good turf grass management will. Disease is reduced by the following cultural practices (which amount to a summarization of this book). Let's run through them.

1. *Establish a good fertilization program.* Too much fertilizer, especially nitrogen, can result in a soft, lush growth of the grass— a condition favorable to some diseases. On the other hand, turf deficient in plant food is susceptible to certain other diseases.

2. *Apply judicious and timely irrigation.* Water deeply and infrequently (once a week is ideal). In order to grow, the fungi spores and mycelium (threads) require moisture and favorable temperatures. This is why grass diseases are most common during rainy seasons, when irrigation is frequent and water remains on the leaves for long periods, and when soil water accumulates and stands for a long time.

3. *Mow frequently.* A minimum of once a week.

4. *Mow most northern lawns at 2½ inches.* (Southern grasses are more presentable at a much lower mowing.)

5. *Do away with thatch.* Don't let excessive thatch accumulate in your lawn.

6. *Reduce shade areas.* Do this by thinning and careful pruning.

7. *Provide good drainage.*

8. *Reduce compaction by aerification.*

9. *Grow a particular grass variety for a particular climate.* In fact, it's best in the cool region to grow blends of two or three Kentucky bluegrasses. The mixture will have better ability to pull through adverse conditions that might damage a single variety. Don't fool around with a variety that is not suited to your locality. Nonadapted grasses will always give you trouble.

10. *Get the most disease-resistant grass.* It, or they, will be the top buy for your new lawn.

Finally, if good cultural practices are not controlling a particular disease, then I recommend the use of certain effective fungicides. But don't wait till midsummer to treat. Begin preventive spraying in the spring. If you wait until midsummer, the disease will have increased in severity and caused damage. It will then be necessary to apply the fungicides more frequently and at higher rates. In essence, properly maintained grass is less severely damaged by diseases and is always able to recover more quickly than poorly maintained grass. This is due to the ability of healthy grass to form new shoots and roots to replace those damaged or killed by disease. Although environmental factors like climatic conditions remain outside the control of man, we can carry out some effective cultural practices to help prevent disease.

Some other problems (nine—count them!) that can give homeowners bad headaches (though they aren't considered here to be diseases) are worth mentioning. This is a good place to put in these problems, because many times homeowners confuse them with diseases.

Mosses. The presence of mosses usually indicates low soil fertility, excessive shade, and compacted, poorly drained soils. Before you do anything, get a soil test made. Use ground copper sulphate at 5 percent in 3 gallons of water per 1,000 square feet, or a couple of ounces of hydrate lime in 3 gallons of water. After killing the moss, renew the affected areas or spots by hand-raking away the moss residue and seeding with good, shade-tolerant grass.

Algae, or green scum, forms as a greenish or brownish scum on the soil where shade has thinned grass and the soil is wet. The slimy scum sometimes forms a tough crust, which seals the soil and smothers grass. The presence of algae in a lawn indicates either that conditions are too shady or that the soil is compacted and poorly drained or both. Renovate the affected area by aerifying, and by pruning any possible landscape that creates shade problems. Algae may be stimulated by too much fertilizer spread in shaded areas of the lawn. Lime or a copper-containing fungicide will give only temporary relief. Tersan LSR and Fore fungicides also help.

Wilt. This condition is the result of a loss of moisture in the leaf blade faster than it can be replaced through the roots. At the first indication of wilt, grass will have a bluish color and footprints will remain on the surface of the turf. Although this symptom seems to be barely measurable, grass will feel unusually warm to the touch, compared with the temperature of the surrounding grass in shade or where grass is stronger and deeper rooted. Wilt occurs usually during very dry and windy hot weather. After watering, grass may not spring back to normal as might be expected. Wilted grass recovers very slowly. But nevertheless, water wilted grass as soon as possible; otherwise, it will go brown—in a hurry.

Wilted grass usually lies down flat and may not perk up for 24 hours, even after watering. I have seen shorter-cut lawn grasses wilt completely and die off in spots all over the lawn. This has happened even after the grass was heavily watered. If heavy traffic is continued on wilted grass, it may die.

Desiccation. This dehydration is a winter dryout. The worst injury from desiccation occurs in the North to lawn grasses, especially those located on knolls, berms, hillocks, and other exposed areas. The best example I know is Lethbridge, Alberta, where the warm chinooks often keep snow off lawns and golf course greens for long periods of time. In Lethbridge, a long time ago, we lost several good greens one winter to desiccation despite heavy watering in January.

Dry, cold winds draw so much moisture from the soil that the dormant grass shrivels and dies on those exposed, elevated areas that are the first to become free of snow. First the affected grass turns brown, then, by the time good spring growing weather sets in, almost white.

To prevent winter dehydration, soak the soil in late fall and again in January if there is no snow cover (or heavy rain). Also water all your shrubs and trees at this time, especially the evergreens.

If you place the neighbors' old Christmas trees on windswept knolls and high spots to collect and hold some snow, you can reduce the problem. Also, try a lath snow fence cut in half and placed at the top of the knoll. This fence will help keep the Christmas trees and branches from rolling down to street level. Laying down straw or hay to prevent desiccation is not my cup of tea. Often, if snow remains for a long time, disease such as snow mold develops and "knocks off" the grass. Suffocation of the grass must also be considered. Aerification late in the fall in North America where desiccation is a problem is not recommended. Aerify in late summer or very early fall so that moisture infiltration by heavy irrigation and rainfall will soak the soil. Keep watering heavily once a week all the way into early winter. Aerifying the lawn too late in the season can cause problems, because it will increase drying out in and around the deep holes that haven't healed. This is true especially if weather conditions in the winter are dry and snowless.

Winter injury. Homeowners should be careful with their lawns when the soil is frozen and bare of snow. I suggest that the turf not be subjected to any traffic, especially before the ground freezes. This caution also applies to frosts in fall and spring on young grass. Walking or riding bicycles on turf when grass leaves and stems are frozen will result in rupture of leaf tissue. Black green marks appear a couple of days or so after traffic damage. Constant traffic will prolong the period of recovery when the ground is frozen, and could even cause permanent damage. So be careful. Keep the kids on the sidewalk—ha!

Canine damage. Female dogs piddling on lawns produce small patches of yellow grass 8 to 10 inches in diameter. These patches usually turn brown and die, but the border of the patch will later become extremely green. This is one way to tell dog urine damage from disease—by the very green border of grass. (No mushrooms.) Heavy watering sometimes helps alleviate dog damage, if done when the initial yellowing first appears. If this is your lawn problem, either get a male dog or walk the female out to some *long, long grass.* Better still, mow your grass long—2½ inches or more.

Localized dry spots. This condition will occur sporadically in your lawn from compact soils, infrequent and inadequate heavy irrigation, uneven bumpy terrain, lack of rainfall, and excessive thatch, which repels water and proper air circulation. Localized dry spots cause much sprinkler runoff, thus disrupting good sprinkler patterns. Excessive thatch is in my opinion the major cause of localized dry spots. Aerifying your lawn in two different directions every fall is an excellent way to control this condition. We will come to aerifying right after the next two lawn problems.

Soil compaction. Certain soils compact easily, especially in areas of heavy foot traffic. This compaction prevents adequate penetration of moisture and nutrients and proper root system development. Saturated, waterlogged soils where traffic is heavy pack easily and bake hard in hot weather. The soil becomes so packed that water will not penetrate the surface. Grass then thins out, paths form, and eventually bare spots and weeds result. To correct this condition, loosen lawn by perforating the soil with an aerifier (not a spiker) once a year—right after Labor Day—in several directions. Water heavily right after aerification, but first sprinkle fresh seed all over the lawn. Don't worry, the water will wash the seed into the holes and you'll have good germination. It's a good idea to fertilize and seed the bare spots before watering.

Buried rubbish and debris (the opposite of treasure) in your yard. A thin layer of soil over buried junk (the great American tragedy of an expensive home, but inadequate topsoil) such as stumps, plaster, cans, concrete, and boards dries out extremely quickly in the hot weather. These dry spots sometimes look to the homeowner like some sort of disease. If this is your problem (frequent in many new lawns), dig out and remove the junk and then fill in the hole with good soil. Pack and tamp the soil as you fill the hole, especially large holes, and then, for good measure, cap this area 2 inches higher than the surrounding area and resod with a good piece of grass. No matter how well you pack soil, it will settle, especially after watering or heavy rains. If you're seeding, leave the area open for a week or so to settle, and then seed. It will always sink, believe me.

Q.—If you had one outstanding lawn maintenance to recommend to the homeowner, what would it be?

A.—It's aerification. Mechanical lawn aerifying is the major cultural practice that is not used as much as it should be by homeowners. This is a shame. I like this wonderful aerification machine better than any of the other lawn improvement devices now sold on the market, such as spikers, vertical mowers, and thinning and slicing devices. The aerification machines that cultivate without disturbing the grass rank as the most important improvement technique available today. Now I'll tell you why I am so high on aerification. Grass has the same basic requirement as any other crop. Like other crops, the turf requires cultivation. To remain healthy and resist wear, grass plants must be supported by a deep and well-developed root system. Aerification helps the soil because it improves soil structure by mechanical manipulation. An aerifying machine punches holes in the soil 2 to 4 inches deep, and with curved "spoons" or hollow tines, removes plugs or cores of sod and soil and deposits them on the lawn surface. These numerous holes (spoons or tines are of different diameters, from ½ to ¾ of an inch, and the better machines remove about 36 cores per square foot) relieve compaction. Here, compaction is considered the layering and surface crusting as well as thatch compaction at the soil surface. These holes provide better moisture percolation by providing drainage channels through which water may move and air may circulate. The more you aerate, the better oxygen-carbon dioxide relationship is achieved in the soil. The holes also improve fertilizer penetration and direct plant food, along with water and oxygen, to where they are needed and can do the most good—deep in the soil. This, of course, provides space for increased root development, and that, my dear homeowner, is the whole secret of a vigorous lawn—an adequate, healthy root system. Many times, I have examined the root system after aerification as compared to the spaces that weren't aerified. The difference in the amount of roots is unbelievable, and I never cease to be amazed by the terrific root system generated by aerification. In addition, aerification breaks up thatch and encourages the decomposition of dead matter. After completion of aerification is a good time to lime your soil, but only *if* soil tests definitely indicate a need. Putting grass seed into the aerifying holes is a smart way to establish an even better lawn, especially if you have poor-quality turf as a result of summer drought, weeds, insects, disease, or just plain poor maintenance. The seed, believe me, will germinate in the holes much better (especially on banks and slopes) than where you here and there "hen" scratched the bare soil. (Some Kentucky bluegrass may not possess sufficient vigor to produce a good root system in scratched or raked soil.) Best of all, by the time the seed sprouts, it has already established a good root system and is protected in the aerified hole.

Aerifying a lawn is a smart way to end the season and prepare the lawn for winter and the next mowing season ahead. There is an old saying, What you do for your lawn today will determine its condition a year from now. Aerify each fall even though your lawn has no compaction or other problems—yet. If nothing else, aerification gives the grass roots a new lease on life.

Aerify right after Labor Day so the holes can heal over before winter, when possible desiccation problems develop. Fertilize and reseed first, then water well also right after aerification. Really soak the ground.

In the cool region, fall is the best time to aerate because the soil is drier, the temperature and moisture conditions are more favorable (and more predictable), and of course, you have more time. Early spring aerification is not desirable because the soil is usually waterlogged. Soils should never be worked when hot or saturated. Remember, Mother Nature has already "aerified" your lawn by heaving and thawing the ground during late winter and early spring, which leaves the ground loose and porous. Aerify in late spring if you have to, but be careful and water in heavily. Prevention of drying around the holes is critical during the first few days after aerification. Summer aerification by homeowners is not recommended. Not by me, anyway. It's too hot and the healing is slow.

I recommend that you aerify your lawn once a year in two directions, from different angles. The more holes you poke, the better. A minimum of once a year for aerification is your best bet. The benefits of aerification decrease if done only once in several years, because too much turf remains undisturbed. Don't worry about the unsightly plugs deposited on the lawn surface. Don't pick them up. You still have a few weeks of mowing, and your lawn will grow over and hide them. Many of the plugs will be pulverized by your lawn mower. Irrigation and rainfall will also help break up the cores. However, it is advisable in order to speed up breakdown to mow in two different directions a few hours after the aerification (let the plugs dry out first; they will break up better) while the full cores are still lying on top of the grass surface. Once the plugs break up, they will act as top-dressing by filling in the depressions and voids in the grass, thus helping to keep the turf surface level. Utilizing the soil cores as a top-dressing also assists in decomposition of the thatch.

At this point, I want to clear up a misconception that confuses a lot of homeowners. Spiking a lawn does not aerify it. Spikers and aerifiers are different machines and accomplish different purposes. Aerifying, as I have stated, relieves compaction and makes deep holes by pulling out soil plugs and depositing them on the lawn surface. Spiking also makes holes, but *compounds soil compaction problems* by pushing soil down deep with hundreds of solid spikes—not pulling it up. So I don't recommend spiking a lawn. Spiking has some value on golf courses, but on a home lawn it's nothing more than a compaction tool. Spiking increases compaction; it does not relieve it. And you certainly don't need to compact your lawn.

Finally, there is the question of cost of an aerifier unit. Those that make a 16-to-20-inch swath run about half the cost of a good riding mower. This cost can be a disadvantage to most homeowners. But look at it this way. It takes more of everything, including time and money, to keep grass growing on poor soils, so economy of maintenance can be achieved as the quality of your lawn improves. Therefore, an aerifier is a good investment. I also am glad to say that there are tool and machine rental stores all over the nation. These stores handle good lines of turf equipment. Also, many good lawn and garden centers rent aerifiers and other tools. However, I have one bit of caution that goes for any lawn machinery. Practice handling the unit before you actually start working on your lawn. The aerifiers that are walk-behind, self-propelled models, or that can be drawn behind a small tractor or a riding mower are heavy, and you must carefully maneuver turns. Be especially careful on slopes and banks and terraces. Also, don't run over metal or solid objects (like sidewalks and gravel) with the aerifying spoons or tines. If you do, you'll bend or crush them and will have to replace the damaged ones.

Q.—(This is asked by many homeowners.) How do we keep up with all the relevant progress in new lawn grasses, pesticides, and fertilizers that are most suitable for our area?

A.—Certainly not by watching, reading, or listening to advertisements, though they are a good way to arouse your curiosity. Periodically, write to your local county extension advisor for pertinent new turf information. Visiting your local golf course superintendent and gleaning fresh turfgrass news from him is also time well spent. Anyone concerned about his grass and who loves beautiful turf is a friend of ours. Amen.

II

Conclusion

THE AMERICAN HOME LAWN has come a long way since the pioneer days of rippling prairies and sod houses. The modern home lawn, thanks to agronomy, has improved tremendously since those long-ago days of pasture-type "lawns" (shoulder high), peekaboo wildflowers, and fertilizer ground from buffalo bones. Today, many home lawns tend to be showplaces, manicured meticulously and groomed to perfection throughout the growing season. However, the majority of home lawns continue to get only "natural" care thoughout the year except for one surge of intensive care in the spring, which lasts as long as spring fever lasts. Sometimes there is a mild burst of genuine enthusiasm after Labor Day, but more often it's confined to spring. Once the summer starts, lawn work is done begrudgingly and without much ambition by most Americans. Actually it is during this crucial time that the vast majority of American lawns experience the most stress and should rightfully (do plants have rights?) have more maintenance attention paid to them. This really is the whole secret of a perfect lawn—attentive and loving care to the turf grass throughout all the growing months, not just when we get spring fever.

In my opinion, modern man in the past decade has slowly been losing his ancient sense of working with Mother Nature, with the earth, with his sense of horticulture. To me this is as certain as the fact that our children are losing their palates to "franchise dining" and good nutrition. So in a way I am happy that owing to the high cost of food and the general dissatisfaction with consumer products, there is now a tremendous revival of both home and community "inflation" gardens. Almost 50 percent of them are worked by first-time gardeners. Call it a quiet, green revolution. Other countries never stopped food gardening as we did right after the Second World War. Besides getting fresher and tastier produce cheaper with these "inflation" gardens, we are reverting to a wholesome link with the soil; without this link, I think we can never exist happily.

In this last chapter, I would like to answer some questions that need to be set straight.

Q.—Someplace I read that an average lawn of 5,000 square feet (50′ x 100′) produces enough oxygen day in and day out for a family of four to survive indefinitely. Is this true?

A.—Recently many so-called experts have been making incorrect statements about turf ecology. One statement that comes up frequently concerns what you have been reading. I am sorry to say, though, that this statement needs closer examination. Let me ask you what happens during the winter or at night when Mother Nature's miracle of photosynthesis is stopped. Do we all perish, especially in the four-season zones? Of course not. The reason we don't is that our biggest source of oxygen is from the oceans—from plankton, algae, and other aquatic plant life. (That's why I worry every time there is a massive oil slick!) Very little comes from cultured plants, but the little oxygen that they do give out is part of the world amount that is necessary for man to survive. No plants must be destroyed carelessly. We must hang on to everything we've got. Do your part.

Q.—I am sick and tired of mowing, watering, and fertilizing grass. I've "had it" with lawn maintenance and paying high prices for something that dies out every summer. What do you think of using artificial turf in a yard?

A.—To homeowners who want it, I say go ahead—if you don't care about walking on a surface that gets hot like asphalt and is especially uncomfortable when you walk out in the yard barefoot or try to sunbathe. Only the color is different. Remember, there is no "air-conditioning" (transpiration) from artificial turf. Use it if you no longer care to see robins pulling out fat worms. Go ahead and install artificial turf if you hate mowing; but you'll feel and look silly vacuuming your manufactured lawn, which will take four times as long because they aren't making commercial home-type vacuums wider than 21 inches as yet. And when soft rains fall, my friend, use it if you don't catch yourself saying, "It's good for the grass." But then, if you're going to install artificial turf, why stop there? Why not go all the way? Plant artificial flowers, shrubs, and trees (we do it now, ugh, at Christmas), and hang stuffed birds here and there along with some artificial stuffed squirrels to give it that "natural" look—you know, along with flamingos and deer on the lawn.

One thing more. Have you checked the price of synthetic turf and the cost of installing it? I think you should. You'll find that you can install almost ten natural lawns for the price you'll have to pay to install the ersatz turf.

P.S. I hope nobody throws any burning cigarette butts on your artificial turf. And be careful of dog litter!! And chewing gum.

Q.—There has been much in the news about the alleged fact that plants respond to people talking to them. What do you think of these studies? Should I talk to my grass? Will it grow better?

A.—I truly believe that any living thing can be communicated with, eventually. Much more reliable research will have to be done with plant life before this "theory" can be proved conclusively. But until then, I do believe this. When you get close to any plant (be it a house plant or grass) and stick your face close to its foundation while talking, you'll notice several things that you may not have noticed before: bugs and disease. For example, springtails, aphids, mealybugs, and whiteflies, and in the grass, sod webworms and cutworms. You might even notice some infection on the leaf blades that you hadn't seen before. In other words, while you're speaking to the plants (in a soothing voice I hope, just in case), you will be noticing problems that you didn't observe before, and thus you may spray and take care of the plant's trouble. The plant, of course, responds with better health and appearance. So go ahead, talk all you want, but keep your eyes open while you're talking.

There is one other thing to remember—carbon dioxide. Actually, a person sitting in a room could possibly stimulate a plant's growth by the normal exhaling of carbon dioxide, and the harder a person breathes, the more this compound can stimulate the plant. Carbon dioxide is vital to all plant life. This fact, then, might very well prompt someone to assume that doing heavy exercise and breathing hard in front of plants is the best thing you can do for them. I agree. However, if you really want to arouse a plant, try sex! Make love in front of your plants. That really releases a lot of carbon dioxide, and everybody is stimulated! As Robert Browning said, in *Pippa Passes:* "June reared that bunch of flowers you carry, From seeds of April's sowing." (No pun intended.)

Q.—My wife and I realize this question is unusual, but we would like you to answer it—seriously. You see, we like to enjoy ourselves outdoors, *au naturel*. But with so many busybodies around, we find it hard to frolic in our backyard in complete privacy. It seems that Lake Forest, Illinois, at this point is not yet ready for our act of . . . well, courage. Is it possible to erect a suitable protective screen as well as some very soft grass that will enable us to indulge in our favorite sport?—and I don't mean golf.

A.—Shades of Masters and Johnson! And it's great for the grass! But frankly, such a usage has never been explored in turf literature. In my various writings I've discussed lawn bowling greens and putting greens, but never a rutting green. Well, why not? Hence, this last piece is for lovers only (and for sunbathers) —a "sensual" environment.

Here's how to grow the best grass, with a prying-proof protective screen, for frolicking in Nature's splendor in your own backyard. My recommendation is an arborvitae hedge. These small ornamental trees should be planted close together in a double row, or what we agrostologists call a staggered planting line. It looks like this:

When nearly mature, the tall and green arborvitae will make an almost impermeably thick hedge to shield you from slinky Peeping Toms and Tomasinas. To make sure you also have a good defense against Creeping Carls, plant a multiflora rose hedge, which is lower-growing, just inside the hedge line. Believe me, now nothing will see through or get through. Just don't roll too near it. However, here's a word of caution I hope you'll take. Until the arborvitae grows good and high, do your frolicking at night. And then you'd better get in touch with an entomologist to advise you on how to get rid of insects. Of course, if you're impatient, a quicker screen is a high stockade fence.

From *personal* experience, the best turf grass for this type of sport is creeping bentgrass (or velvet bent). It's a "springy" and soft grass that I usually don't recommend for the average home-owner. But your situation is different (and interesting), so I think it calls for this grass's special mattress quality. In addition to being the Englander of grasses, creeping bent is as smooth as a Spring-maid sheet (and remember, it's "a buck well spent"). Buy creep-ing bentgrass from a sod nursery if you can't wait for it to grow.

If you don't have a creeping bent lawn, don't despair. An up-right, cool-season grass, such as Kentucky bluegrass, will do just as handsomely. But I recommend that you don't keep it low-cut at bristle height (for obvious reasons). Let it grow long so it flops slightly, as when touched by a gentle wind. About 3 inches. This is the height I've been advocating strongly throughout the book, never realizing until now that there might be another great reason for this ideal cut. So now you have it! An *au naturel* glade, a delightful minimeadow, or—in your case—a climax prairie (agrostologically speaking). And why not? Grass and suchlike have been going on for . . . well, what do *you* think Eden was paved with?

Appendix

U.S. EXTENSION SERVICES

Address letters to:	Turf Grass Specialist, Co-operative Extension Service,
ALABAMA	Auburn University, Auburn, Alabama 36830
ALASKA	University of Alaska, College, Alaska 99701
ARIZONA	University of Arizona, Tucson, Arizona 85721
ARKANSAS	Post Office Box 391, Little Rock, Arkansas 72203
CALIFORNIA	University of California, 2200 University Avenue, Berkeley, California 94720
COLORADO	Colorado State University, Fort Collins, Colorado 80523
CONNECTICUT	University of Connecticut, Storrs, Connecticut 06268
DELAWARE	University of Delaware, Newark, Delaware 19711
DISTRICT OF COLUMBIA	Federal City College, 1424 K Street, N.W., Washington, D.C. 20005

FLORIDA	University of Florida, Gainesville, Florida 32611
GEORGIA	University of Georgia, Athens, Georgia 30601
GUAM	University of Guam, Post Office Box ⚡ EK Agana, Guam 96910
HAWAII	University of Hawaii, Honolulu, Hawaii 96822
IDAHO	University of Idaho, Morrill Hall, Moscow, Idaho 83843
ILLINOIS	University of Illinois, Urbana, Illinois 61801
INDIANA	Purdue University, Lafayette, Indiana 47907
IOWA	Iowa State University, Ames, Iowa 50010
KANSAS	Kansas State University, Manhattan, Kansas 66506
KENTUCKY	University of Kentucky, Lexington, Kentucky 40506
LOUISIANA	Louisiana State University, Baton Rouge, Louisiana 70803
MAINE	University of Maine, Orono, Maine 04473
MARYLAND	University of Maryland, College Park, Maryland 20742
MASSACHUSETTS	University of Massachusetts, Amherst, Massachusetts 01002
MICHIGAN	Michigan State University, East Lansing, Michigan 48823
MINNESOTA	University of Minnesota, St. Paul, Minnesota 55101

MISSISSIPPI	Mississippi State University, State College, Mississippi 39762
MISSOURI	University of Missouri, 309 University Hall, Columbia, Missouri 65201
MONTANA	Montana State University, Bozeman, Montana 59715
NEBRASKA	University of Nebraska, Lincoln, Nebraska 68503
NEVADA	University of Nevada, Reno, Nevada 89507
NEW HAMPSHIRE	University of New Hampshire, Taylor Hall, Durham, New Hampshire 03824
NEW JERSEY	Rutgers—The State University, Post Office Box 231, New Brunswick, New Jersey 08903
NEW MEXICO	New Mexico State University, Las Cruces, New Mexico 88001
NEW YORK	New York State College of Agriculture, Ithaca, New York 14850
NORTH CAROLINA	North Carolina State University, Raleigh, North Carolina 27607
NORTH DAKOTA	North Dakota State University, Fargo, North Dakota 58102
OHIO	Ohio State University, 2120 Fyffe Road, Columbus, Ohio 43210
OKLAHOMA	Oklahoma State University, Stillwater, Oklahoma 74074
OREGON	Oregon State University, Corvallis, Oregon 97331
PENNSYLVANIA	The Pennsylvania State University, University Park, Pennsylvania 16802

PUERTO RICO	University of Puerto Rico, Rio Piedras, Puerto Rico 00928
RHODE ISLAND	University of Rhode Island, Kingston, Rhode Island 02881
SOUTH CAROLINA	Clemson University, Clemson, South Carolina 29631
SOUTH DAKOTA	South Dakota State University, Brookings, South Dakota 57006
TENNESSEE	University of Tennessee, Post Office Box 1071, Knoxville, Tennessee 37901
TEXAS	Texas A & M University, College Station, Texas 77843
UTAH	Utah State University, Logan, Utah 84321
VERMONT	University of Vermont, Burlington, Vermont 05401
VIRGINIA	Virginia Polytechnic Institute and State University, Blacksburg, Virginia 24061
VIRGIN ISLANDS	P.O. Box 166, Kingshill, St. Croix, Virgin Islands 00850
WASHINGTON	Washington State University, Pullman, Washington 99163
WEST VIRGINIA	West Virginia University, 294 Coliseum, Morgantown, West Virginia 26505
WISCONSIN	University of Wisconsin, 432 North Lake Street, Madison, Wisconsin 53706
WYOMING	University of Wyoming, Box 3354 University Station, Laramie, Wyoming 82070

Index